Love, Queenie

Also by Mayukh Sen

Taste Makers:
Seven Immigrant Women Who Revolutionized Food in America

Love, Queenie

Merle Oberon, Hollywood's First South Asian Star

Mayukh Sen

W. W. NORTON & COMPANY

Independent Publishers Since 1923

For information about permission to reproduce selections from this book, write to
Permissions, W. W. Norton & Company, Inc., 500 Fifth Avenue, New York, NY 10110

For information about special discounts for bulk purchases, please contact
W. W. Norton Special Sales at specialsales@wwnorton.com or 800-233-4830

Manufacturing by Lakeside Book Company
Book design by Brian Mulligan
Production manager: Louise Mattarelliano

ISBN 978-1-324-05081-0

W. W. Norton & Company, Inc.
500 Fifth Avenue, New York, NY 10110
www.wwnorton.com

W. W. Norton & Company Ltd.
15 Carlisle Street, London W1D 3BS

10 9 8 7 6 5 4 3 2 1

To my late father, Sakti Sengupta,
for fostering my cinephilia,
and my mother, Kasturi Sen,
for tolerating it

Contents

*Merle Oberon with Clark Gable at the 8th Academy Awards,
where Merle received a nomination for Best Actress in a Leading Role
for her performance in* The Dark Angel *(1935).*

Introduction

AT THE START OF 1935, MERLE OBERON FEARED HER HOLLY-wood career was over. It had barely begun just a few months before, when she had arrived in America via England. The passenger records from her voyage across the Atlantic the previous November stated the facts clearly: She was twenty-three, unwed, and born in the city then known as Bombay, India.

She had already established herself as an actress of repute back in England under the aegis of Alexander Korda, head of the influential London Films. After signing a contract with the production company in 1932, she became its resident so-called exotic, playing foreign creatures conceived as stereotypes: Think castanet-clicking Spaniards and mysterious French noblewomen. Whenever questions arose about why her tan never seemed to fade, she parroted the cover story that the company invented for her: that she was born to well-heeled white parents on the Australian island of Tasmania. The suits at London Films, believing she was light-skinned enough to pass for white, willfully erased the fact that her mother was South Asian, and that Merle had grown up in poverty in what was then Calcutta. Back in Merle's birth country, her tormentors had taunted her about her "chee-chee" accent, a pejorative for Anglo-Indians, the subordinate racial category to which Merle belonged by dint of her mixed South Asian and white heritage. Her handlers banked on no one challenging the new biography they fabricated for her, and the British public took Merle at her word.

But she didn't have any such protections in America, where she was more or less alone for the first few months. Hollywood's gossip columnists were far more vicious than those in England; upon her arrival, they began to print speculations that her mother was a "Hindu." *Hindu* was a byword in the American vernacular for any South Asian, regardless of religious creed; it was also a distinct, government-sanctioned racial category as of the 1930 census. This was a time when the fear of the Hindu—sometimes spelled as "Hindoo"—ran riot in America. Earlier in the twentieth century, anxieties about the "dusky peril" posed by South Asian immigrants threatening the sanctity of white labor gripped the American psyche, feeding a climate of bigotry that held steady in the years that followed. The Immigration Act of 1917 kept immigrants from South Asia (along with other parts of Asia belonging to what lawmakers termed a "Barred Zone") from coming to America at all. Six years after the passage of that law, the Supreme Court ruled that any South Asian immigrants already residing in America's borders would be ineligible for naturalization henceforward; the government also revoked the citizenship status of South Asians who had already become citizens, rendering them stateless. By the time Merle arrived in the States, Americans were content to imagine South Asians as turbaned mystics or uncivilized primitives. Yet, simmering beneath these romantic stereotypes was a xenophobic belief that they were fundamentally unassimilable.

Making matters more dire, Merle also just happened to arrive in Hollywood the same year that the industry began rigid enforcement of the Production Code—colloquially called the Hays Code—a set of conservative axioms meant to tame an industry that political bluenosers saw as a playground for sin. The rulebook curbed the on-screen depiction of such perceived moral indignities as miscegenation—defined within the text of the Code as being between Black and white races, but interpreted broadly enough to apply to non-Black performers of color more generally. Had audiences known Merle was anything other than white, she would have been exiled to a career of playing temptresses and domestics, a supporting actress on a film's narrative margins.

So Merle moved surreptitiously in those first few months in Hollywood. She put herself through the miserable rigors of starring in an American musical, *Folies Bergère de Paris*, in which she'd play a French baroness. But the film's makeup artists accentuated her amygdaloid eyes and taffy-pulled her hair to elongate her scalp. This ignited the abject disappointment, even disgust, of critics. "Miss Oberon, through most of her sequences, looks precisely like a Malaysian, which is just too bad," the *Washington Post* moaned upon the film's release in early 1935. Her appearance inspired further doubts about her purported white heritage. Hollywood's homegrown sorority of actresses, all of them white, harbored mistrust about whether this brown vamp was really from Australia. As a result, Merle had little social life. Parties, when she managed to score invites to them, were dances of humiliation. She spent all of Christmas crying, thrown back into the seclusion of a childhood in India feeling unwanted because she thought no one wanted to be friends with a mixed-race girl.

She was all but ready to leave town when she heard that the powerful producer Samuel Goldwyn was looking to cast the lead role in a remake of a 1925 film called *The Dark Angel*, a love triangle set in England during World War I. Merle knew that the principal role in that film, for an ivory-skinned and virginal English beauty named Kitty Vane, could, if she played her cards shrewdly, give her the chance to expunge the stain of *Folies Bergère de Paris* from public memory and thus revise her screen persona. A scrapper from her youth, Merle channeled her desperation into action. Goldwyn had a pineapple-blonde actress in mind for the part, Madeleine Carroll. Merle had known Carroll, the star of a 1931 British film, *Fascination*, in which Merle had a thankless one-scene role as a flower seller of dubious racial origin ("What an exotic-looking creature! Are you Egyptian?" one character chirped upon seeing her). So Merle's crusade for Kitty Vane went into overdrive. She started to tell Goldwyn that watching the 1925 version of *The Dark Angel* as a girl in Calcutta had been one of her most formative moviegoing experiences, even saying it had been the first movie she ever saw. Others involved in production weren't convinced of her fitness for the role: The attached director, Sidney Franklin, said she was "too Oriental." United Artists officials said she was only fit to play a Hindu. But Merle doubled down on her efforts. "I would die if Carroll got part," she cabled to Korda, her boss in England, in March 1935.

Goldwyn, an immigrant from Poland, was a parvenu to Hollywood like Merle. He was so charmed by her persistence that he didn't listen to the naysayers when he rubber-stamped her as Kitty Vane that spring. Goldwyn believed so firmly in Merle's potential that he even eked out a deal to share her with Korda in England, an arrangement that would have her straddling the cinemas of two countries, unusual for a star of that era. Goldwyn signed Merle with the full knowledge that she was South Asian. Should anyone threaten to reveal that secret, he was ready to muzzle them by paying them off.

Merle thus began to calcimine herself: Off came the greasepaint from her previous roles, the loud strokes of mascara that had been hiding her grape-green eyes. Though *The Dark Angel* would be made in black and white—which could cloak her from scrutiny about her heritage, and aid her in passing—Merle made the mistake of suntanning on the California beaches too much while shooting, buttering her brown skin. She could not fight what was in her blood. The studio made her go to a beauty salon and undergo skin-bleaching treatment for an entire day so that her complexion would lighten enough for the cameras. This was a painful trade-off, part of a punishing artistic process for a role that had the potential to make her a Hollywood star. But Merle's command of her craft became so assiduous that she even trained herself to cry at will. Goldwyn's magical promise to give Merle a goody-two-shoes makeover sparked press interest in the project, and she now had a firm answer for journalists who confronted her about being "Eurasian," as they called it back then: "I detest 'exotic' women! They represent everything I'd hate to be and that I'm scared to death of becoming," she told the *Los Angeles Times* that September. The efforts paid off: Critics were taken with Merle's about-face when reviews started hitting papers that month. She had transformed herself from a coppery foreigner to the embodiment of Hays-era purity.

And she could act. "Miss Oberon, abandoning the Javanese slant of the eyes for the occasion, plays with skill and feeling," raved the *New York Times* critic Andre Sennwald.

So praised was Merle's performance that it would bring her to the pomp and glitter of the Biltmore Hotel on the night of March 5, 1936, for the eighth annual Academy Awards—a ceremony that had gained a new nickname that year, the Oscars—as a nominee for the Academy Award for Best Actress. Merle was far unlike her fellow nominees in terms of pedigree; two of the frontrunners, Bette Davis and Katharine Hepburn, were already proven quantities in Hollywood, and Hepburn already had gained an Oscar. Merle was quite young, too, having turned twenty-five just weeks before the ceremony. She was also South Asian, though most in the public—aside from those few who had their suspicions—saw Merle only as white. Prior to that point, the acting categories of the Academy Awards had been occupied exclusively by white performers. No performer of color had received such recognition before, certainly no Asian woman like herself. That night, she tangled her arms in those of Clark Gable, the suave star whom she was seeing casually, as they arrived to the applause of fans who'd swarmed outside the hotel. Her diaphanous gown fluttered around her five-foot-two frame, with a spindly band of pearls dangling from her neck. They sat next to Goldwyn and his wife, Frances, at a round table. The category in which she was nominated would be announced last.

It was long past midnight when Merle heard the winner's name: Bette Davis. Merle let the disappointment run through her as she lost her first, and final, Oscar nomination. So few people in that room knew the symbolic significance that her mere presence as a nominee would come to have in subsequent years. Within the Best Actress category, that pattern of nominating only white actresses would continue for nearly two more decades, Merle being the sole disruption until 1955. After her, it would take eighty-seven years for another Asian woman—per the Census definition of the term, referring to those of East, Southeast, or South Asian descent—to receive a nomination, and eventually win, for Best Actress. Merle surely hadn't dreamed that she would write herself into history that night, or that others would later try to erase what she had achieved. But the fact that Merle Oberon was Asian at all was a secret she guarded with her life. This was less a choice than a necessity, and it came at great psychic cost to her. When the klieg lights dimmed after a day's work, her public performance ended, and the truth was hers to live with, alone.

★

SHE WAS UNLIKE ANY star I'd ever seen. It wasn't only her look, resembling no Crawford, Davis, or Garbo I recognized from that era: the inkjet hair, the charmingly crooked snaggletooth that would jut out whenever she smiled, the bronze skin that reminded me of my own. It was her voice. She spoke clipped and practiced English that, on occasion, would slip, revealing a hint of the city that had made her. I knew that accent well: It was the same I'd heard among my father's Bengali family from Kolkata, the city where she'd grown up. This connection made my response to her feel more real, more true, than any I'd felt toward other performers from that period.

I was a teenager when I first came across Merle Oberon as Cathy in William Wyler's *Wuthering Heights* (1939), the film for which she is arguably most remembered today. It was around 2009 or so, and I was a senior in high school in suburban New Jersey. By that point, she had been dead for three decades, but I felt bound to her by city and skin. I knew the broad contours of her biography: that she had been born into poverty as a mixed-race, Anglo-Indian girl in British India in the early twentieth century. That, upon immigrating to London as a teenager, she ditched the name Queenie Thompson and within a matter of years reinvented herself as Merle Oberon, becoming a star of Anglo-American cinema under that name. That she concealed her maternal South Asian lineage and passed for white because the prejudices of the era demanded she do so, maintaining until her 1979 death the studio-constructed fiction that she'd been born to European parents in Tasmania.

As a teenager, I had enormous empathy for Merle Oberon's struggle.

Most gay boys I knew tended to fawn over other divas of the era, but my chosen idol was Merle: I understood, as a teen who was still coming to terms with his sexuality, what it meant to hide a part of yourself for your safety, to secure a life where you might want to make your dreams possible. Her ascent was also meaningful to me as a South Asian, for Merle found purchase in a world where our likes were rarely acknowledged. That alone made her so much more than her tragedy. I knew, even then, that projecting a performer's offscreen biography onto their onscreen work was a simplistic way to read art. But when I saw Merle on screen, I saw the hurt in her gaze. I also felt an admiration for her survival, a disbelief that she could summon the will to make art despite her pain.

After embracing Merle Oberon's majesty early in my cinephilia during the late aughts, I was dismayed to learn that mine was a minority opinion. The narrator of the great James Baldwin's *If Beale Street Could Talk* (1974) discounted her as "a nothing actress" with a "disquieting resemblance to an egg," reflecting a general consensus. David Thomson, a writer whose work fomented my ambition to enter the profession of film criticism, lamented that "she was often a dull actress" in *The New Biographical Dictionary of Film* (originally *A Biographical Dictionary of Cinema*), which I considered a holy book. Some were even more savage. An academic who ran a blog dedicated to the Academy Awards—back when there was a cottage industry of what I and many others called "Oscar bloggers"—dismissed her: "What use was Merle Oberon, really? Her face has a hard, flat quality onscreen that seems to repel the audience's identification, and she seems insufficiently open to the actors around her." It stung to see her entire existence as an actor written off so snidely by people I considered tastemakers.

Life took me away from writing about film and toward other subjects, but my mind always returned to Merle Oberon. In the few times Merle's name did manage to permeate the zeitgeist, I saw her regarded with cruelty. People, both within and outside the South Asian diaspora, sullied her as a self-hating race traitor whose considerable achievements were better left unacknowledged. These critics seemed to have little understanding of what it was like to be Anglo-Indian in South Asia during the early twentieth century, how the studio system in Hollywood's Golden Age left actresses like Merle with next to no agency, how restrictive US immigration legislation against South Asians made her entire existence on American soil precarious. Her story, I thought, clamored for a South Asian perspective that contextualized her condition, her choices, and her eventual triumphs. I vowed that one day, if the tools were available to me and the public interest was sufficient—I would write a book on her life.

MY RESEARCH FOR THIS BOOK involved a combination of tracking down Merle's surviving family members from India (now living outside the country), along with scouring press coverage of her—interviews, film reviews, gossip columns—during her lifetime; combing through her highly curated private papers—and the papers of her Hollywood contemporaries—at archives (namely, the Academy of Motion Picture Arts and Sciences' Margaret Herrick Library in Beverly Hills); reviewing immigration and travel records; and reading the biographies and memoirs of people who knew her when she was alive.

As I began writing this book a few years ago, there was one biography of Merle Oberon in existence: Charles Higham and Roy Moseley's *Princess Merle: The Romantic Life of Merle Oberon* (1983). (Her life has also inspired fictional treatments such as Michael Korda's 1985 novella *Queenie*. He had been Merle's nephew from her first marriage.) Published a few years after her death, *Princess Merle* fractured the myth of her Tasmanian birth by stating that she was, indeed, a woman of mixed South Asian and white heritage born poor in what is now Mumbai, India. Major news outlets, podcasts, and books have repeated claims from that book with nary a whiff of suspicion for four decades running. But the name Charles Higham will ring alarm bells for anyone with a passing knowledge of showbiz history; even the most cursory of Google searches will reveal that he had a tendency toward fabulism, presenting outlandish and thinly sourced claims in his biographies of such figures as the Tasmanian actor Errol Flynn and the American mogul Howard Hughes. Reviewers, journalists, even obituary writers castigated Higham for these transgressions. But *Princess Merle* never generated the scrutiny that Higham's books on Flynn and Hughes did, for Merle did not have the stature of those men in public memory. As I became aware of the extent of Higham's questionable methods, that prior biography became less a guidepost than a text for me to refute. (Moseley, his coauthor, has not been the target of such allegations about fabulism.)

The book also contained errors. Unmentioned in that book— perhaps because neither Higham nor Moseley knew about it—was the fact the woman Merle thought of as her mother was actually her grandmother. This became public knowledge nearly two decades after the release of Higham and Moseley's book, though there has been no proper biography of Merle Oberon in America since, necessitating a more up-to-date approach. The girl whom Merle had been told was her half sister was actually her biological mother, whose rape at the hands of her stepfather resulted in Merle's conception. The disclosure added another layer of tragedy to Merle's story, situating her in a cycle of trauma that reached across generations and oceans. Her mother, who bore her as a teenager, had to carry on the public performance that her daughter was really her half sister, all while, a world away, her daughter had to deny her South Asian roots and pretend she was white.

Through my reporting, I have amended some of the other claims that Higham and Moseley's book introduced. Merle's family challenged Higham and Moseley's assertion that Merle was part-Māori (they clarified that she was one-quarter Sinhalese, though British India still classified her under the blanket of "Anglo-Indian"), or that her full name at birth was Estelle Merle O'Brien Thompson (it was simply Estelle Merle Thompson, according to her family and her baptismal certificate). My research, too, changed the widely circulated version of Merle's filmography drawn from Higham and Moseley's biography of Merle; for example, there is no evidence she appeared in the film they alleged to be the first entry in her list of screen credits—1928's

The Three Passions—and even if she were cut from the final reels, this film came out a year before Merle left India. (A revised filmography follows the epilogue of this book.) I also tugged at certain threads that weren't otherwise present in that earlier book and warranted deeper inspection, surfacing reports of her forced sterilization as a teenager and alleged spousal abuse she survived.

There is, unsurprisingly, so much that ended up on the cutting-room floor of this book for the sake of narrative propulsion. It's not as if I could include all the film roles she intended to play but eventually had to cancel (the 1948 ballet drama *The Red Shoes* was intended to be a vehicle for her); every mention of "exotic," "sloe-eyed," "slant-eyed," or "Oriental" that preceded Merle's name in coverage of her; or the coded descriptors attached to her: "a pagoda that knows how to cook," "girl bride of Genghis Khan," "imperturbable young Buddha." We aren't even scratching the surface here, but this truncated list can provide a small sense of what Merle was up against in her climb up the Hollywood hill.

Still, a larger existential question haunted this project: How do you capture the truth of someone who was an unreliable narrator of her own life, who lied so often about herself for survival? Merle's papers contained little about her life in India beyond a few photographs, while most of the figures in her life who might have held knowledge about her connection to her birth country are now dead. There is so much that even the most punctilious research cannot yield: details about her relationship with her grandmother, for example, and her mother. Her family in India isn't certain whether Merle ever knew the identity of her real mother, but they think it's unlikely, and I have not found any persuasive evidence that would contradict their belief. The letters that Merle and her biological mother exchanged throughout their lifetimes are, apart from the snippets of one that appears in this book, now irretrievable. This roadblock posed quite a formidable challenge, and making peace with these lacunae became a somewhat painful, but imperative, part of the process of writing this biography.

I also sought to contextualize Merle's story within its relevant historical backdrop, which I hope will illuminate how hard she had to fight to create a new life for herself. America was a country that locked its borders to South Asian immigrants like her (as well as immigrants from other parts of Asia) until 1946, after which quotas dictated how many South Asian immigrants were allowed into the country. Currents of discrimination still coursed through the public bloodstream in the years that followed. Plus, she began acting in a time when Hollywood, like the nation that birthed it, took great pains to exclude performers of color, including those who were South Asian. Because she acted for four decades, Merle also witnessed the collapse of the highly regimented studio system within which she came up. This book maps her against these changing headwinds. It also considers her alongside the few other South Asian contemporaries who were navigating Hollywood as well, showing the collective struggle to which she belonged.

Merle's relationship to her birth country, and her South Asian heritage, were far more complex than most abbreviated renderings of her story would have you believe. But I don't want to overcorrect and create a Lysoled portrait of Merle, spinning her story into some blandly inspirational narrative about how one woman "turned shit into sugar." This book aims to neither excuse nor condemn, but to arouse empathy. As you read, I hope you might start to question the demands the public places on stars in life and in death, and how those demands intensify when those performers come from underrepresented groups as Merle did, meaning that they—individuals trying to survive an exploitative system—have had to carry an extra, symbolic burden of being the most unimpeachable torchbearer for their race. My intention is not to disturb the memory of this actress who captured my imagination all those years ago but to bring some greater peace to it. It is so easy to judge Merle Oberon from the smug and righteous comforts of a twenty-first-century remove, to lazily point a finger at her by saying she let her people down by pretending to be someone she wasn't. But I have no desire to smear her. I want to see her.

A Note on Naming Conventions

You will notice that this book's initial chapters refer to our subject as "Queenie," her preferred name in her youth, while subsequent chapters denote her as "Merle," honoring the re-christening she underwent as her film career began. Such marquee-friendly name changes were required of many film stars, but, in this particular case, that shift represented a meaningful break from the past of racial shame she wanted to leave behind. Still, there remained stray moments in her adult life abroad—such as when she corresponded with her mother, whom she believed to be her sister, in India—in which she continued to call herself "Queenie." Her existence involved a constant series of negotiations between her contradictory private and public selves (the former firmly locked in India), which the language in this book seeks to reflect.

In addition, early references to the cities and countries in South Asia relevant to her story will, in the interest of remaining faithful to her era, adhere to the language of that period. The Indian city today named Mumbai was then Bombay, for example, while what is now Kolkata was once Calcutta; Sri Lanka, where her mother was born, was then called Ceylon. The entity known as India at the time of her birth in 1911 now encompasses such countries as Bangladesh and Pakistan. Finally, some may wonder why I refer to Merle as "Anglo-Indian" despite the fact that she was actually of partial Sinhalese extraction (with roots in what is now Sri Lanka, not India, putting her closer to Sri Lanka's mixed-race Burgher community). Interviews with her family made clear that labeling her as "Anglo-Indian" is accurate to the historical and geographical context of her upbringing in India rather than Sri Lanka. Describing her as Anglo-Indian, her family clarified, is also truthful to how she self-identified in her early life.

Love, Queenie

Chapter 1
My Name Is Queenie
(1911–1929)

*Fourteen-year-old Merle Oberon—then known as
Queenie Thompson—dressed as a dancing rose in 1925
in Calcutta (now Kolkata), her hometown.*

*T*HE DREAM BEGAN EARLY, WHEN SHE WAS STILL A LITTLE girl. She would pose and comb her hair as she sat before the mirror in her family's shabby home in the South Bombay area of Khetwadi. Constance Joyce Selby, the teenage girl she thought of as her sister, would wonder why she was so preoccupied with this vision of herself;

so would the woman she believed was her mother, Charlotte Selby. Shouldn't she be focusing on school? But Queenie, as they called her—a derivation of Charlotte's pet name for her, "my Queen"—responded with firm conviction: She didn't care about her studies. She wanted to be an actress.

In truth, Queenie had it all wrong about her family. Constance Joyce wasn't her sister, but rather her mother. She was a half-Sinhalese and half-British girl with brunette skin and an aquiline nose who'd been born in the Ceylonese city of Colombo. She had given birth to Queenie in Bombay when she was only fourteen. Meanwhile, Charlotte, a Sinhalese woman from a hill station near the Ceylonese city of Kandy, was actually Queenie's grandmother. Constance Joyce's stepfather, Arthur Thompson—a white British mechanical engineer from the English town of Darlington—had raped her, resulting in Queenie's conception. To avoid a scandal, Charlotte scooped up her daughter's child and raised her as her own, all while telling Queenie that her mother was her half sister. Constance Joyce played along with this painful charade. The truth would imperil their already tenuous position as Anglo-Indians in surrounding society. Though Charlotte's ethnic roots were in Ceylon (now Sri Lanka, outside what was then known as India), such distinctions about the provenance of one's South Asian genes did not quite matter according to the hierarchies of British India, where Constance Joyce and Queenie fit the constitutional definition of Anglo-Indian because of their South Asian blood; they certainly saw themselves as Anglo-Indians. Queenie's father absented himself not long after her birth and returned to England, leaving her with no memory of him. Charlotte told her that he had been a soldier, or tommy, so that was what Queenie always believed.

This is the violence into which Estelle Merle Thompson was born on February 18, 1911, at St. George's Hospital in Bombay, where the family had been living for five years by that point. She would thereafter observe February 19—the date listed on her baptismal certificate—as her birthday throughout her public life. The year of her birth was, in a stroke of coincidence, the year that the Indian census revised the definition of the term *Anglo-Indian*, which had previously been an umbrella label for any British person residing in the British Raj. That classification would, from 1911 onward, denote a person of mixed European and South Asian ancestry. It was a more dignified designation than the previous *Eurasian*, a term that had become associated with government-backed prejudice. This semantic change, codified in law, was the result of organized campaigning among a chorus of Anglo-Indians who wanted to align themselves with an idyllic homeland abroad, a place many of them had never even seen.

British India was, after all, a largely hostile environment for Anglo-Indians like Queenie. The census recorded 100,451 Anglo-Indians that year vis-à-vis a mammoth population of 315,156,396 in the country—a tiny fragment—though that figure might not account for the sheer number of Anglo-Indians who sought to pass as white Europeans. To do so was a calculated way of bettering an otherwise unfortunate lot in Indian life; being Anglo-Indian was, in many cases, not necessarily a privilege in the bustle of Bombay. Theirs was a community that the ruling class preferred not to acknowledge: Anglo-Indians were breathing evidence of Britain's imperial malfeasance. Meanwhile, other South Asians who sought freedom from British rule had different reasons for rejecting Anglo-Indians. The more vocal of the lot saw Anglo-Indians as pathetic patsies who bowed in subservience to their British autocrats. This was especially true of upper-caste—specifically Brahmin—Hindus, who would look down on Anglo-Indians as a spurned breed, saving their harshest contempt for Anglo-Indians who toiled away in menial positions on, for instance, India's railways. What further alienated many Anglo-Indians was the growing tide of Indian nationalism, fettered to the fever for independence, that would have left little space for Anglo-Indians to exist in the nation that would emerge from any fight for freedom.

With this culture of exclusion came a language of derogation toward Anglo-Indians that would never really escape Queenie, even after she left the subcontinent: *Half-caste. Country-bred. Blacky-white. Chee-chee. Kutcha-butcha* (half baked). *Café-au-lait. Eight annas* (referring to the fact that there were sixteen annas to a rupee). Economic opportunities for Anglo-Indians—especially for those whose complexion did not allow them to access the precarious privilege of passing—was often scarce, a material circumstance that Queenie knew all too well. She grew up in abject poverty. Charlotte worked as a nurse, a low-paid position that meant she was routinely absent. Sometimes she would need to leave Queenie in the care of preteen girls who would dote on her as if she were a little sister—bathing her, feeding her, doing her hair. With the woman she thought of as her mother gone so often, Queenie would play-act being a mother of a dozen kids, fantasizing about being present for them in a way Charlotte wasn't.

Racial and material discrimination were facts of life for Queenie, who, like Constance Joyce, was seen as Anglo-Indian, not white, to those she came across. As long as she remained in India, she had little hope of harnessing whatever privilege her lighter skin tone could give her. You could even hear it in the way she spoke the patois of what was then called Hindustani, with an accent typically ridiculed for its singsong cadence. This alone would guarantee her exclusion. The best Queenie would have been able to hope for was to go abroad, which might allow her to cross color lines more easily than she could in India. Queenie was determined to overcome the prejudice in India that came from both class and racial fronts in any way she could. Determined to make it big.

This ambition propelled Queenie forward as she grew older. Constance Joyce splintered off from the family, yoking herself to a man from Goa years her senior whose family riches glittered to her eyes. Constance Joyce had felt abandoned by her own mother, who seemed so absorbed by the child she had been forced to relinquish. Before she left for married life and distanced herself from her mother and her daughter, Constance Joyce would take a token of Queenie with her as a treasured lifelong possession: a pair of earrings, two scrawny gold hoops, that Queenie had worn at three, a tiny remembrance of the daughter she could never publicly claim as her own.

Together, Queenie and Charlotte moved to Calcutta during Queenie's early adolescence, around the time she was six. The city had been
the footstool of the British Empire up until the year of Queenie's birth,
after which the capital became Delhi. Calcutta was no less friendly to
Queenie's ilk than Bombay had been. There, she and Charlotte were
once again felled by poverty. Charlotte's flat on Mangoe Lane, in one of
the more destitute parts of the city, was workaday and unremarkable,
with a floating curtain partitioning the kitchen from the sitting room.

In Calcutta's prestigious La Martinière boarding school, Queenie
continued to feel the brunt of intolerance toward Anglo-Indians. A
Christian school, La Martinière was the province of the pampered
and elite, which Queenie certainly was not; Queenie was known as a
foundation pupil, a Christian girl admitted to the school based on her
indigency. Other girls' families paid for their attendance, but Queenie's didn't, which made her, in short, a charity case. Paying students
reminded her of that every day, constantly mocking her. Even her
uniform, a plain white smock, was different. Girls her age teased her
about what they called her "chinky" eyes—using a racial slur for East
Asians—and commented that she would be rather pleasant-looking
were it not for that perceived "defect."

During this period, the teenage Queenie began to drift toward the
refuge of performance, finding salvation in the Calcutta Amateur Theatrical Society, or the CATS, a troupe for acting hobbyists that had
thrived since the nineteenth century. She'd dance in the chorus for
productions such as *Aladdin* and *Sinbad the Sailor*; she'd serve in the
singing trio for *The Geisha*, a British musical comedy. She'd dress up
as a rose and roam around the city in costume, posing in front of Calcutta landmarks such as the Victoria Memorial and pretending to play
safari on the Hooghly River.

But Queenie's real aspiration was to enter the movies. During her
childhood, moviegoing was an active part of life in Calcutta across
all social strata: The first permanent movie theater in all of South
Asia was, in fact, Calcutta's Elphinstone Picture Palace (eventually
called the Chaplin Cinema), erected in 1907. Though the nucleus of

British India's burgeoning film industry was in Bombay, Calcutta had a budding feature-film industry of its own. But demand outpaced production by the 1920s, so the majority of films on Calcutta's screens—films that Queenie would've seen—came from Hollywood. The Calcutta of her youth was also home to many future silver-screen actresses. Queenie would sometimes play tennis with Rose Musleah, a Jewish girl—another minority—who would later become a prominent leading lady in Indian cinema under the name Miss Rose. Acting generally had the reputation of being a taboo career path for proper women in those days, akin to sex work. Thus, talent from marginalized communities—Jews and Anglo-Indians—dominated early cinema before the vocation of screen acting became less stigmatized. But for Queenie, whose Calcutta upbringing had been so miserable, the possibility of starting a film career overseas would have been a far more exciting prospect than staying in a country she felt didn't want her.

Charlotte supported Queenie's ambitions as she grew older, and in fact had begun to realize that her dreams were worth stoking, given their poor financial straits. Queenie's hopes became her own, and Charlotte began to act like a stage mother. Starting to detect that Queenie's fast-blooming beauty could potentially attract powerful men who might aid her acting career, Charlotte encouraged Queenie to use her good looks to her advantage. But Charlotte also realized this plan could backfire easily, jeopardizing Queenie's future. She had seen her own daughter give birth to Queenie when she was so young. What acting opportunities might an inadvertent pregnancy foreclose for Queenie, this girl who wanted so badly to make it in the movies? Better to have her sterilized.

As Queenie approached seventeen, Charlotte took her to a doctor and, without telling Queenie what was about to happen to her, ordered the doctor to sever and partially remove her fallopian tubes. Young Queenie was unaware, in that moment, of the damage this procedure would wreak upon her body, leaving her with a desire to have children she would struggle for years to fulfill; the realization would only come to her in adulthood, by which point the trauma—physical, psychological—was irreparable.

★

BY THE TIME SHE turned seventeen, Queenie was out of school and had found work as a receptionist for a firm known as Halley Brothers. She would go to movies often, losing herself in the silent weepies, like *The Dark Angel*, which played on the city's screens. She would spend evenings attending performances of *Joy Bells*, a touring English show that had stopped at Calcutta's Empire Theatre. As she sat in the crowd, Queenie fixed her gaze on a white singer and dancer. Queenie would go to these performances again and again, entranced by the sight of this girl's freedom and grace. Before watching the show for the third time, she purchased a bottle of violet perfume from Houbigant, an extravagance on her meager receptionist's salary, and knocked, shyly, on the dancer's dressing-room door after an evening performance.

"My name is Queenie Thompson," she said, barely lifting her voice above a whisper. After years of torment at La Martinière, Queenie knew her place, knew not to overstep her boundaries when speaking to white Europeans who would only regard her with disdain. "I have seen your show three times from the gallery, and I think you're wonderful. Someday I hope to go on the stage and be just like you." That cacophonous, cut-glass clang that came out of Queenie's mouth horrified Phyllis Beaumont. With just one look at Queenie, Phyllis immediately pieced together that she was what Brits derisively called "a chee-chee girl." But another dead giveaway came with that voice, whose accent told its own unhappy story. Phyllis thought Queenie was gorgeous, with her slender figure, striking eyes, and blackberry hair. But she knew that the simple matter of Queenie's parentage—written so clearly on her face, heard so loudly in the way she spoke—restricted any possibilities in Calcutta. To Phyllis, Queenie was an Eliza Doolittle in need of a Henry Higgins.

That pity was the scaffolding on which Queenie's friendship with Phyllis was built. Queenie's need for acceptance reached straight into

Phyllis's heart. They were born a few months apart, with Queenie being slightly older. Queenie began to socialize with her regularly, despite the differences embedded in their skin. Phyllis felt she had little to lose by palling around with an Anglo-Indian girl, since a stage performer wasn't exactly a profession that commanded respect. Ecstatic that someone had created space in their life for her, Queenie, eager to impress, regularly brought her new friend bouquets after evening performances. Queenie found new employment as a switchboard operator for the Calcutta telephone company not long after she began her friendship with Phyllis, and she had become her household's breadwinner; Charlotte was no longer working.* Queenie was just scraping by, and Phyllis chided Queenie for living above her means by bringing her gifts. Yet Queenie acted as if she might one day be able to afford such luxuries.

Queenie was shy about revealing her own class background. She would always ask to visit Phyllis at the tony Grand Hotel, where her friend stayed, never once inviting her to the ramshackle flat in the Chowringhee neighborhood, where she and Charlotte now lived. But Queenie otherwise made Phyllis privy to her every insecurity, along with her questions about who she was. Queenie would confide in Phyllis about her long-gone father, for example, who had made a beeline for England, lamenting that she'd never known that half of herself. Charlotte was the only parental figure she knew and could identify with. Queenie had grown up believing that this dark-skinned Sinhalese woman was her mother, contributing to the urgency of her anxiety that, no matter how much work she did to assimilate, she might never belong.

The connection between Queenie and Phyllis was genuine, not purely transactional. As "working girls," they would spend weekends—especially Sundays—with one another, and evenings found them

---

* Various archival sources locate Queenie at different jobs in her late teens: The artist and filmmaker Derek Jarman would claim she had worked as a secretary for his great-uncle Tommy at one point.

in public restaurants and cafés. Queenie's status as an Anglo-Indian barred her from the more exclusive British establishments. At the few venues where Queenie could get through the door, though, white Englishmen would take a liking to her, dining and dancing with her. Firpo's, a highly popular restaurant, was a favored haunt, and she was fast developing a reputation as one of Calcutta's finest beauties. Around this time, she fell into the orbit of film industry power brokers like Mark Hanna, who was representing Paramount in India, flirting with the possibility of entry into cinema. Though Queenie would try her best to conceal her mixed heritage around the men she encountered in such circles, some would distance themselves from her when they suspected she had South Asian blood: Open consorting with an Anglo-Indian girl would have spelled social doom for them.

But with her new friend's affirmations, Queenie shed her teenage diffidence, accepting that her unique beauty was a tool she could deploy for survival. She and Phyllis would have picnics, wander the Calcutta Botanical Garden, and visit the city's racecourses. At one such race, Phyllis introduced Queenie to Ike Edwards, an English jockey who instantly cottoned to Queenie. She in turn indulged his flattery, sensing this older man could be her ticket elsewhere. Queenie began telegraphing her sexual availability to him. For Queenie, doing so was potentially her way out of India; she was eager, bordering on desperate, for a better life than the one that circumstance had given her. Also, immigration and resettlement could increase the possibility of concealment. Abroad, she felt she would have a better chance of submerging herself into white British society than in a place like Calcutta.

Thankfully for Queenie, a jockey's life was inherently peripatetic, and the approaching summer monsoon season meant that Edwards, unable to race against the wind-driven downpours, would be leaving the subcontinent soon and returning to England. This was Queenie's chance. She couldn't easily secure a passport because she was Anglo-Indian, a bureaucratic snag that threatened to keep her in Calcutta permanently. Yet she worked her charms so strategically that she got

Edwards to agree that they would pretend to be husband and wife, and that he would pay for her passage from Calcutta.

Queenie's aim all along was to take Charlotte with her. Together, the two women decided that Charlotte would need to play the role of a servant in Queenie's life. It was the only way for them to live under the same roof abroad, no matter how painful this masquerade would be for them both. So in 1929, Queenie sailed for England with Edwards, who left her with a return ticket should she ever want to go back to India, a country that had created her but apparently resented her. She cashed in that ticket for some new clothes, and Charlotte arrived soon thereafter. Their new life had begun.

Chapter 2

I Have No Mother

(1929–1932)

GAUMONT-BRITISH PICTURE CORP. Ltd. present

LESLIE HENSON

with

HEATHER THATCHER

AUSTIN MELFORD

CONNIE EDISS

•

directed and adapted by

VICTOR SAVILLE

RELEASED BY REGAL FILMS LTD.

A WARM CORNER

Lobby card for Victor Saville's A Warm Corner *(1930), a film in which Merle—then still Queenie—was an uncredited extra.*

WHEN QUEENIE FIRST GOT TO LONDON IN 1929, ADJUST-ment wasn't easy. Her financial condition resembled her straits back in Calcutta, and she quite possibly relied on sex work—becoming what some referred to as "a girl of the streets"—to survive. Whispers about these beginnings would stigmatize her for years to come, even well after her lifetime. One snarky British journalist would, long after her death, refer to her snidely as "Queenie the half-caste slut." But she had to make a living for herself and Charlotte. They did not even have a washroom of their own in the flat they shared, and the shower only spit out cold water. Queenie would sew her own dresses, chintzy knockoffs of items she'd see in department-store windows. Sometimes, she would even subsist on crackers and water. Despite being in a new country, Queenie still felt like an outsider because of her race, just as she had back home. She'd stare at the images of blue-eyed blondes on candy boxes, thinking she would've given anything to look like those white girls. Her life would be so much easier.

In London during the 1920s, immigration of Anglo-Indians like Queenie from British India was sporadic, though not exactly sparse: Thousands had flocked there for employment or in search of connections to an ancestral homeland. By 1930, an estimated five thousand Anglo-Indians had settled there—many of them, like Queenie, seeking assimilation into white British society. Gone were the spotless skies and sizzle of India's sun, having given way to the shiver of the British winter. In the absence of an organized Anglo-Indian community, these migrants often had to depend on the family unit. Charlotte and Queenie only had each other.

Steady work was hard to come by, too, for Anglo-Indians like Queenie—especially in films. As she roamed this new, unfamiliar city, she would watch for advertised auditions for extras and then muscle her way into casting calls, only to be turned away. At such tryouts, a gaggle of fifty or so girls would sometimes crowd into places like the Café de Paris, in Piccadilly, one of the city's swankiest haunts. In those days, London was home to a constellation of nightclubs just like those that Queenie had known in Calcutta—and, as had been the case back home, these spaces were sometimes unwelcoming to Anglo-Indian girls like Queenie, who would draw stares when she entered the room. The Café de Paris was high society's stomping ground. A-list musicians performed in a rotunda positioned below street level while hostesses would glide across the room, goading white-tie–wearing men to dance and order champagne. The club attracted royals of every imaginable title—enough to make the performers feel like plebeians. Other venues, like the 400 Club in Leicester Square, were even more grand and glamorous; one couldn't even set foot in there without wearing proper evening dress, which Queenie couldn't afford. But Queenie yearned to go to venues like the 400 Club, to spend time among the rich and influential. Fastening herself to powerful men, just as she was able to do in Calcutta with Ike Edwards, would be one way to convert that fantasy into reality.

Any shoulder-rubbing Queenie did at her auditions paid off by the time she turned nineteen, in 1930. After yet another fruitless casting call at the Café de Paris, a man who worked there asked her whether she'd be interested in a gig at the café. Queenie had too much pride to accept the offer, at least at first, but she was so desperate for basic provisions that she eventually relented. This job gave her two pounds per week; it also gave her dinner. So began Queenie's work as one of five hostesses at the Café de Paris, a coveted spot.* The Café de Paris's duenna gave Queenie and her fellow hostesses strict mandates: They would have to eat meals at their own table on a balcony. Though their job required them to mingle with clients using their sex appeal, intercourse was out of bounds. Even if it was obvious to anyone with functioning sight that Queenie was of mixed race, her beauty, so arresting, overrode any concerns that her looks may have engendered.

Along with her hostess work, Queenie continued pursuing a so-far-nonexistent screen career, but her race remained a roadblock. When she first tried to begin her film career in the early 1930s, Britain's national cinema was in tatters. Filmmakers in the 1920s had found themselves dwarfed by the muscle and might of America's bustling film industry, whose output had been seizing the attention of moviegoers—particularly the British working class—since the end of World War I. In fact, only five percent of the films shown in British theaters in 1926 were actually made in Britain. That worrying statistic resulted in the passage of Britain's 1927 Cinematograph Films

---

* Queenie cycled through a carousel of different names while working at the Café de Paris: Estelle O'Brien, Mary O'Brien. It seems her adoption of the O'Brien surname, which was not on her birth certificate, had begun by this time, perhaps as a strategic way to ally herself more closely with whiteness.

Act, an attempt to rescue the country's film industry from obsolescence. Among the results of that law was a spate of "quota quickies"—inexpensive films churned out briskly to prevent American films from cornering the British market. These quota quickies were sometimes attached to Hollywood films. Serious filmmakers who had come up through the silent era now found themselves competing against hungrier upstarts who, eager to make a pound from quota quickies, prized profit over art. The 1927 act did its part to stimulate an ailing industry at first, with a cluster of new production companies materializing just before the turn of the decade. But after that initial period came the development of sound, which, with its immense threat to silent cinema, led to a brief slowdown in 1930. The 1927 act was starting to look like more of a stopgap measure than a viable substitute for a healthy national filmmaking apparatus, and British cinema was once again in need of a course correction.

It was in this artistically barren environment that Queenie, after five months of working at the Café de Paris, scratched her way to her first screen test opposite the established actor Carl Brisson. She had never before seen the inside of a studio; nobody had explained the mechanics of moviemaking to her. She entered a large, crowded room and spotted Brisson sitting in the center. She reached out to shake his hand. He grabbed her hand, pulled her into his lap, and started making aggressive advances upon her. She recoiled in horror, fighting back with a chair, unaware that this was how things worked in the industry she so desperately wanted to join. She had no idea that Brisson's violative behavior was, in fact, part of the required scene in her screen test. All anyone else could do was laugh at her immaturity. Queenie's humiliation was their entertainment.

Sloughing off the indignities, Queenie briefly considered making dancing her career, so she began dance classes at the academy of Victor Silvester, who was charmed by this pretty flower from India. She became one of his most promising students, only for her to burst into tears when she failed an especially tricky ballroom dancing exam.

Meanwhile, back at the Café de Paris, men who would become

familiar to Queenie later in life encountered the unpolished version
of her. A British soldier named David Niven, who would break her
heart in Hollywood a few years later, sat in the crowd, as did the actor
Douglas Fairbanks Jr.—a subsequent friend, and the son of a future
costar—and the director Victor Saville. It was Saville who first threw
a crumb at her: Smitten with this hostess's beauty, he cast her as an
extra in his film *A Warm Corner* (1930). Queenie was delighted. Yet this
was one of a handful of parts—if one could even call them that—of little consequence that she would essay in the early 1930s as she awaited
her chance for a breakout role; extras like her didn't get screen credits.
She put herself through the downtrodden starlet's diminishing rite of
passage by going to the cinema hall to watch movies she remembered
she'd been in, unable to find herself on-screen.

As Queenie reached for a real foothold in the film industry, she
began to date a few well-connected men associated with the Café de
Paris who potentially could help her reach her goal. There was almost
always a clear power differential in her relationships with these suitors,
as they tended to be older, wealthier. She fell for Leslie Hutchinson, or
"Hutch," a Grenada-born Black singer and pianist who performed at
the venue. He was more than a decade her senior and saw her determination to succeed as a winning trait, not to mention her beauty.
But she was also young, naive, and had not come into herself yet, thus
untouched by vanity—qualities Hutch would have found alluring. She
likewise found a companion in the white American socialite Charles
Sweeny, two years older than Queenie. She was always very conscious
of having a lower status than most women men like Sweeny dated
because of her class and race, and Sweeny was skittish about being
associated with an Anglo-Indian girl whenever she asked him to take
her to venues like the exclusive 400 Club. But Queenie was a charmer.
She knew Sweeny liked her, so she made sure he honored her requests.
Other diners there would slip notes to Sweeny, telling him that he
was with the most beautiful girl they'd ever seen. When Queenie told
Sweeny about her acting aspirations, though, he had misgivings. He
told her she had to change her name, for starters. Maybe something

Shakespearean. On a whim, he suggested *Oberon*, alluding to the medieval king of fairies in William Shakespeare's *A Midsummer Night's Dream*. She liked the sound of it.

As Queenie continued her work at the Café de Paris, she took a sincere interest in the artists whom the café lured—and not just for romantic purposes. She would often arrive early for her evening shifts to listen to the crooning of the American singer and actress Ethel Waters. As a Black woman, Waters had had to fight hard to earn respect in the American entertainment business. The two women would speak frequently. Waters was struck by this pretty thing who looked "Javanese" to her. Queenie told Waters of her ultimate fantasy.

"Do you think I could make good in Hollywood?" Queenie asked Waters one night. "Should I take the gamble and go there?"

Waters paused for a beat to study Queenie's face. She could see a fundamental sweetness that could carry Queenie far. "I think you'll make good," Waters replied. "Go to America. Take the chance." Though it would take some time for Queenie to heed that advice, that vote of confidence lingered in her mind. She began to calculate a brighter path to fame, dreaming of being elsewhere.

★

THOUGH WATERS MAY NOT have been aware that this ethnically ambiguous girl was South Asian, there were dangers for Queenie in being in America. Phobias about South Asian immigration had infected the American public mind since the start of the century—so much so that the country had enshrined that discrimination in law. "Have We a Dusky Peril?" blared a 1906 headline in the *Puget Sound American*, a newspaper in Washington state. The article decried the entry of "Asiatics with their turbans" who spurred white Americans to worry about their security, labeling the invaders as "Hindu" (a catchall term for South Asians regardless of religious affiliation). These immigrants were Punjabi Sikh men who had immigrated to Canada by the thousands and, fleeing the racism they encountered there, traveled across the border into the American city of Bellingham, Washington, only to find prejudice there, too. "Thousands of worshippers of Brahma, Buddha, and other strange deities of India may soon press the soil of Washington," the article warned, fanning prejudicial flames.

Violence sprang from this rhetoric: A year later, mobs of the city's white lumber-mill workers went door to door to the homes of South Asian immigrants, breaking windows, beating them, and driving them out. Such naked bigotry led the 1911 US Immigration Commission, a government committee, to label South Asians "the least desirable race of immigrants thus far admitted to the United States." This in turn set the stage for the passage of the Immigration Act of 1917, which prevented the legal entry of immigrants from an "Asiatic Barred Zone" that included South Asia. Adding to the injury of this law was a unanimous 1923 Supreme Court ruling that decided South Asian immigrants were ineligible from becoming American citizens because of their race. The man at the center of that case, a Punjabi immigrant named Bhagat Singh Thind, engaged in a desperate and ultimately ham-fisted attempt to retain his citizenship, weaponizing his high-caste identity as evidence of his Aryan purity in a bid to situate himself within whiteness. That failed: The ruling against him stalled legal, documented immigration of South Asians to America for more than two decades, while South Asians who were already in America found themselves denaturalized. Some even died by suicide as acts of protest.

This was the hostile backdrop against which the Anglo-Indian actor William Henry Pratt—better known to filmgoers by his stage name of Boris Karloff—began his Hollywood career in 1919. He was one of the few South Asian performers who had managed to make any progress against the hostile headwinds of the Anglo-American film industries at the same time Queenie was itching to get her start. Growing up in England, he and his siblings, born to two Anglo-Indian parents, were subject to bullying due to their dark skin; upon immigrating to Canada—and later America—as an adult, he would remake himself as Karloff. The election of a stage name was not an uncommon phenomenon for working actors, but Karloff's re-baptizing had the added effect of preemptively waving away questions that his clay-brown complexion instigated. Karloff would pretend that his mother, who was white and South Asian like Queenie's, was Russian, as if his Slavic-sounding surname might explain what magazines and newspapers of the era called his "swarthy" looks. He banked on the gullibility of moviegoers, and his gambit worked: Karloff assumed roles of various races throughout his career, all while keeping his own heritage confidential. In such films as Stuart Paton's *The Hope Diamond Mystery* (1921) and James Young's *Without Benefit of Clergy* (1921), Karloff even played South Asian characters (such as a "Hindu servant") alongside white actors who greased their complexions to match his, a practice known as "brownface."

Cosmetic techniques like brownface were common in American cinema during that time. Films such as Phil Rosen's *The Young Rajah* (1922), for example, featured the Italian-born actor Rudolph Valentino, a leading star of that era, with a bronzed face and wearing a jeweled turban as an Indian prince. The film reflected Americans' general cultural posture toward South Asians, believing them to be otherworldly mystics possessed of spiritual gifts so puzzling that they barely seemed human. Americans' slack-jawed fascination with South Asians during the early twentieth century was often plainly xenophobic, with a heady dash of racism. Karloff slogged his way through violent, dark roles until parts with real substance came in the early 1930s, when he played monsters like the patchwork humanoid in *Frankenstein* (1931), and menacers like the long-slumbering Egyptian priest Imhotep (and his human avatar, Ardath Bey) in *The Mummy* (1932), and finally became a star. His casting capitalized on viewers' impressions of him because of his skin tone: He was an imposing outsider who had to earn American sympathy.

Despite such limited opportunities for South Asian performers, Hollywood would have been an ideal place for someone like Queenie to set her sights, just as Karloff had before her. The most popular actresses among British moviegoers in 1931 all tended to be Hollywood stars. At the very top was Norma Shearer—who would play a major role in Queenie's life just a few years later—along with Constance Bennett, Marie Dressler, Ruth Chatterton, Janet Gaynor, and Greta Garbo. It seemed, that year, that British cinema was unable to manufacture its own stars on the same scale as Hollywood, despite the surfeit of talent within its borders.

Queenie became aware of this when a director named Miles Mander spotted her at another routine audition, struck by her amber skin and the long, fake-astrakhan-lined overcoat she wore. He took her out to lunch, where Queenie told him of her ambitions to be a movie star at any cost. Impressed, he wrote a small part for her in a film where she miraculously survived any cuts: *Fascination* (1931), a drama in which she appeared for under thirty seconds as a woman dressed in a ghostly veil selling flowers to rowdy nightclub revelers, all of them white. Queenie seemed fearful, unsure even of where to fix her eyes when standing before the camera. She had few lines, delivering them so quietly she was practically inaudible. "What an exotic-looking creature! Are you Egyptian?" a character exclaimed of her. (Her mother was Spanish, she replied.) Mander, despite giving her a puny part, believed in this girl and tried to introduce her to every other director he knew in England, but none would bite. Filmmakers just didn't know what to do with someone so distinctive. In a sea of flaxen-haired beauties who dominated British screens, she was hard to classify.

"Queenie? Queenie Thompson? Where are you?"

The assistant director's voice summoned her onto the underlit stage at the British and Dominions Imperial Studios, just north of London. Mornings there began early, around 7 a.m., when a crowd of about twenty actors would hover at the door in front of the set. All that was required of an extra like her was someone who could show up on time and work for scant pay. Despite her piecemeal accumulation of bit parts by the time she began working on this tiny film called *Ebb Tide* (1932), Queenie was meerkat-shy before the camera. She could hold court in extravagant settings such as the Café de Paris, but sustaining composure before a set and crew was a different matter.

Queenie plopped her petite frame onto a piano in a makeshift bar-room. Beside her was an actress she'd never met, a moon-faced British debutante named Joan Winnifrith, who would adopt the stage name Anna Lee the same year as *Ebb Tide*'s release. Almost two years younger than Queenie, she, too, was a film novice, though she was equipped with some formal acting schooling—certainly more than Queenie could claim to have. Queenie's only acting teacher was the camera.

"We're supposed to sit on the piano and pretend to sing," Anna told Queenie. "I'm rather nervous. Are you?"

"Yes," Queenie replied. "I always am."

Queenie's task that day seemed simple enough: The two women were supposed to dangle their legs back and forth as they sat on the piano. They were playing sex workers. Queenie was then to jump off the piano during the scene, scamper up a staircase, open the door at the top, peer inside, and scurry back down while Anna stayed put. Easy. The take began. Queenie, fidgeting, did as she was told, hopping down from the piano and rocketing up the stairs. But the door wouldn't budge. Queenie's response was visceral, immediate: She began to cry. Anna completed the bit instead while Queenie muffled her sobs.

After shooting concluded that day, Queenie was shivering while waiting for a bus as rainwater dampened her flimsy cloth coat. Anna came across her and, taking pity, offered her a ride back to London and supper at the flat where Anna lived with her godmother. Anna handed her a lap rug as Queenie got into the car. After a few moments of silence, Queenie quietly asked Anna if there was a bath in her flat. There was, to Queenie's relief: She had been fantasizing about sitting in a lagoon of balmy bathwater that would rise to her neck. In her girl-ish excitement, she was unable to contain the singsong lilt to her accent that she'd managed to suppress on set. Anna could hear the difference.

Upon reaching Anna's home, Queenie hung her soggy clothes to dry before the fireplace and slid into one of Anna's dressing gowns. Then, the two sat at the dinner table with Anna's godmother. Queenie took two helpings of everything, pouncing at the roast beef and York-shire pudding as if she hadn't eaten a meal since birth. When Anna's godmother asked Queenie where she was from, Queenie was honest: She came from Calcutta. But she clammed up when Anna's godmother asked Queenie whether her mother was with her. Queenie wasn't sure what to say. "I have no mother," she responded, her gaze downcast. Anna didn't press her on the matter. Queenie then took her postpran-dial soak in the palatial tub, perfumed with lavender bath salts. Tying up her dark hair, she told Anna that, one day, she would have a big bathroom of her own, as large as this one.

Queenie would frequently go over to Anna's flat to take baths, and they became best friends in the weeks that followed, with Anna supplanting the void Phyllis Beaumont had occupied in Queenie's Calcutta life. Despite Queenie's timidity before the camera, she had continued to use her sexuality to advance her prospects, just as Char-lotte had encouraged back in India; this collision of traits struck Anna as incongruous. How was this fragile deer of a thing the same woman who wanted to become a globally famous actress? On their long walks through Kensington Gardens, Queenie disclosed the scale of her ambi-tion: She wanted to be a star, the greatest in the world. "I don't care what I do or who I have to sleep with to get there," she said. "But *I will get there.*" Anna wasn't comfortable with the idea of having sex with someone you didn't love just for the sake of your career. But this was a reality of life Queenie had accepted. She also knew that subduing her heritage was part of this game. Queenie would keep mum about her racial origins with her new best friend.* One day, Queenie ran into Anna while walking past Harrods, the department store, with

---

* Anna Lee claimed that she herself was among the casualties of Queenie's climb to stardom: Queenie would become more of a stranger to Anna in the decades that followed, by which point Anna would piece together that the quiet brown woman she'd seen was really Charlotte. In her memoir, Anna wrote of coming to terms with Queenie's distance, understanding why Queenie would want few reminders of her past. Still, Anna was present at her old friend's eventual funeral in 1979, indi-cating that there was still fondness present.

Charlotte, who was draped in a sari. Before Anna had the chance to speak to Charlotte, Queenie interjected, explaining that this brown lady was her maid. She didn't speak any English, Queenie added, hoping that Anna would take her at her word.

★

THE STUDIO CANTEEN AT the British and Dominions Imperial Studios thrummed with hopefuls that morning in early 1932. Having come there for a screen test, Queenie was waiting in line for tea when an actress named María Corda, more than a decade her senior, got lost in the story of her face. Corda's career as a film actress had reached a dead end at that point; her Hungarian accent had the harsh clank of metal, making her ill-suited for the talkies. Privately, she thought of Queenie in hideous terms: this "little black half-caste Indian girl." But even within the smog of her racism, Corda couldn't deny that Queenie was a knockout. The woman grabbed her ex-husband, a man with whom she was still in love (so much so that she would often bicker with him in his office). Alexander Korda was the founder of London Films, a company that he had begun in February; his brothers, Vincent and Zoltán, were also involved in the venture. She pressed her nails into his arm so hard he spilled coffee on his trousers. "There she is, you fool! Look at that face!" Corda said. "It's worth a million pounds. *There* is your damned Anne Boleyn."

Korda, a bespectacled man nearly a foot taller than Queenie, was prospecting for an actress who could inhabit the crucial role of the doomed sixteenth-century queen in his forthcoming film, *The Private Life of Henry VIII*. As he studied this twenty-one-year-old girl, Korda realized his nagging ex may have been right. He'd hit pay dirt. Korda sidled up to the table where Queenie sat and introduced himself to her. "I want to see if there's anything behind this face of yours," he told her.

A shrewd businessman, Korda was a foreigner to Britain who had managed to make something of himself, despite the tumbledown circumstances of his childhood. Born as Sándor László Kellner in 1893, in the village of Pusztatúrpasztó (in what is now Hungary), he grew up a peasant. He lost his father at thirteen, leaving him, his mother, and two younger brothers in poverty—not unlike Queenie—forcing him to effectively become a father early in life. When he began his career as a journalist in his home country, he was still a teenager. Nonetheless, his work soon put him close to Budapest's film industry; he edited a weekly program for the film company Projectograph and founded his own film journal before sliding into directing films. It was through this that he met the enterprising stage and film actress María Falkas, marrying her in 1919 and turning her into María Corda. (She wanted to retain an identity of her own rather than having any of her success attributed to him, hence her decision to replace the K in her husband's family name with a C.) Korda himself went through a series of revisions to his birth name throughout his early life before he eventually began to call himself Alexander Korda around the time of his marriage. This new name allowed him to obscure his Jewish origins in a virulently antisemitic era. Sublimating his identity in this way, Korda understood, was obligatory for creative survival. Any evidence of his Jewish origins could so easily deprive him of further career opportunities if he were to leave his home country—which he did.

By the time Korda got to Los Angeles in 1926, Hollywood had become the Mount Olympus of moviemaking, and what was known as the star system was slowly taking shape. A year after Korda's arrival, the increasingly pervasive use of sound—a new way for audiences to connect with performers—facilitated the creation of a grooming machine that turned on-screen talent into canvases for projection of an audiences' fantasies. The regimen of studios carefully manufacturing performers for celebrity would become standard by the following decade, when sound had all but overtaken American cinema. By 1930, Korda started working at the studio Fox, and he was particularly impressed by the star system. He saw how the studio passed off a Montreal-born girl named Yvonne Lussier as "Fifi D'Orsay," molding her into a French bombshell despite her having never lived in France, the country where her studio biography claimed she was born. What she gained with this colorful falsification, though, was a career.

Studios in Hollywood were self-sufficient behemoths, which inspired Korda to fashion a company of his own that could compete with America's big fish when he returned to Britain in the early 1930s, following a falling-out with his Hollywood bosses. British cinema was in shambolic shape compared to Hollywood's vigorous ecosystem across the pond, and Korda would eventually help change that. By the time he encountered Queenie, Korda had a deal with another prominent American studio, Paramount, to make quota films for British audiences, thus meaning that London Films was, in essence, an arm of Paramount tied to Hollywood. Aside from these workmanlike quotas, Korda also arranged a deal with the reigning British film distributor at that time, Gaumont-British, guaranteeing the screening of his non-quota films in theaters.

Brief small talk with Queenie that day was enough to convince Korda to sign her as a contract player, with the intention of building her into a star, as American studios often did to young actresses. But Queenie required more than garden-variety nurturing. The possibilities for full-fledged stardom for her would be limited because of her race, especially if she wanted eventually to go to America, a place she'd dreamed about ever since Ethel Waters planted the seed. And London Films would have to iron out a few kinks in her biography: her place of birth, her racial heritage, her class background. Queenie had brought her original file card, which was required of her at most auditions, and she'd written she was born in India. That was a problem, justifying the invention of an origin tale that fully recast her as white. Korda had also become fully enamored of the British Empire and its might, seeing its territorial conquests as a great national achievement for his adopted country; this attitude would only have increased his eagerness to erase Queenie's racial identity.

With the help of his London Films team, Korda decided to cook up a studio biography for her that would state that her father had been English, her mother French and Dutch. As for her birthplace, Korda and his team found an attractive point of origin for her in the heart-shaped Australian island of Tasmania. Once at the foot of the British

Empire, it was remote enough in the English imagination to register as what the era considered "exotic," just as Russia was for Boris Karloff. In this fabrication, India would remain within the frame, but not in such a way to suggest ancestral ties to South Asia: Now, Queenie's British Army officer father had died before her birth, after which she and her mother would move from Tasmania to Bombay to live with family, followed by Calcutta. (The associations with La Martinière and Calcutta Amateur Theatrical Society, or CATS, survived the studio's many strategic elisions.) Then, her uncle would take her on holiday to England, where she decided to stay. Done and done.

This elaborate studio fib was rarely consistent, contracting and mutating throughout Queenie's career; sometimes her father had died in a shooting accident, other times of pneumonia. In the press, her parents would become Irish, then English and French, then French and Irish. But London Films correctly assumed that few journalists would possibly have the energy to cross-check such claims for verification. Queenie was twenty-one when she signed with the company, negotiating the future of her career with a man eighteen years older who was handing her a better life. Her childhood in India had been pockmarked by pain and exclusion, and the opportunity to distance herself from the memory of a birth country she felt had shunned her would have had its own psychological allure. This Tasmania yarn would also give her the chance to fulfill her young life's great ambition: to become a famous actress.

With the matter of her origins then settled, Queenie and Korda then tried to finagle a stage name from her given one. Over the course of three weeks, they rotated through a gallery of them: Merle O'Brien (borrowing from Queenie's middle name). Merle Ashby. Stella Auberon. She pleaded with Korda to stick with Merle O'Brien, but he rebuffed the idea, insisting that O'Brien made her sound like any old bobby, or police officer, in New York. They tried more permutations. Queenie thought Merle Auberon was the next best option. They sanded away some more before landing on the spelling *Oberon* that her old boyfriend, Charles Sweeny, had proposed to her early in their romance, a compromise between Auberon and her desired surname of O'Brien. It was thus decided: From that point forward, Queenie Thompson, the impoverished Anglo-Indian girl from Calcutta, would live the rest of her public life as Merle Oberon, the white woman from Tasmania.

Chapter 3
Anne *Sans Tête*
(1932–1933)

Merle Oberon as Anne Boleyn in The Private Life of Henry VIII
(1933), the film that established her as a star in Britain.

THE NEWLY MINTED MERLE OBERON PLUNGED INTO DEEP
waters early on with London Films. She had considerably less experience than her fellow new contract players, some of whom had cut
their teeth on the stages of London's West End; all she'd done was
trill in the CATS chorus. This made her rather unusual for the era,
as most film aspirants had had some formal stage training. There
was also a class element dividing her from other talent: Would-be
actresses tended to be brought up in financially secure environments,
unlike Merle. Despite the pains Korda had taken to airbrush India

out of Merle's backstory, he felt that she fit the specific type of the so-called "exotic," the kind who could entice audiences in seductive roles befitting her saturnine looks. He thus slotted her into the cast of *Men of Tomorrow*, a drama in which she would play a collegiate vamp named Ysobel d'Aunay. Korda wasn't convinced that she could handle a broader variety of roles at this larval stage, which irked Merle: Now that a production company had given her a shot, she wanted desperately to be a star. When Merle tested for the role of a secretary in the film company's inaugural title, *Wedding Rehearsal*, Korda—who was directing—felt that she was unsuited for the part of a timid-seeming wisp of a girl hiding behind granny glasses. The actress Ann Todd, a banana blonde, landed the part instead.

But Merle's fortunes turned when Todd was injured in a car accident just as filming was set to commence in May 1932. His hands tied, Korda eased up and let Merle step into the role, which required little from her beyond radiating meek charm. The film followed a nobleman whose nagging grandmother sought to marry him off; he comically averted any prospects who came his way, oblivious to the fact that his grandmother's fey secretary, Miss Hutchinson, was besotted with him. "Hutchie," as the film called Merle's character, was a drab duckling of a girl who would undergo her swan transformation as the film progressed, ditching her glasses to reveal the true looker who'd been lurking beneath all along. She and the nobleman would marry at the story's end.

For all her desperate ambition to land the part, Merle became nervous about this golden opportunity. She kept to herself on set, for she was so different from all the other hoydenish girls at the studio. She hadn't yet wrangled her accent, an embarrassment for her that would have made white Brits cringe, but the film, mercifully, gave her very few lines. (Years later, aided by a vocal coach, she would paper over her natural drawl with a polished Mayfair accent.) But at least she had that "money face" that had mesmerized María Corda, and the film lavished Merle with so many close-ups that reviewers couldn't help but take note of her when the film started screening that fall. Despite the film's failure to register at the British box office, the press gushed about this "bright and fresh" ingénue from Tasmania (a claim journalists bought wholesale). Yet there were foreshadowings of the omens that would haunt Merle as she tried to establish herself in her career. A few in the press did notice her "slightly slanting 'Sylvia Sidney' eyes," referring to the American actress of Jewish descent who had donned "yellow-face"—a stepsister to the practice of brownface that was prominent in both British and American cinemas—to play a Japanese woman for the lead role in *Madame Butterfly* (1932). There was danger in this comparison: Merle could forever be typecast, doomed to play the role of "the other."

Anxious to prove her versatility early in her career, Merle jumped right into *Men of Tomorrow* that summer, playing an Anglo-French vixen who would try to crowbar an Oxford student away from his faithful wife. This was the first of the London Films quota quickies for Paramount, and it would be lost in the following years; no known prints exist today. Korda did not want this film to be any thoughtless factory-churned product but rather a picture that would give his talent roster juicy material, which is why he hired Leontine Sagan, one of the few female directors Merle would work with during her career. Sagan's daring film *Mädchen in Uniform* (1931) had concerned the topic of same-sex affection at a girls' school, and it indicated that Sagan had a real singularity of vision. Despite hiring Sagan for this very reason, though, Korda was too much of a control freak to give her much artistic latitude. The two of them clashed: He wanted the film stripped of the psychological complexity that had animated Sagan's previous title; he expected a more anodyne movie concerned with the innocence of youthful love. For this new university setting in *Men of Tomorrow*, Sagan wanted to insert scenes that implied homosexuality, but Korda felt such thematic matter conflicted with the mandates of commercial cinema. Merle emerged from the scrum unscathed: The positive reaction to her work in *Men of Tomorrow* only seemed to confirm that London Films had a justified confidence in her. But the film, like *Wedding Rehearsal*, was a box-office disappointment. Subsequent months would bring a slowdown at London Films: Gaumont-British, dissatisfied with Korda's arrogance, told the company it would be ending their distribution partnership in December 1932.

London Films would begin 1933 trying to rescue itself from ruin, downsizing personnel to stay afloat. Though few could have predicted it, Merle would be a key player in keeping it alive.

THE PRIVATE LIFE OF *Henry VIII* would permanently alter the fabric of British cinema. The film—which eventually had a budget in the ballpark of $550,000, steep for a British production at the time—had initially been a tough sell to potential investors who were gun-shy about funneling money into a costume drama from a company nearly in arrears: A film about sixteenth-century Tudor England couldn't possibly right the ship for British cinema. After a series of dispiriting meetings with businessmen, Korda managed to convince an Italian financier to provide some money for the film. He also squeezed out a deal for United Artists—a Hollywood studio that primarily distributed the work of independent producers—to release the film in the United States. Korda found a prize asset in Charles Laughton, who would be his leading man; though he was British, Laughton had been under contract with Paramount in the United States, meaning that global audiences had some degree of familiarity with him. With all this support, the production became an inordinately intricate affair, unlike most projects that sound-era British cinema had ever seen. Korda's brother, Vincent, designed sets that vividly resurrected the period, while costumes—including, for Merle, a black dress with theatrically baggy sleeves, a necklace with the letter "B," and an ornate hairpiece—were scrupulous in their detail.

When filming began in May 1933, though, twenty-two-year-old Merle was incensed to learn that her role as Anne Boleyn amounted to a paltry few pages in the script. She had naively assumed this part would be of equal, if not greater, stature than her previous ones under Korda, even hoping that it might fast-track her to stardom. But

Boleyn, the second wife of Laughton's loutish King Henry VIII, would die roughly sixteen minutes into the film, guillotined before a crowd on false charges of adultery. The rest of the film would chronicle his four successive marriages. When Merle stood next to the four white actresses who'd play his other wives, she felt inadequate, wishing she were as pretty as they were. But she was determined to make a silk purse of this throwaway role. ("If I don't, they may get rid of me in a sub-title the way they got rid of Catherine of Aragon," she told a journalist a few years later, referring to the way the film shafted the king's first wife.) So Merle studied Boleyn, studied her life: She visited Boleyn's room in the Tower of London, read everything she could. She immersed herself in Boleyn's thoughts, imagining herself on the scaffold where the queen had been executed. She trained herself to cry without glycerin, the film world's synthetic shortcut for tears.

The set had its fair share of chaos. Laughton, an irascible man more than a decade Merle's senior, could be as temperamental as the king he played. He would sometimes wait for the crew to ready a shot before, with a wave of a hand, declaring himself not in the mood to proceed. In comparison, Merle was a proverbial nobody among the cast, and most of her scenes were shot near the end of the five-week production period. The crew had to exert extra sweat trying to light her properly because of her skin color, considerably darker than those around her. The film would begin on the morning of Boleyn's execution. "Will the net hold my hair together when . . . when my head falls?" she said as she preened before mirrors, fussing over the netting keeping her coiffure in place. Despite Merle's private protests about her truncated part, the role was designed to arouse the pity of the audience, and thus inevitably memorable. Her character joked that her name would forever be "Anne *Sans Tête*," meaning Anne without her head; she wondered aloud, in one moment dripping with vanity, "Isn't it a pity to lose a head like this?" Her character's fate was the most outwardly morbid element of a film that trafficked in the lighthearted. With its extreme close-ups of Merle's glassy eyes and quivering lips, the film bent over itself to underscore Anne Boleyn's exquisite agony. Merle's raw and empathetic screen presence elevated what could easily have been a negligible role. In those short scenes, she managed to suggest an entire emotional world for Anne Boleyn: delicate and strong, helpless and defiant in a single breath.

The experience of making *The Private Life of Henry VIII* helped Merle gain confidence in her own abilities. Still, she felt a flash of disappointment when she spoke with people who had watched the film after its release that fall. They told her they hadn't managed to spot her in the film. "Were you late? Did you see the execution?" she would ask them. "That was me." Merle worried that whatever she had done to make this role matter had not been enough, but once critics had their say, she had little reason to stew about the size of her role. Reviewers on both sides of the ocean recognized *The Private Life of Henry VIII* as a major work that startled British cinema awake from its stupor, crediting Merle as a chief factor in this cinematic triumph. Some critics praised the "spiritual insight" she brought to the role, while others noted that she touched "near perfection" in her portrayal. The rapture that Merle's performance spurred in both countries neutered any of her embarrassment about what had seemed like an anemic cameo. Even the film's financiers couldn't have foreseen that this girl would capture the hearts of audiences with her role. Something about Merle's unusual presence, so refreshingly disparate from that of other British screen actresses at the time, galvanized the moviegoing public starved for home-brewed talent.

Merle was not the sole beneficiary of the film's good fortunes: One journalist would later argue that Korda's success from *The Private Life of Henry VIII* was "as revolutionary to the British film industry as was the coming of the talkies." In March 1934, Laughton would receive the Academy Award for Best Actor for his brilliant work, while the film itself became the first British picture to garner a nomination for the Academy Award for Outstanding Production (what would later become Best Picture). That same year, United Artists extended and widened its distribution agreement with London Films, thus tying Korda—and, by extension, Merle—closer to Hollywood. What Ethel

Waters had told Merle—that America was worth a shot—seemed within reach after the film's release. Hollywood began circling; studio executives who'd previously ignored Merle's British screen tests took a second look. Britain's media pinned their hopes on "the woman who launched a thousand tears," as they called her, seeing her not just as the country's biggest movie star but as a potential crossover talent—a rare bird in those days. When Merle posed for a December 1933 issue of the British journal *The Sketch*—her bare chest obscured by a sheet, her eyes purring into the camera—the headline even trumpeted this faux-Tasmanian girl as "The Most Promising Player in the World."

With *The Private Life of Henry VIII* having raised her stock, Merle went back to the Café de Paris, the very place where she'd been a hostess a short time ago, now as a guest in the well-heeled crowd. The salary she collected from her parts under London Films allowed her to afford to dress in pricey Schiaparelli clothes and accessories. And, after years of living in that embarrassing flat without a bathtub, she moved into a posh home on Gloucester Place and took Charlotte with her, continuing the arrangement of star and servant they'd hatched in search of a better future.

Chapter 4

My One Ambition

(1934)

Merle Oberon with Leslie Howard in
The Scarlet Pimpernel *(1934).*

THE PRIVATE LIFE OF HENRY VIII BROUGHT MERLE CLOSER TO a life she and Charlotte hadn't thought possible. Alexander Korda, realizing he had a likely box-office heavyweight on his hands, loaned Merle out to filmmakers outside of London Films. He had imagined himself as a Hollywood mogul, so he ran his company much like an American studio, keeping his charges under strict orders. But he quickly learned that Merle was a star of another breed, one unwilling to slavishly remain faithful to her boss if doing so might keep her from reaching her full potential. Korda would have little choice but to share her. The British actor John Loder, who had played a secondary part in *Wedding Rehearsal*, had been poring over the rushes, or raw footage, for *Henry VIII* when he found himself spellbound by Merle. He recommended she test as the female lead for *The Battle*, an English-language production set in Japan during the Russo-Japanese War of the early twentieth century. After Sylvia Sidney (of *Madame Butterfly* fame) turned down the role, Loder felt that Merle would make a fine Marquise Yorisaka, a Japanese woman whose husband would ask her to tempt a British military attaché, only for her to develop genuine romantic longing for the enemy. Merle flew to Paris, where the film was shooting, and dazzled in her screen test. She clinched the part.

Merle's schoolmates at Calcutta's La Martinière had put her down because of those "chinky" eyes of hers; now, that feature proved an asset. The film required Merle to embody not only a cipher but a stereotype: that of a Japanese naïf whose pretense of docility masked her duplicity. She would be donning yellowface as Sidney had done for *Madame Butterfly*, her eyebrows obliterated to skinny pencil marks, her hair lacquered with a coconut-oil pomade and pinched in a tight bun, her eyes winged at their tips. The practice of yellowface was so normalized that participation was a condition of screen stardom. If Merle might have found the part demeaning, the system within which she worked left her with little power to voice any protest. From a distance, the part teemed with superficial parallels to Merle's own story: This was a woman coached to adopt Western habits—like smoking cigarettes and shaking hands rather than bowing when introduced to someone new, by a man (in this case, a husband) with far greater social capital than she had. Merle understood this woman's predicament well. Wanting to put her own stamp on the part, Merle even made a point of mixing flecks of gold dust into her makeup for the film, an embellishment she would later say gave her "a certain scrubbed look which I wanted my Japanese lady to have." Her skin's porcelain gloss, viewed on the black-and-white film, heightened the sense of exoticism others projected onto her.

Merle's commitment to her craft, though, registered as arrogance to the French crew. Another actress, Annabella, had played this role in the French version of the movie filmed and released earlier. Others on set suggested Merle watch those French-language scenes to save them some rehearsal time. But she declined: Merle, fearing she might internalize and inadvertently mimic Annabella's mannerisms, sought to establish herself on her own terms. This earned her an unflattering French nickname on set: She was *Merde* . . . in a word, *shit*. But Merle was proud of her performance in the film, unusually so. She felt that whatever training she'd begun to develop in *Henry VIII* she had sharpened with *The Battle*. On-screen, Merle kept her eyes perpetually downcast, her neck craned to a permanent bow, her gait staccato, suggesting occasional flickers of inner life within her character's containment. Her line readings had a soporific quality. (This was a film whose characters regarded Japanese people as "savages," its women as "slaves.") Though Merle's technique as a performer was not yet sophisticated enough for her to ably sustain elements like, say, a Japanese accent—a likely condition of the fact that she was also still trying to curb her Anglo-Indian accent—critics showered her with hosannas, revealing the period's appetite for this type of racial caricature. Merle proved herself to be not just "an exotically attractive creature, but an imaginative actress," one wrote; she was "convincingly Oriental," said another.

These reviews suggested that Merle was well on her way to becoming a serious actress, but bruising affronts to her talent lay in wait. Soon after *The Battle*'s completion, Korda gave the American director Bernard Vorhaus his blessing to borrow Merle for *The Broken Melody*, a low-budget production in London. She would play a poor Parisian landlord's daughter who had fallen in love with a tenant. Vorhaus considered Merle one of the most jaw-droppingly ravishing women he'd ever set his eyes on, an Aubrey Beardsley *Arabian Nights* illustration come to life.* She was quite clearly different from other stars working

---

* Beardsley was a Victorian illustrator known for his precise and decadent aesthetic, tinged with eroticism.

on British sets at the time. This gave Merle the most dialogue of any previous role, and she struggled to domesticate her speaking voice to match the conventions of the era. She couldn't help but have her accent slip out in certain lines and phrases: *tunes; time; courtyard*. And filming *The Broken Melody* came with other humiliations. The production budget was so horrendously tiny that, while filming, Merle fell from a makeshift fire escape, tearing her clothing and revealing her breast. She tried to take the incident in stride, seeing no shame in her sexuality. But the crew would play the rushes over and over again, ogling the momentary exposure of her body.

THE MORE TIME MERLE spent with London Films, the more it seemed British cinema would typecast her as the foreign soubrette. Korda's next role for her, in *The Private Life of Don Juan*, did not ease these concerns. Filmed in the spring of 1934, it had an astronomical budget close to $700,000—higher even than *Henry VIII*'s—indicating lofty artistic aspirations, an attempt to replicate the runaway success of that predecessor. This was a Seville-set comedy in which Merle was to be, in the argot of the film's credits sequence, "Antonita—a dancer of passionate temperament." Merle was once again asked to humanize an ethnic stereotype, that of the fiery Spaniard. "I thought I was dreadful in it," she'd say years later to a journalist. "I must feel a part, and for some reason I never could feel that one." *Don Juan* tanked at the box office upon its release later that year.

But this film was a significant step forward for one reason: It included an on-screen kiss for Merle. That kiss would have been verboten had viewers of the day known that Merle was South Asian, given the standards of the era that precluded on-screen interracial kissing. In the previous decade, the Chinese American actress Anna May Wong, a star of American film who had increasingly soured on the stereotypical roles offered to her on her home turf, migrated to Europe for rosier prospects. Yet England, one of her chosen refuges, wasn't devoid of occasional minefields. She would play the love interest of the white

English actor John Longden in *The Road to Dishonour* (1930). Absent from any frame of that film, however, was a kiss on the lips between the two principals, due to a mandate from the British Board of Film Censors, a body that allowed Longden to do just about everything short of kissing her. He could sit at Wong's feet, hug her, even peck her hand. But kiss her on the lips? Never.

And Hollywood was even more allergic to such displays of affection between white actors and performers of color. The very year of *Don Juan's* release saw the trade body known as Motion Picture Producers and Distributors of America enforce the Production Code, or what was called the Hays Code, across Hollywood studios. The Code had been written in response to a series of sex and crime scandals that had disturbed Hollywood during the 1920s and tainted the industry in the public eye. Devised by the reactionary Joseph Breen, this censorious set of rigidities governing American studio films barred any suggestion of miscegenation, still illegal in the majority of American states, along with such unmentionables as homosexuality. The text of the Code specifically outlawed intimacy between Black and white characters. (What is perhaps Hollywood's most famous chronicle of racial passing, John M. Stahl's *Imitation of Life*, came out that year and posed a real test to censors unsure of how to deal with the topic of a light-skinned Black woman passing for white.) The nature of the Code's chilling effect was such that there was widespread resistance to depictions of interracial romance between white actors and *all* performers of color, Black or otherwise.

Both British and American cinemas, then, were becoming ever more fraught terrain for the likes of Merle. Openness about her South Asian ancestry would have carried the risk of any leading roles evaporating. To offset any questions about her race at this chrysalis stage, Merle poured her efforts into growing her reputation as a public beauty. She stood for pictures so often that one tabloid joked she was England's most photographed woman. She posed in ads for Ovaltine, for Lux soap, for Potter & Moore's Mitcham Lavender Powder-Cream, a product that she claimed gave her skin the radiance

necessary for roles such as Anne Boleyn. Appearing in these advertisements was common for any up-and-comer in the film world, but
for Merle, this kind of visibility—particularly when it came to ads for
complexion care—had the bonus of allying her with whiteness. Such
positioning would serve her well in America, where the growing
encroachment of the Hays Code, as well as immigration law, would
make life so precarious. Despite the risks, Merle knew that Hollywood might offer her career the chance to soar that Britain could not.
Her success in *Henry VIII* started to seem like a one-off; British cinema's opportunities still paled in comparison to America's. As Merle
mulled over a transition to Hollywood, Korda pushed her into *The
Scarlet Pimpernel*, which was to begin shooting in August 1934 after
the *Don Juan* production wrapped. In it, she would play another foreigner, this time the French wife of an English baronet. But in that
downtime between production schedules, Merle would escape to the
French Riviera, a detour that would, without warning, expedite her
transition to Hollywood.

★

SHE HAD MET HIM once before earlier in the year, in England, but
Merle sparked to Joseph Schenck once they reconnected in Monte
Carlo that summer. Schenck was one of the most well-known—and
well-liked—men in Los Angeles. He was the president of United Artists, with whom Korda had that distribution deal, and a cofounder
of the associated production company Twentieth Century Pictures,
which had been formed in 1933 and had its films distributed by United
Artists. During the years that followed the Great Depression, Hollywood became highly consolidated and corporatized, resulting in the
emergence of what was known as the Big Five, a quintet of studios
comprised of Paramount, MGM, Fox (Korda's former employer, which
would merge with Twentieth Century to form Twentieth Century–
Fox in 1935), Warner Brothers, and RKO. In this vertically integrated
configuration, these studios controlled the three crucial stages of film
production, distribution, and exhibition. All of them owned movie

theater chains that allowed them to dominate the market, guaranteeing steady audiences for the films they produced. Rounding out this ecosystem were the Little Three: Universal and Columbia—production companies that, while not owning theater chains themselves, nevertheless had robust distribution strategies—and United Artists, a distributor that released films for independent filmmakers through the theaters that the Big Five owned. These studios also employed thousands under contract: directors, producers, performers.

As for Schenck, he had a reputation, as one newspaper put it, for being "a phlegmatic but outspoken fellow" whose fifty-two years aged him beyond an emerging screen talent like twenty-three-year-old Merle. He also had his eccentricities: He loved playing golf so much that he wore golf knickers to work, despite reportedly being terrible at it. He, like Merle, was an outsider to the film world, having come to the United States from his Russian homeland when he was in his teens. Schenck had worked in a drugstore and even built an amusement park before he became involved in the film business. Now, he was Korda's superior.

Merle knew they were an odd pairing. He was so much older than she was; he came from a universe where she did not yet belong. But as she got to know him, Merle recognized that Schenck could offer the same opportunity for betterment she'd seen in Ike Edwards: a man who could open the world to her and give her the life she desired. Schenck was freshly divorced from the actress Norma Talmadge, and Merle was a hot prospect primed to make inroads in Hollywood, a domain over which he reigned. Despite their apparent mismatch in demeanors—when they cavorted about Monte Carlo, Merle dressed casually in shorts and a sleeveless blouse, Schenck in a dour suit and tie—Schenck was moonstruck. In a whirlwind courtship, he asked Merle to marry him that very summer. Merle, realizing what this man might be able to do for her career, said yes, though on a trial basis, hoping it might buy her some time to calculate whether this decision was really to her benefit. In this world, even romance had a transactional component.

Merle agreed to spend a few months away from Schenck before their marriage in Hollywood that fall. The hoopla surrounding the unlikely twosome propelled her profile in the American film industry, exposing her name to a galaxy of power players who would soon become major figures in her life. Schenck cabled the influential producer Samuel Goldwyn, who released his films through United Artists, about his pairing with Merle; their engagement also put her prominently in front of the producer Darryl Zanuck, Schenck's fellow Twentieth Century Pictures founder. Zanuck was, like Korda, an ambitious upstart. He had previously been with Warner Brothers, one of the Big Five, leaving in 1933 to form Twentieth Century with Schenck. Sensing money in Merle, Zanuck arranged a deal with Korda to borrow Merle for Hollywood films under Twentieth Century. Zanuck decided to cast her that summer as the lead in her first Hollywood film, the musical *Folies Bergère de Paris*. The expectation among the Hollywood commentariat was that, by the time filming began for *Folies* later in 1934, Merle would be "Mrs. Schenck," as the papers began calling her. But after saying yes to Schenck's proposal, Merle soon learned he wanted that film to be her last, much to Merle's dismay. His harsh requirement for her marriage was that she cease acting altogether. He felt a woman belonged in the home. As she began shooting *The Scarlet Pimpernel*, Merle started to resent Schenck's notion that this acting thing of hers was a hobby for amusement. That film, however, would give her yet another reason to reconsider her betrothal.

★

THE SVELTE LESLIE HOWARD was the perfect embodiment of the Scarlet Pimpernel, an English baronet named Sir Percy Blakeney who led a secret parallel life as a masked hero rescuing French noblemen from execution during the French Revolution. The British-born Howard's lanky carriage did not immediately suggest swashbuckling chivalry, but he had his own brand of charisma that made him intoxicating to watch, particularly in this role. Merle was enthralled by him when they began shooting *The Scarlet Pimpernel*, based on an early twentieth-century play and novel by the writer Baroness Orczy. The film was directed by the rather green American Harold Young, a former supervising editor for London Films installed to helm this film after the first director—another American named Rowland Brown—clashed with Korda over a lack of creative freedom. Merle would play Blakeney's wife, Marguerite, a Frenchwoman who had been an actress before marriage. Their union was an unhappy one: Marguerite would feel neglected by a spouse who was absent so often that she began to suspect he had contempt for her, not knowing that he was the same gallant man of mystery about whom she kept hearing.

Eighteen years older than Merle, Howard had been acting for nearly two decades across both stage and film. He had the affect of a stern intellectual, and he found Merle to be a woman of considerable self-possession who knew what she wanted and how she might get there with her streak of fierce independence. He also admired her liberal political slant. Yet there were practical impediments to their pairing—namely, that he was married, though he had already made a name for himself as a womanizer. No matter. It wasn't long before Merle fell fully, thoroughly in love with him, waiting for the telephone to ring so she could hear his voice. In public, they would paw at one another, so much so that some of Korda's staffers would even tell them to tone down the playfulness.

The electricity between Howard and Merle carried over to the filming of *The Scarlet Pimpernel*, where Merle made her character's need for her husband's love—and her renewed passion for him after discovering his heroics—so moving that they formed the emotional fulcrum of the film. In lesser hands, this role could have been that of a flowerpot: Merle was gussied up in vivacious attire, with bosomy, low-cut dresses that emphasized Marguerite's ability to use her good looks to get her way in the world. It would take Merle as long as fifteen minutes to squeeze herself into some of the costumes. She would sit on a dais while posing for a portrait in her first scene, a total vision sneaking bonbons into her mouth. The black-and-white cinematography of Harold Rosson added a coat of mystery to her beauty: The locks of her hair resembled licorice, her nose curved like her mother's. No prior film had bottled Merle's star quality quite as tightly. Beyond just seeming like an opaque temptress, though, Merle managed to project her character's humanity. Despite her impressive work, Merle hated herself in the film once again. "Leslie's superb, but my Heavens! I'm awful," she told a journalist. She felt herself strumming the same notes in each movie; she was forever the vulpine siren, unable to escape the strictures she felt Korda had imposed upon her. Merle's ungenerous self-assessment didn't align with the critical approbation of her. Reviewers by and large considered it her finest performance to date when it was released in late 1934. Commercially speaking, the film even outgrossed its high budget.

Despite being the toast of British cinema, Merle could not stay in London forever. America, and the variety of roles available to its leading actresses, still would have seemed more artistically fertile ground for her. Based on the strength of this work, the momentum of her career would have made it foolish for her to bow to Schenck's dictate that she give up acting. Just as *The Scarlet Pimpernel* finished production that fall, Schenck, sensing Merle had cooled on their imminent marriage, journeyed to London. For Merle, the peculiarities of their pairing had crystallized in her mind's eye, and she was finally able to become honest with herself: He'd do more harm than good for her. The gulf in their ages really *was* too wide, for one. And she couldn't come to terms with his conviction that a woman's place was in the domestic realm. (There was also the minor issue of her affair with Leslie Howard, now in full throttle.) She felt she was too young to retire. Movies were her calling.

When she told Schenck this, he understood. This was Merle's first Hollywood coup, asserting that she would not let any man trample over her ambitions. The dissolution of Merle's engagement didn't impact her agreement to star in *Folies Bergère de Paris*. "And now my one ambition is to be a really good actress," she told a British journalist in a piece published in November 1934, galvanized by her dissatisfaction with her performances and wanting desperately to better her craft. Merle still had something to prove—not just to the world around her, but also to herself.

Merle would sail for America in mid-November of that same year. Her passage would mark the end of the make-believe arrangement she and Charlotte had sustained for five years; Charlotte was in her fifties now, dealing with a cocktail of illnesses, and she would not follow Merle to America. Merle wasn't certain when she'd see Charlotte again, but she made sure to allocate as much money as she could to ensure Charlotte's good health and a pleasant life. She left Charlotte in the care of a nurse, while also seeing to it that a local family would provide her company on lonely weekends. Despite these comforts, Charlotte, having finished playing the dual roles of mother and maid to a granddaughter who was now rocketing to fame, would begin to pine for India. She would write letters to her daughter, Constance Joyce, in India, saying that Merle was now in Hollywood making another picture. And she would see Merle's movies when her health allowed. As for Merle, this would be the longest she'd be without the woman she had thought of as her mother. No matter how far she traveled—no matter how often she insisted to journalists that she'd been born in Tasmania to white parents—Merle still thought of India as home. The passenger manifest indicated India as her birthplace as she set sail for New York, despite the dangers that disclosure would have exposed her to, given the restrictive immigration law against South Asians. Pretending to be an Anglo-Saxon girl who'd simply been born on the soil of the subcontinent was her best available option for safe travel. Merle had left India in search of something better. But she still couldn't fully let it go.

Chapter 5

To See My Mother Again

(1934–1935)

Merle Oberon and Samuel Goldwyn on the
set of The Dark Angel *in 1935.*

NEW YORK MADE MERLE FEEL LIKE A SMALL THING, WITH its skyscrapers and important people. She arrived there in late November of 1934, greeted by photographers who snapped her posing like a princess on her luggage upon docking. A more elaborate procession would await her when she traveled to Los Angeles by train near the end of that month. Leslie Howard's manager fetched her at the station, where an army of paparazzi hounded her, all eager to get a glimpse of this new stargirl. She felt she'd stepped into a fairytale, as if she were playing tourist, mesmerized by the whirligig of Hollywood and anxious to meet stars who had once just been names on a marquee. Her circle of trusted allies was small, and she had no mother figure here. Plus, she realized that most people in Hollywood knew about her purely through her association with Joseph Schenck, and though Schenck remained cordial with Merle, there was lingering resentment toward her from others in the industry for the very public way she'd broken off their engagement. Merle's frustration, even fear, that people did not take her seriously as an artist carried over from England to America, too, and she did everything she could to combat the perception that she was only some accomplished man's arm candy.

A knot of rumors followed her in transit, after all: That she had arrived in Los Angeles with a $50,000 wardrobe. That she was a husband-snatcher. That she was "a ruthless vamp and a girl who made the Northwest mounted police look like amateurs when it came to getting her man," as Louella Parsons, the notoriously acid-tongued doyenne of Hollywood gossip, put it so indelicately in a December 1934 profile of Merle. Celebrity gossip of this sort had been taking up real estate in newspaper columns as far back as the silent-film era, but by the 1930s, it had become a thriving industry in Hollywood, with the scoop-hungry Parsons being the pioneer. As a newspaper reporter in the 1920s, Parsons championed one otherwise maligned actress, Marion Davies—the mistress of the newspaper magnate William Randolph Hearst—so relentlessly that, with Hearst's help, she eventually began writing a nationally syndicated column on the latest industry happenings. By 1934, Parsons had become a figure of considerable influence, but she had counterparts across the country. Walter Winchell, for example, was a columnist who would report on New York goings-on, as was Ed Sullivan. There would be challengers to Parsons's position later in Los Angeles. Notable among them would be

Hedda Hopper, a proudly conservative former actress whose widely syndicated column gave her a national platform. The glamorous, British-born Sheilah Graham also had a syndicated column of her own that same decade. Merle had no way to know she would become a fixture of the columns of each woman, that Parsons and Hopper would even become her friends. But she would soon learn that she would need to curry favor with them, a requirement of her survival in an industry that could very easily have outed her.

Disarming them with her charisma wouldn't be easy at first, however, especially since columnists like Parsons already had fixed preconceptions of Merle. Merle's arrival in America generated such interest that Parsons lined up a lunch with her to profile her, par for the course for new studio-backed arrivals. A quick study of character, Parsons could smell how desperate Merle was to make new friends. While she and Parsons dined, Merle would scan the room for American stars such as Joan Crawford, Jean Harlow, Carole Lombard— women who occupied the very position Merle so desired. But to Parsons, Merle couldn't dream of competing with such women for one reason: Merle "is not beautiful. Her cheekbones are high; her eyes are not the large expressive orbs that we associate with screen beauty." To Parsons, Merle lacked apple pie appeal.* "But she has charm, great charm, and an engaging personality that must be irresistible to the many men who are reported to have found her attractive," Parsons added as a consolation, a sign of how far Merle's personality would carry her with women like Parsons who may have been put off by her unconventional appearance. Sheilah Graham, meanwhile, was repulsed by Merle's slatternly looks upon their first meeting, the wooly hair that had undergone overexposure to the sun. This casual cruelty, trading on the language of exclusion,

---

* That said, it should be noted that such assessments constituted a minority opinion. It's tough to find mentions of Merle's name in that era's papers without the words *exotic*, *beautiful*, or some combination of the two preceding it. Still, Louella Parsons's word carried great weight in its day, and one can only imagine how that may have contributed to Merle's feelings of isolation in such an unhappy time.

was a veiled way of suggesting that Merle did not fit Hollywood's established—white—rubric of beauty.

The female stars who dominated Hollywood in that era were, perhaps unsurprisingly, almost exclusively white. In the Great Depression years, movie stars had become hallowed idols in the American public eye, on par only with athletes. During a time of such economic gloom, their trajectories epitomized a dream of material possibility; it was thus no surprise that these aspirational images reflected the hostilities of America's broader racial hierarchy. In the years prior to Merle's arrival in Hollywood, the biggest female box-office draws in America included Marie Dressler, Norma Shearer, Joan Crawford, Janet Gaynor, Jean Harlow, Mae West, and Greta Garbo. All represented different types, and thus the compulsion to retrofit them into one mode would be inaccurate—Dressler, for example, was in her sixties and considered portly by that era's standards, while West, who played proud and sexually confident floozies, was a perennial challenge to Code censors. Hollywood was not necessarily allergic to foreign talents, either; Garbo had been born in Sweden. But the throughline that united these women was their whiteness.

Merle, with her looks at best ethnically ambiguous, represented a threat to that hegemony. Reporters in those days wrote about her features as if they were items on a cheeseboard: her "olive" skin, her "almond" eyes. More skeptical journalists attacked her with the possibility of unmasking. That December, the *Los Angeles Times* film critic Philip K. Scheuer, for example, openly asked Merle whether she was, indeed, Eurasian. Preserving her safety at what was essentially the start of her Hollywood career, she point-blank denied such an accusation. "I am French-Irish," she stated defiantly. Her mother, she said to Scheuer—contradicting herself—was "English on the paternal side and French-Dutch on the other." Scheuer belonged to a coterie of film critics whose assessments of films were populating American publications in the 1930s, a decade when film criticism was in its infancy as an established career. Reviews ran routinely in trade publications like *Variety* and the *Hollywood Reporter,* along with newspapers like the *Los*

Angeles Times, the *New York Times*, and New York's *Daily News*. The line between film criticism and gossip reporting occasionally became muddied; Scheuer was among the most prominent film critics working in Hollywood, though as a condition of his job, he occasionally dipped his toes into the same gossipy waters where women like Louella Parsons resided. Merle's insistences to Scheuer about her whiteness were firm, but the suspicions were unabating. When the *Washington Post* casually stated that her "parentage is one-half Indian (Hindu, not Dakota)" as a throwaway line in an article about rising Hollywood stars during her first few months in America, Merle was helpless, unable to interject with a rebuttal. She wasn't used to the forensic level of scrutiny in Hollywood compared to England, where she didn't have to field questions of this sort about her race; the notion of having a private life did not seem to exist in America. Merle would slowly come to understand that she would have to accept the constant glare of the spotlight rather than trying to dodge it if she were to have a Hollywood career.

Keep in mind that the overarching societal fear of "the Hindu," informed by restrictive immigration law that prevented the entry and naturalization of South Asians like Merle, still strangled the American mind. Boris Karloff had been able to dodge immigration law because of his birth in Britain, but Merle, born in Bombay, wouldn't be able to do so quite as easily. There were a handful of immigrants who flew under the radar of laws restricting South Asian immigration to America, or at least tried to, after the Immigration Act of 1917. Merle—whose South Asian ancestry, had the public found out about it, would have been enough to classify her as nonwhite and compromise her place in America—was one. In that period, other South Asian immigrants who had entered America after 1917, many of them Bengali Muslims, would acclimate to America by integrating into preexisting African American or Puerto Rican populations in neighborhoods like Harlem; meanwhile, male Punjabi immigrants who had already immigrated to America prior to 1917 would marry Mexican women in Southern California after subsequent immigration law made it impossible for their families from back home to join them in America.

But for Merle, assimilation into Hollywood's whiteness was the most realistic path toward acceptance in the industry. This was a necessity for her to have a career: Brownface still dominated the American screen when it came to depictions of South Asians. The year of 1935, when *Folies Bergère de Paris* would be released, saw the production of two Indian-set films, *The Lives of a Bengal Lancer* and *Clive of India*, in which non–South Asian actors would darken their skin to play South Asian roles; some would be outright villainous, as was the case with the former film's treatment of Mohammed Khan, played by the white actor Douglass Dumbrille.

No matter how strenuously London Films had coached Merle to stick to that line about her Tasmanian birth, plumes of suspicion about her ancestry—informed by America's broader cultural attitudes toward South Asians—surrounded Merle. Seeing her as a foreign interloper trying to edge her way into a town where she didn't belong, industry folk gave her a wide berth, omitting her from important party guest lists for those first few months. Jean Harlow was one of the only women to treat her humanely. Merle otherwise had a miserable Christmas season in 1934; all she could do was cry. Like some callow critter who naively thought things would be different, she dutifully made the rounds at industry gatherings to which she *was* invited, but she felt as she had as a seventeen-year-old girl in Calcutta: that nobody wanted to be her friend.

One night, Merle was on her way out of a party where she had felt cold-shouldered by everyone—as usual—when her heel caught the hem of her dress, sending her tumbling to the floor. Everyone stared. Some suppressed their snickers. But one woman in the crowd felt nothing but sympathy for her. Her heart went out to "Merlie," as she called this sad girl, from the second she saw her on the ballroom floor. This woman was Norma Shearer, nine years Merle's senior. Born in Canada, Norma was already among Hollywood's top actresses in both critical and commercial terms, with an equally influential husband in the powerful executive Irving Thalberg of MGM, one of the Big Five. Norma's supremacy in the industry had not come easily to her; a series

of setbacks in the prior decade, when she was trying to establish herself in roles of substance, had been quite similar to what she saw Merle
facing. Norma, who had begun her career in silents, was one of the few
actresses to retain her status as a box-office draw through the transition to the talkies. Like Merle, she lacked much in the way of theatrical
training, making her a rarity in Hollywood's bushel of stage-reared
talent. And she, like Merle, had a family secret that could vaporize her
career at any moment. Norma's sister, Athole, struggled with undi-
agnosed bipolar disorder. Norma would do her best to attend to her
sister's needs out of the public eye, for the stigma surrounding mental
illness ran so deep that even Norma would have been likely to face
disparagement by association.

Merle quickly found a sisterly ally in Norma, seeing in the older
woman the kind of star she hoped to become. Norma, for her part,
recognized her younger self in Merle, whose struggles were akin to
Norma's own early career travails. In some ways, the two women had
what the other so wanted: Norma possessed a proximity to power that
Merle desired, while Norma saw Merle—who already had a portfolio
of paramours and knew how to use her beauty for her own career
gain—as a sexually free being in a way Norma wasn't. Together, the
two women felt complete. The trust between the two flowered organi-
cally over Merle's otherwise lonesome first few months in Hollywood,
and Norma would become Merle's best friend. They grew so close that
Merle confided in Norma the most damning truths of all: that she'd
left behind a maid in London who was really the woman she knew
to be her mother, that she'd been born in India, that she was Anglo-
Indian. Norma understood what it was like to hide a part of yourself
that others would, unfairly, see as a handicap. To succeed in spite of
what you could not control. To avoid letting it define you.

★

MERLE'S ROLE IN *FOLIES Bergère de Paris*, for which filming stretched
into January of 1935, neither calmed the myriad questions regarding
her racial heritage nor slaked her thirst to become a well-regarded

actress. At first, she was dazzled by the mechanics of American film-making: She couldn't believe she had a bungalow that doubled as a dressing-room—and with wheels! "It is like living in an Aladdin's lamp palace all the time," she told one journalist. Darryl Zanuck was going to great lengths to groom her, spending exorbitantly—an estimated $20,000—for her makeup and wardrobe. But the experience went south soon, as it became more apparent that this role might forever narcotize Merle in the part of the "exotic" other, not unlike what she had been trying to escape by leaving England. In this film, based on a fanatically popular Parisian play, she would be the Baroness Gene-vieve Cassini, the wife of a philandering banker who cheated on her frequently. The role was a trifle, and it wasn't much different from those earlier supporting parts that had buried her in cosmetic artifice. Her hair was slicked to heighten her forehead. Her eyebrows were once again crayoned to faint parentheses. The far edges of her eyes were taped with strips of fish skin to give them a slant. This, combined with her own gold-dusted makeup that she would later say made her resemble "a girl from Mars," made Merle an object of derision when the film hit theaters that year. "This girl, the strongest femme lumi-nary in England, makes her first Hollywood appearance in this film, and it seems curious that she should have been brought clear across the ocean and continent for the assignment," *Variety* complained that February. More than one journalist said she looked as if her satiny face were a mask, not that of a human. The word *Oriental* ossified around her name. To reviewers, she was "Chinese," "Javanese"—take your pick from the continent of Asia. Anything but white.

Merle recoiled when she saw the film, hating the exaggerated slant of her eyes. Her racial ambiguity had been her stock-in-trade back in England, but America had a more unforgiving topography. She con-fused people. It didn't help matters that such films as *The Scarlet Pim-pernel* and *The Battle* (retitled *Thunder in the East* for Americans) were both in American movie halls around early 1935, while *Don Juan* was fresh in the country's memory. Merle's omnipresence in American theaters—in a year when eighty million Americans were visiting the movies every week—contributed to the impression that this greasy tropical creature was too incongruously different from any other female star to appeal to American audiences. It seemed, following *Folies Bergère*, that Zanuck's costly experiment in fashioning a new star in Merle had bombed, and she was no longer sure she would remain in Hollywood at all. She was homesick for London. Merle's personal life did not give her a compelling reason to stay: She asked Leslie Howard to leave his wife and child for her, wondering whether their relationship was more than a mere fling; he rebuffed her. Merle withdrew into herself so completely that she didn't think she'd ever be in love again. She was gearing up to defect from Hollywood in early 1935 when she learned that a producer named Samuel Goldwyn was hoping to cast a fresh-faced girl of the English countryside in a new film he was making. Merle thought she'd be perfect.

SAMUEL GOLDWYN WAS—LIKE ALEXANDER KORDA, like Joseph Schenck, like Merle herself—an outsider to the world of movies who yearned for assimilation. Though he'd been born in Warsaw as Szumel Gelbfisz, his enterprising spirit drew him to America in his teens. He remade himself many times over, first as Samuel Goldfish and then as Samuel Goldwyn. He sharpened his business acumen as a glove salesman before deciding that this new trade called moviemaking might be worth his while. As the founder of the independent company Samuel Goldwyn Productions during the 1920s, he developed a reputation as a king of star-makers. Talents he'd reared included Vilma Bánky, a Hungarian girl whose photograph he came across in a Budapest shop window, according to Hollywood lore. He launched her in America with *The Dark Angel* (1925), a silent vehicle in which she played a good-hearted girl named Kitty Vane, whose two childhood friends were jockeying for her affection in World War I–era England. The way Goldwyn saw it, the role of Kitty Vane was an actor's feast; he considered it the greatest ever written for a woman. Hearing that he now wanted to remake this movie she'd seen back in Calcutta as a talkie, Merle realized that working under Goldwyn could propel her career forward. To start, she worked to secure Myron Selznick, a top agent of the era, to represent her. He took a chance on her, despite the disaster of *Folies Bergère*, helping her worm into Hollywood's corridors of power.

For the role of Kitty, Goldwyn had initially wanted the English actress Madeleine Carroll, a wheatish-blonde Brit who'd been the lead in *Fascination* (1931), the film in which Merle had played the Egyptian-seeming flower seller. Worse, Goldwyn had seen Merle on the lot of *Folies Bergère*, a movie that didn't exactly convince him she could be this country-bred princess. She wanted to prove him wrong. And so, looking for a reason to stay in Hollywood, Merle cannonballed her way into the race for the role. She began soft-soaping Goldwyn by going through Korda, cabling her boss in Britain to say she'd just *die* if Carroll were to get the part. Word then traveled to Goldwyn, who was taken with her moxie. Goldwyn sensed a hunger he could capitalize on, a willingness to genuflect to the demands of the American movie market. But she had more people to persuade: *The Dark Angel's* attached director, Sidney Franklin—who'd directed Norma Shearer in a handful of films (and would later direct one of Hollywood's most notorious examples of yellowface, 1937's *The Good Earth*)—had seen Merle in *Folies Bergère* and found her too "Oriental" to play a typical English girl like Kitty Vane. Franklin wanted "a girl that could give me a great performance by acting ability," as he cabled Goldwyn, disbelieving Merle. Goldwyn's staff was iffy on her, too, thinking that she'd poison that virginal role with her "exotic" and "sexy" attitude. They thought she was only equipped to play, well, a Hindu by virtue of her appearance. Though Merle had gained more confident control over her accent by this point, she could only do so much to change her looks.

Goldwyn overrode these doubts, for he had long been on the hunt for a female star who could compete with the likes of Greta Garbo, jewel of MGM. He felt that Merle's sheen of exoticism with her dark features provided an exciting contrast to most other female stars inhabiting American screens, though those foreign qualities would not, he felt, deter audiences outright: Strip her of the maquillage and Merle could very well pass for a small-town English girl, Goldwyn thought. He had tried to pull a similar magic trick once before, with a blonde actress named Anna Sten, who had been born in what is today Ukraine, but she was a box-office nonstarter. So Goldwyn wheedled Korda to share Merle under a joint contract and make films for them both, beginning at an impressive $60,000 per picture. Goldwyn was determined to make Merle a transnational star unlike any Anglo-American cinema had witnessed. For an actress to skate between two English-speaking national cinemas was uncommon in that period; she had the added benefit that, no matter which country these films were made in, they would be distributed by the same company, United Artists, so long as London Films continued its partnership.

Korda was initially cool on the prospect of letting Goldwyn have so much access to a performer he considered his discovery, but Merle, wanting to make inroads in Hollywood, made sure she got her way. Korda also gained a firmer sense of Merle's gumption during this episode. She was flouting the unspoken rules of this system in which Korda would have wanted to control the talent in his stable and dictate the terms of their careers. But Merle's bid for the role in *The Dark Angel* was almost a statement of intent to Korda: Not even he could slow her drive. Korda's businesslike posture toward Merle was starting, in these moments, to give way to a feeling far deeper and more complex, though Merle still regarded him with hero worship. He was nothing more than her much older boss.

When Goldwyn took Merle on for *The Dark Angel*, he didn't think she was yet a great actress. "Now I believe I have discovered a rich vein of gold ore," he told the press about her, as though she were his loot. "But I shall not be satisfied to keep it as it is. I shall transform it into its pure, true form. I shall strip it of all the spurious metals and refine it into its elemental purity." Upon signing Merle, Goldwyn was well aware that Merle was Anglo-Indian. Starching her image would be one way to keep the truth at bay.

★

Offscreen, Merle's association with Goldwyn—along with the sisterhood that Norma had offered her—helped her integrate into the industry's upper crust. Slowly, at twenty-four, she was able to reverse her reputation as that friendless girl who'd landed on American shores only a few months earlier. Merle lived in a beachfront home in Santa Monica, the steps lapped by the waves. Next door was Norma, who would take her to parties at the beach houses of actresses such as Marion Davies. She won over attendees like Louella Parsons, who'd previously been so unkind to Merle in print. In her spare time, Merle fished—a pastime in Bengal—whenever she got the chance. She rose at 7:30 each morning to take her two Dalmatians, Entwhistle and Trubshawe, onto the beach. This was the kind of place she'd always fantasized about. It still amazed her that her neighbors were interesting to millions of people. "In my wildest dreams I never imagined myself living near these celebrities, of whom I used to read in magazines," she would write, incredulously, in a one-off newspaper article she penned. "Watching them on the screen, how could I hope to know them in real life?" Merle could slip into her bathing suit, hop over the fence, and swim in Norma's pool next door. She got to watch movies before they even hit theaters in Norma's projection room. Merle and Norma were practically fused at the hip, and Merle had a fast-developing affinity toward her young son, Irving Thalberg Jr.

Harboring dreams about one day marrying a man and having children of her own, Merle found a hopeful prospect in the up-and-coming David Niven, a former British Army lieutenant she'd met years earlier when she worked at the Café de Paris. He wasn't much like Leslie Howard; David was more of an easygoing outdoorsman with a goofy attitude, traits that appealed to the childlike part of Merle. (Almost a year older than Merle at twenty-five, he was clueless about how to be an adult. He looked like a fourteen-year-old when he tried to smoke cigarettes.) He also had a libido to rival Merle's. Upon arriving in Hollywood, David phoned her by chance, thinking she wouldn't have time to see him. Merle, eager to bounce back from Leslie Howard, immediately suggested they get a meal. She'd show him the ropes in this industry where he sought to make a dent, teaching him such basics as how to read a script before a camera. She escorted him to parties, too, as if he were her lapdog, and people called him "Mr. Oberon." Even though Merle served as David's de facto mentor, she felt she could be herself around him.

As she began filming *The Dark Angel* in May 1935, Merle was getting nervous about whether she'd really be convincing as a bangers-and-mash British girl. The casting announcement didn't go over well with the moviegoing public. "That girl should be the exquisitely dainty, ethereal type, not an Asiatic adventuress," one angry fan, remembering Vilma Bánky, wrote of the Kitty Vane role to the magazine *Picture Play*. Such aggression led Merle down a path of introspection from which she would not easily recover. Her sense of her own racial identity growing more tenuous by the day as she absorbed herself in this part, she sought to assert her whiteness in whatever way she could. For the purpose of convincing the public that she was, indeed, the right actress for the role, Merle began to distance herself vigorously from her racially ambiguous persona. She told journalists of the metastasizing insecurity about the word *exotic* that they had attached to her. What did *exotic* mean to her? "Smell of burning incense," she told one *Los Angeles Times* reporter. "Jasmine blossoms. Or heaps of gardenias all over the place. Pretty sticky. And a long, slinky black velvet dress." That word *exotic*, she said to another journalist that year, made her think of actresses like Anna May Wong, one of the few other Asian women in Hollywood at that time—and publicly known as such, unlike Merle, whose Asian heritage was a matter of speculation instead of accepted fact. For Merle, Wong was a useful foil, a prop she could use to establish her place in Hollywood.

Around that time, Wong was back in Hollywood gunning for the lead role of an adaptation of Pearl S. Buck's Pulitzer–winning novel *The Good Earth* (1931) as the Chinese farmer O-lan, only to discover that the role was off-limits to her because the white actor Paul Muni had already been cast as the male lead. She then tested for a more ancillary role before she recused herself from the casting process entirely, wanting no part in the circus she saw forming before her. "I do not see why I, at this stage of my career, should take a step backward and accept a minor role in a Chinese play that will surround me entirely by a Caucasian cast," Wong told a journalist. Given all that Wong was publicly battling just to have a career, Merle wanted everyone to know that she wasn't anything like her. Merle would rather have dropped out of films if she had to don another siren's costume. This was the psychological price of Merle's conditioning at the hands of the burgeoning star system in Hollywood: It warped her self-image.

But this revision of persona allowed Merle the luxury of a full commitment to her craft, which was developing considerably. During one week in which she had to cry, cry, cry constantly on the set of *The Dark Angel*, Merle ended up fainting and staying home to recover. At another point, she accidentally spent too much time in the California sun, allowing her natural complexion to emerge. When Merle returned to the set, the crew was horrified at how brown her skin had become. How would the camera be able to handle her? The film's cinematographer, Gregg Toland, was by that point Hollywood's most famous cameraperson, and Goldwyn's standby. He specialized in depth-of-focus photography as a gateway toward realism. Other cinematographers of the era lit their stars as if through a mosquito net to emphasize their youth, their beauty, their glamour. Toland eschewed this and other conventions; he wanted to achieve truth through his cinematography. Thus, the crew forced Merle to go through an entire day of skin bleaching at a beauty shop. In that decade, several cosmetic creams—Black and White Soap, Palmer's Skin Whitener Ointment, Elsner's Pearl Cream—were on the American market, targeting usually though not exclusively Black Americans. These products often lacked regulatory oversight; some contained harmful mercury. Merle was in no position to refuse. If this is what it took to become a well-regarded actress, so be it.

★

By the time of *The Dark Angel's* September 1935 release, review-ers were agog at seeing Merle shorn of her foreign plumage, calling her "something new under the cinema sun." Though watching the film today makes clear that Merle didn't quite have the candlepower to overcome her character's fuzzy lack of definition—she was doing her best to enliven a pencil sketch of a role, a paragon of purity—critics of the day were too distracted by her about-face to air protests. Thank goodness, they felt, she'd abandoned that bizarre helmet of shellacked hair she'd once sported for a wavy bob. "Merle Oberon plays her Occi-dental role as well as she plays Oriental roles, and is quite as beautiful and alluring," observed one reviewer. (Most other critics also pre-ferred her so-called Occidental avatar.) They admired her elocution, high praise for a girl who'd been wary of even opening her mouth because of the "chee-chee" accent that everyone had ridiculed. Such notices served as a significant marker of her progression, suggesting that she could indeed leave behind her Indian past. One reviewer even said that she was demure, wholesome, the kind of girl with gowns fit for Sunday school. This was clearly a star-making performance, aided by the Goldwyn publicity machine. Audiences readily agreed, with the box-office receipts for the film being further cause for celebration.

Near the summer's end, as Merle rode aboard a train snaking its way from California to New York for the film's premiere, Goldwyn cabled her with news of early responses. "The talk about the change in your screen personality is something that will make history," Gold-wyn wrote to her, with a touch of prescience. Alexander Korda, mean-while, told the publicity chief of London Films, John Myers, to arrange a reception for her, with a slightly proprietary attitude: "We all have to be very proud of her achievement as she was with us from the very beginning," he said to Myers. Around the time of the film's release, Korda continued to firm up his presence in Hollywood in a way that would have aided Merle's career: He became an equal partner in, and owner-producer of, United Artists.

As reviewers threw praise Merle's way for her conversion, the gulf between her public and private worlds was growing larger. Merle was posing in even more advertisements for Lux Toilet Soap and Max Factor, touting her fair complexion.* Nonetheless, there were still times when Merle yearned for India and the girl she used to be. She missed having people call her Queenie. Only a few people on this side of the world still did that. Within weeks of the film's opening, she realized she needed to return to London, at least for a bit, to reconnect with her past. "I am coming over for six weeks or two months," she told one journalist for the *Evening Standard*, a London newspaper, via telephone in September, "mainly to see my mother again."

---

* These advertisements would remain a crucial part of Merle's public image until the early 1950s, coinciding with the downturn of her Hollywood career and the gradual darkening of her skin with age.

Chapter 6

Papa Goldwyn, Father Korda

(1935–1937)

David Niven, Merle Oberon, Norma Shearer, and Irving Thalberg
in February 1936.

THE BRITISH PRESS WENT ALL OUT TO TREAT MERLE'S VISIT
as an occasion equivalent to a royal homecoming; her success across
the Atlantic had become a matter of national pride. She made stops
for soirées at her old haunt, the Café de Paris. Merle was aware that,
in secret, some in England were wondering indignantly what a girl
from a scorned corner of the Empire had done to deserve such attention. Still insecure, she feared that they were right: that she'd gotten lucky, that she'd fallen in with the right crowd at the right time,

that Samuel Goldwyn and Alexander Korda were the responsible parties for any fortunes she enjoyed. Merle still labeled her birthplace as Bombay, not Tasmania, on passenger manifests, despite the potential jeopardy to her career. The attachment she had to that homeland, the real one, remained.

After spending precious time with Charlotte, Merle darted back to New York at the end of October, reuniting there with David Niven. She realized then that he wasn't the monogamous type, as that sex drive of his could get him into trouble; he had carried on various affairs while she'd been away. But the affection between them was untarnished: He persuaded her to purchase a car so they could make a cross-country road trip from New York to Los Angeles rather than travel by train. She agreed, happily, having earned enough money to fund the trip (unlike David, still struggling). Such was her fame at this point that, when they stopped at a Chicago hotel one night, Merle had to don a disguise: She wore a black wig and dark glasses and called herself Mrs. Thompson, as if she were back in India again.

Samuel Goldwyn nearly keeled over when the couple returned to Los Angeles. He worried that Merle's public cavorting with David might infect the chaste image that Goldwyn had been crafting for her. Goldwyn's next project for her was an adaptation of the firebrand playwright Lillian Hellman's controversial 1934 play *The Children's Hour*, whose initial text concerned lesbianism. The bowdlerized film adaptation was scrubbed of what the Hays Code termed "sexual perversity," where the themes of lesbianism were revised into a milquetoast heterosexual affair. Merle would play an American woman named Karen, who would open an all-girls school with her college pal, Martha (Miriam Hopkins). One obstreperous student named Mary would claim, maliciously and erroneously, that Martha was having an affair with Karen's fiancée, Joe (Joel McCrea). The scandal would close the school, irrevocably damaging the lives of Karen, of Martha, of Joe. The director of *These Three*, as the film would be called, was William Wyler, an immigrant like Merle, born in what is today France. A punctilious director, he would hack away at takes to achieve whatever picture of perfection existed in his mind, even if he could not articulate what, exactly, he wanted from the actors working with him.

It was during the filming of *These Three* that Merle found herself growing insecure, bordering on vain, about her star status. She panicked that Bonita Granville, the preternaturally talented young actress playing the diabolical student Mary, was getting too much of Wyler's attention. Merle did not yet have the experience, or confidence, to express these worries to Goldwyn herself. (She was twenty-four when the film began shooting, but she still had some childlike affectations; one quirk she couldn't shake in this period was her predilection for flopping around set in bunny slippers.) Merle asked McCrea to complain on her behalf to Goldwyn, who wouldn't budge. "I'm having more trouble with you stars than Mussolini is with Utopia," he crowed, referring to the Italian leader's pillaging of Ethiopia. Merle then tried to reason with herself: A real star would know when to leave her ego aside, when to cede the stage. She decided to relax. As a result, her skills as a dramatic technician—one who could cry at will, yes, but also detect a character's underlying soul—became more surgically precise, emerging in the eventual film, which opened in 1936. Yet Merle's fears were not entirely unfounded: The reviews for her were respectable, though not euphoric, as they were for Granville.

After this minor kick to her psyche, Merle received the validation she craved in February of 1936 with the announcement of the nominations for the Academy Awards. The awards had been established in 1929 by the Academy of Motion Picture Arts and Sciences, with the noble goal of becoming Hollywood's most prestigious form of recognition. (Merle's best friend, Norma, already had one of the coveted statuettes on her mantel.) It was this year when the award received the colloquial nickname of the "Oscar." That same year, however, saw the Academy Awards developing a spotty reputation as a crude game of politics where studios would try to jostle for dominance, rather than allow the awards to remain unbiased barometers of artistic excellence. For Merle, the Academy Awards would have represented everything she hoped for, acceptance from a hallowed elite.

So, in 1936, Merle happily found herself nominated for the Academy Award for Best Actress for her role in *The Dark Angel*. Merle was effectively an undergrad competing in the varsity division, and everyone in Hollywood knew it: Her fellow nominees included big shots such as Katharine Hepburn and Bette Davis, while her minimal stage-acting experience, unlike that of every other Best Actress nominee that year, also separated her from the pack. (CATS didn't really count as theatrical work; that was kids' play, and columnists often reminded her of that. "I'm still laughing," one wrote in derision when noting this factoid in her résumé.) But this lack of obvious credentials made her achievement all the more remarkable. The nomination was also a testament to the effectiveness of Goldwyn's relentless publicity campaign to scrub Merle's image—and whiten it. Until that point, the Oscars had been the exclusive domain of white performers, a reflection of the white-dominated industry itself. The Oscar celebration that year would be a sparser affair than usual: Three labor unions—the Actors Guild, the Writers Guild, and the Directors Guild—were encouraging their members to boycott it out of annoyance with the shabby way they felt studios were disrespecting their craft. But Merle went anyway, unwilling to forgo the biggest night of her career. The ceremony was finagled into a tribute to the director D. W. Griffith, a Hollywood stalwart by this point who had also attracted his fair share of criticism for racist depictions of African Americans, and the glorification of the Ku Klux Klan, with 1915's *The Birth of a Nation*.

Though Merle was still seeing David Niven at this point, she ripped a page from his philandering playbook when she began briefly dating the debonair Clark Gable, a star contracted to MGM, and she made him promise to accompany her to the ceremony as her date, protests be damned. That night in March at the tony Biltmore Hotel, Merle showed up with Gable—who was a nominee in the Best Actor category for the dramatic film *Mutiny on the Bounty*—wearing a white chiffon gown confettied with gold flecks and lined with sable. Upon their arrival, the throng of fans who had pooled in front of the venue applauded them. The ceremony seemed to drone on until her category came at the night's end. Bette Davis of *Dangerous* (1935) was the winner, having won in a sympathy vote after a high-profile snub the previous year for her role as a no-nonsense waitress in *Of Human Bondage* (1934), opposite Merle's former inamorato Leslie Howard. Merle was flush with dejection. From then on, the Oscars would become a spectator sport for her. Despite the loss, however, she had made cinema history, infiltrating a club that was never designed with the likes of her kind in mind.

★

AFTER REACHING WHAT HAD seemed like her career's summit, Merle experienced the most chilling of comedowns when a man from her biological father's hometown of Darlington, England, contacted her with the threat of blackmail. He said he knew that she'd been born in India, not Tasmania, and that she was mixed-race, telling her he'd approach the media and divulge the truth unless she—with her newfound, Oscar-nominated fame—gave him money. Desperate for recourse from a potentially career-ending scandal, Merle sought the counsel of Goldwyn. He took care of matters with efficiency, paying the man off in exchange for silence. As long as she was under Goldwyn's guardianship, Merle would have a layer of protection against such extortive attempts. But there were other menaces that even he could not control.

Hollywood was changing rapidly in 1936. Just as the talkies had begun to usurp silent cinema in the late 1920s, black-and-white movies were now starting to die off at the expense of Technicolor. The three-strip invention would have presented a treacherous new obstacle for a performer like Merle who had been able to use black-and-white films as a shield from scrutiny about her skin tone. She'd learned her lesson about tanning for black-and-white cinema after *The Dark Angel*, but color was a different beast. In this period of considerable change, even Merle's fellow actresses were generally reluctant to abandon the security of the familiar black-and-white cinema for Technicolor. But implicit in any hesitation expressed by actresses was the threat of replacement: If a star like Merle said she wouldn't act in a Technicolor film, Hollywood could easily find another girl eager for the chance. The public clamored, however, for an energetic new technology that might enhance the spectacle of moviegoing. (Some studios even saw Technicolor as an ideal format for representations of far-flung locales in South Asia, and travelogues set there would appear in the years that followed, visualizing the splendor and majesty of that bejeweled region.) For Merle, passing would thus become more imperative than ever in this time of tumult. Avowal of her South Asian roots was not an option.

Well aware that she would need to capitalize on any momentum that her Academy Award nomination had engendered, Merle spent the spring months of 1936 doing color test after color test. What would she do otherwise—stop acting? As Merle put herself through her paces, David O. Selznick (the brother of her agent, Myron Selznick), an independent producer of considerable repute, dangled before her a biopic of the English nurse Florence Nightingale. She signed on, but, as time passed, Merle grew frustrated with how long that film was taking to get underway. (It didn't help that another film on Nightingale was under production from Warner Brothers, eventually released in 1936 as *The White Angel*, starring Kay Francis.) As a consolation for the delay, Selznick instead promised Merle she would play the lead in *The Garden of Allah*, a color film in which she'd be a wealthy woman wandering the Sahara. The prospect of baking in the sticky soup of the Arizona heat for the shoot initially put Merle off, but she nevertheless began to ready herself for the role as any professional would, knowing that the part would be necessary for retaining her stature. As shooting was about to begin that spring, though, Merle received upsetting news that shifted any sense of belonging she had felt: Marlene Dietrich, the white German actress whose stardom occurred years before Merle's, had taken a color test for *The Garden of Allah* without Merle's knowledge. The crew loved Dietrich so much that they decided to replace Merle. The reason was simple: They didn't like the way Merle looked in color.

Merle was mortified. The public airing of the reason for her firing made matters even more embarrassing. At first, Merle turned her resentment toward Dietrich, envious of how easy that woman seemed to have it. Having gotten her cinema start in her German homeland during the previous decade, Dietrich had managed to make a name for herself in Hollywood as an imperious woman, incensed with being anything less than the axis around whom an entire film revolved; she often fluttered her eyes and played up her allure to ensure optimal treatment on set, an art that Merle was still in the process of perfecting. There was only so much room for foreign women at the top of the industry, and by receiving this role in *The Garden of Allah*, Dietrich asserted her supremacy over Merle in Hollywood's hierarchy. (Dietrich, for her part, regarded Merle as little more than pond scum, calling her "a real common piece.")

Fighting back, Merle took the righteous and dramatic step of suing David O. Selznick for $125,333.33, on the grounds that her removal from *The Garden of Allah*, as well as the production limbo of *Florence Nightingale*, had not only bilked her of a salary but also damaged her reputation. (As for why the sum was so comically specific, Merle alleged that she had already been paid $10,666.67 of her agreed-upon sum of $136,000 for the two films.) Though this suit was a symbolic gesture on Merle's part—the case would end up languishing for four years, after which she withdrew it—she was sending a clear message to the industry: Money was not all that she desired. She demanded respect, and she was especially unwilling to let anyone believe that she could not make the leap to color films. Such a notion would only feed the speculations about her ancestry that she had worked so tirelessly to dispel. "I can't stand idly by and watch a mere rumor pull down everything I've worked years to build," she frantically told a reporter, challenging the line that unsatisfactory color tests had led to her dismissal. But she also spoke with great courage that she would not let the industry deprive her of the life she'd made for herself. "Once you arrive at the top, you've got to fight every moment to stay there," she said. "That is why I never have and never will allow Hollywood to kick me around."

As Merle waged this very public battle, her two bosses did their best to mollify her. Korda and Goldwyn—feeling even more territorial over Merle after the Selznick fiasco—announced that they would share Merle's work in an extended, five-year joint contract. Merle knew this was a unique arrangement for Hollywood actresses, but whatever uncertainty she may have felt was tempered by Goldwyn's lofty promise that he would, through this contract, make her a millionaire. Yet he and Korda had different visions for her future: Korda wanted her to be the ethnically ambiguous temptress, Goldwyn sought the white English rose. In public, Merle tried to act as though she were content with this division. "I'm in the position of the child of divorced parents, without having any of the heartaches that go with that situation," she would laugh to reporters. "I spend half a year with Papa Goldwyn and just as I'm beginning to get a little tired of Hollywood, I'm rushed off to England and Father Korda."

The reality of the situation was less placid: After *The Garden of Allah* imploded for Merle, Korda cabled her with protective concern, begging her to come back to England while reminding her that she was under contract with him. In Merle's time away from British cinema, London Films had bounced back from the doldrums and begun flexing its muscles. That year, 1936, Korda would upgrade the London Films digs and open a studio in Buckinghamshire, outside London, called Denham Film Studios, which would become the largest set of its kind in all of Europe. It resembled an amusement park, akin to what Merle had become accustomed to in Hollywood, with a boathouse, stables, and seven sound stages with electrically operated doors. The company employed more than two thousand people. Korda's ambitions grew along with this upsizing, and he began to envision putting Merle in the historical epic *I, Claudius*, based on a duo of epic novels by Robert Graves, chronicling the tumultuous life of the Roman Emperor Claudius. Her screen husband from *The Private Life of Henry VIII*, Charles Laughton, would be Claudius, while Merle would play his wife, Messalina, a cunning siren conspiring to kill him.

Merle had her misgivings about accepting Korda's proposal, for Goldwyn still wanted to domesticate her image in America and did his best to keep her there. As Merle mulled over Korda's offer, Goldwyn—who increasingly saw her as one of his most prized assets—threw her a softball in the form of *Beloved Enemy*, a drama about the 1921 Irish Rebellion, told from a British perspective. She would play a wholesome English girl who falls in love with a leader of the Irish resistance (Brian Aherne). To further placate Merle amid her career frustrations, Goldwyn cast David Niven, with whom Merle had resumed her romance after the interlude with Clark Gable.

The shoot for the film became emotionally arduous: One Saturday in September, while on Goldwyn's lot, Merle received a call from Norma Shearer, saying that something was gravely wrong with her husband, Irving Thalberg. He could barely eke out a breath; he was coughing, struggling to speak. A doctor's diagnosis confirmed that he had been cruelly stricken by a case of lobar pneumonia. By the time Merle arrived at Norma's house at 7 p.m., family members had crowded around the door to the bedroom where Thalberg lay ill. Merle looked at her friend, clearly unable to take care of herself, and made sure Norma ate dinner. Two days later, Merle was downstairs in the family's living room when Thalberg died. This huge loss would only make Merle and Norma grow closer.

Upon *Beloved Enemy*'s release at the end of 1936, critics faulted the film for playing fast and loose with history by making Merle the sympathetic embodiment of English morality. Despite this, she gave her most polished performance to date, and today it is one of her filmography's stronger entries (though, with time, regrettably underseen). She was ably charming in the film's early scenes and very moving in the later reels where it seems the two lovers might have to spend their lives apart. Her casting in the film alongside relatively less established actors like Aherne signaled Goldwyn's optimism in Merle's ability to put butts in seats on her name alone. But that plan didn't pan out: Goldwyn was disappointed in the meager box-office sums the film generated.

Filming had also put a strain on Merle's relationship with David
Niven. She had become even more frustrated with his infidelity.
Retaliating against him for his indefatigable sex drive, Merle reciprocated the advances of her leading man, Aherne, a stately and handsome actor from England. But this was a mere power play on Merle's
part, for she really wanted to marry David. She presented the idea
to him as a sort of ultimatum, but he was too skittish to commit to
Merle for good. Youth—he was twenty-six—and its attendant wild-
ness still defined him. He was also intimidated by Merle. He thought
of her as a "Great Big Star," as he would later write in his 1971 memoir. In his eyes, she was already at the top of the industry ladder,
while he was still trying to claw his way upward. But the matter
of her race may have been the greatest hindrance of all. Having
met her back when she was a hostess at the Café de Paris, he knew
that Merle had been hiding the fact that she had grown up as a poor
Anglo-Indian girl in Calcutta. He was unable to see her as the kind
of woman with whom he could settle down and start a family. Miscegenation was, after all, still outlawed in California, and the risk
of authorities clocking her—and making their lives hellish—would
have been too steep.

Despite refusing to take her hand in marriage, David saw Merle off
in New York as she reluctantly departed for London to make *I, Claudius*
at the end of 1936, leaving her Dalmatians in the care of a dog trainer.
Privately, Merle would carry with her the regret that she didn't marry
David. A few years later, she would watch him marry a white British
woman, with whom he sired two sons; still later, he would say that
he forever lamented not marrying her when he had the chance, too
blinded by the overstimulation of his youth. He and Merle would keep
in touch over the years, and when she met one of his sons in the 1960s,
she stopped and admired him. "You are the son I should've had," she
said to him, filled with remorse at what her life could have been.

In this time of great loneliness for Merle, more than mere career
commitments were pulling her back to England. Charlotte was getting older, and Merle wanted to spend Christmas with her.

★

IN MID-MARCH 1937, MERLE'S chauffeur must not have seen the other car careening toward them that day in London as they headed to a costume fitting for *I, Claudius*. She'd always feared something like this would happen. He tended to be a bit wild on the road, and whenever he made a street crossing, Merle would wonder whether she'd make it out alive. This time, she nearly didn't. Their Rolls-Royce collided with a speeding car, throwing her through the window and onto the pavement. When she came to, she had no idea where she was—nor, in fact, *who* she was, though she could hear people muttering around her: *It's Merle Oberon!* Floating in and out of consciousness, she feared she'd reached the end of her life, seeing a virtual tunnel with light. She snapped back to cognizance and found herself being sewn up in an emergency ward of London's Middlesex Hospital. She was alert enough to ask the doctor whether her face was okay, knowing that it was her one bargaining chip.

Filming for *I, Claudius* hadn't exactly been a promenade in the park for Merle. When she had arrived in England the previous November, at first it felt rather nice to settle back onto her old stomping grounds. She could recognize the office boys and carpenters from her pre-Hollywood days, faces that were just a little older now. Korda had roped in Josef von Sternberg—the Vienna-born director who'd helped Merle's rival Dietrich shoot to fame—to direct the film. Korda promised that von Sternberg could make Merle an even bigger star, on a par with Dietrich. That Merle was working with von Sternberg nauseated Dietrich, one of those in Hollywood who suspected that all those rumors about Merle's racial background might have had a whiff of truth to them. "Can you imagine . . . that Singapore streetwalker à la Roman poisoner?" Dietrich scoffed. Indeed, Merle herself feared that von Sternberg—so closely entwined with Dietrich—would be able to see through her cover of whiteness and potentially even expose her.

Her part in this film, soaked in temptation, wouldn't strengthen the case against such gossip. When Merle finally saw the completed script in January 1937, she found her role inadequate, even downright regressive within the context of her career; she had taken the risk of relocating to America precisely because she had wanted to get away from such provocative parts. The script was still being doctored in the early days of shooting, and she began worrying that she barely had a character to play. She liked her diaphanous dresses and her red wig. That was pretty much it. The script had too many isolated scenes of heavy drama without a proper soul stitching those actions together, including random acts of violence like Messalina stabbing the emperor. Merle had a sinking feeling that the film would fail if it ever reached the big screen. London Films, despite having relocated to Denham, was now in disastrous shape, having expanded too quickly; the concept of professionalism seemed foreign to this company whose filmmaking machine was oiled with molasses. Merle began to pine for the efficiency of Hollywood, despite the setbacks she'd had there.

She begged Goldwyn to arrange for her return to California, bemoaning the lack of acting opportunities in the role. "Think Claudius would undo everything you have done," she cabled him in January, asking for his advice not as a boss but as a friend. But there was no real possibility of backing out. Korda tried to bend to her wants, ordering script revisions that might repair her mood. Here was a man whose relationship to Merle had been predicated on his seniority to, and power over, her. By now, though, Korda was starting to show signs of being utterly enamored of Merle romantically, but she still kept him at a professional distance. She also found that her demands were less pressing than the matters of the men on set. Von Sternberg was running into issues with Charles Laughton, whose commitment to his art had become even more studied—some might even say precious—since *The Private Life of Henry VIII*. Laughton would sometimes crawl into Merle's dressing room in full costume, sit in her lap, and cry to her about being unable to find his character. Merle felt sorry for him, but she would also learn how manipulative he could be, for his moods shifted on a dime. Occasionally, when Merle would have trouble accessing her own part, her mask would slip, and "the accent" would emerge. Laughton then would bully her about the ugly sound of her voice, never neglecting to remind Merle of her roots.

Now, as Merle lay swathed in bandages and concussed in her hospital bed, doctors expected that her scars would fade, and certainly that she would live. Yet it would take a few months before she could resume work, hurling a wrench into the *I, Claudius* production schedule. Korda, unable to envision the film without Merle, made the decision to put *I, Claudius* to sleep after her car accident. Only a few frames of this film would remain, some showing Merle appearing as though photographed through gauze, skipping impishly as she holds the camera's gaze.* With time, the shock of the crash would subside. Merle would come to see her survival as a sign that she should be unafraid of death, whenever it might come for her.

* There were rumors that Merle's accident was really a Trojan horse for Korda's desire to terminate the film because of his unhappiness with Laughton's work. Some even joked that he'd staged it just to cut his losses. (It's unlikely the latter is true.)

Chapter 7

An Accent of My Own

(1937–1938)

Merle Oberon posed for a Max Factor advertisement in 1937.

CHARLOTTE SELBY WAS ONLY FIFTY-SIX WHEN SHE DIED ON April 23, 1937, succumbing to persistent diabetes and high blood pressure. Merle was barely out of the hospital after her accident when she received the news. While in London, Merle had been renting a house overlooking Regent's Park, located on the same street where she and

Charlotte had lived when they first got to London in 1929. Charlotte had been in the care of her nurse, Gertrude Webb.

Following the twin blows of her accident and Charlotte's death, Merle came undone. "You see, I'm very much alone in the world," she told gossip columnist Sheilah Graham, bereft, not long after Charlotte's death. The indignities continued as Merle saw this woman's life compressed into a tiny item in the papers, with obituaries using her married surname of Thompson and revising her identity to be that of a white woman who'd married a British Army officer in Hobart, Tasmania. Merle had little choice but to comply with these falsifications. As she mourned the woman who was her one meaningful connection to her heritage in this new world, Merle found a private Hampshire estate where she could set Charlotte to rest. A towering cross marked the remains of the woman who raised her.

In the months following Charlotte's death, Merle lifted herself out of grief's nightmare through her work. Still smarting from the wound of *The Garden of Allah*, she wanted to prove that she could look good in Technicolor. She also took more elocution lessons to iron out any straphanging vestiges of the subcontinental accent that Laughton had weaponized against her, pushing her farther from the land she once called home. In these days, she came to find more of a lifeline in Korda, who was well aware of how rough the previous few months had been on her. Seeing that she was devastated by Charlotte's death, Korda felt a particular responsibility to do right by her after the *I, Claudius* fracas. Merle, in the throes of her bereavement, was starting to find greater comfort in Korda's presence, especially given the recency of her realization that David Niven would never be a long-term companion. With Charlotte gone, Korda was—along with Norma (still in California)—one of the few who knew Merle's desires and ambitions so intimately. He had met her when she was still Queenie Thompson from Calcutta; around him, she had the freedom to be herself, a luxury unattainable in a public life spent passing. Her days became lonesome again. When she would host visitors at her Regent's Park home, she'd bid farewell to them regretfully as she closed the door, wishing she had someone to gossip with before she went to sleep. In the shadow of Charlotte's death, Merle also felt a growing desire to have kids, vowing to adopt a child if she didn't get married within two years. She even missed her Dalmatians back in Hollywood, hoping they hadn't forgotten her. To tide her over, she adopted a cat—any companion to make her feel loved.

Merle decided to stay in London until the following spring of 1938. This was a dangerous choice, for American audiences could be so fickle with their preferences. The British film industry slumped into a recession around that time, and Korda was struggling. *I, Claudius* was the last in an unending line of Korda's overextensions: His company had begun to hemorrhage money, a drastic reversal of the post–*Henry VIII* period in which Korda seemed to be British cinema's savior. British cinema was far from a safe place for a rising talent like Merle, so working there would have been merely a stopgap until she could resume her Hollywood career. Yet, in Britain she had the support of people who adored her, ranking as the ninth most popular female star in a 1937 poll of British moviegoers (Norma Shearer was at the very top of the list). Later that summer, Korda found her a vehicle in *The Divorce of Lady X*. It would be shot in Technicolor, which British cinema was generally slower to adopt than America, but Korda, characteristically following the rhythms of his Hollywood brethren, led the charge in Britain. Having Korda's oversight, then, would function as protection for Merle, ensuring that her debut in color would not result in the outing of her South Asian heritage.

The Divorce of Lady X was a romantic comedy, the kind Merle hadn't done since migrating to Hollywood and tugging at her audiences' tear ducts under Samuel Goldwyn. Sliding between the modes of drama and comedy wasn't unusual for actresses of that era, but audiences— particularly in Hollywood, where Merle still endeavored to make a permanent mark—liked to pigeonhole women. The American actress Irene Dunne, more than a decade older than Merle, was equally adroit in comedy and drama, but films in the former category, such as *Theodora Goes Wild* (1936), firmly established her as a leading screwball comedienne, even though Dunne herself preferred her dramatic work. Audiences in America could react with hostility to attempts at elasticity. Katharine Hepburn, Merle's fellow Best Actress nominee in 1936, starred in a string of box-office duds beyond her usual dramatic fare—notably the comedy *Bringing Up Baby* (1938), which would be released the same year as *The Divorce of Lady X*. Such a cold reception demonstrated how fixed certain roles were for Hollywood actresses, even the best of them. Reputationally speaking, Merle knew audiences saw her as more of a dramatic actress in the Bette Davis tradition; Davis was a performer who would mellow some of her dramatic roles with sardonic notes but whose forays into full-blown comedy films were rather rare.

After Merle's spate of career inertia due to her accident, though, an artistic challenge like this was precisely what she would have needed. Here was her chance to show the world that she was capable of gaiety. *The Divorce of Lady X* was a remake of *Counsel's Opinion*, a 1933 film Korda had done. Merle would play a headstrong woman who, fogged in and trapped in a hotel overnight, must spend the night in the same suite as a no-nonsense barrister who falls in love with her. Her costar would be Laurence Olivier, a titan of the theater four years her senior. Olivier's broad canvas of a face could appear both boyish and rugged, capable of expressing discontent or charm with equal persuasion. Despite his enormous talent, Olivier had not yet adapted his stage skills to the medium of film. Years earlier, he was set to play opposite Greta Garbo in *Queen Christina* (1933), a Hollywood production, only to be fired because he couldn't generate chemistry with her. He retreated to the stage. Merle was a screen veteran compared to Olivier, though she was unaware that Olivier had a low opinion of her as an actress. They may have belonged to different schools of acting— one filmic, the other theatrical—but their divergent approaches fortunately caused little friction during the making of the movie itself.

When Merle saw the color rushes of *The Divorce of Lady X*, she fell in love with herself. "I'm so used to seeing the scene we've shot in black and white that color is like finding unsuspected facets in an old friend," she giddily told a reporter. Her excitement came through in the finished product, where Merle's disarming performance buoyed the candyfloss plot. Not all reviewers agreed with her self-assessment, though, and quite a few predictably focused on her coloring. Indeed, Merle was sheathed in so much makeup—likely a result of Korda's strategic ploy to preempt any questions about her heritage—that she appeared sallow in the film's sea of pastels. No matter how much Merle adored the way she looked, reviewers said that the color form deleted her delicate beauty, injuring the appeal she had in black-and-white films.

DESPITE THE EVENTUAL TEPIDITY of the response to *The Divorce of Lady X*, Merle felt a new screen life blooming within her as she closed out 1937, a traumatic year. "I've been working like a beaver," she happily wrote to Goldwyn. The elation, though, was short-lived. She immediately followed *The Divorce of Lady X* with the filming of *Over the Moon*, another featherweight comedy under Korda plagued by such production snags that it didn't hit theaters until 1939, a reminder of British cinema's ingrown disorganization. There were constant rewrites, even a swap in directors from William Howard to Thornton Freeland due to Howard's squabbles with Korda, who only wanted the best for Merle. Over the course of production, Merle's patience began to fray, and her short fuse surfaced when she demanded the firing of a nervous assistant after he brought her the wrong pair of gloves. Observing this episode was the American singer Elisabeth Welch, who would perform in a cabaret number in the movie. Like Merle, Welch was mixed-race, having been born to a white mother and a father who was Black and Indigenous. She was aware of what many others on Korda's lot knew: that Merle was South Asian. Although Welch was appalled by Merle's behavior, she also understood the nature of her struggle, knowing that the dual mandates of keeping this secret about her racial identity and navigating this high-pressure environment could lead to outbursts that Merle could not control. Such empathetic colleagues were few for Merle.

In *Over the Moon*, Merle would play a kittenish woman who falls into obscene wealth after inheriting her dead grandfather's vast fortune; this "poor little nobody," as the film calls her, would escape the poverty under which she'd spent most of her years, now prancing around in fur coats. While she wrestles with the question of what she wants from life, distant relatives parasitically emerge from the woodwork, angling for a chunk of her money. It was a Cinderella story like Merle's own offscreen saga, except that Merle had tunneled her way out of dire straits through hard work rather than mere dumb luck. The film was on the prolix side, giving Merle pages of tart dialogue that she flew through with great élan, evidence of her growing confidence as a performer. In one scene, for example, she rattles off a monologue in under a minute, carrying on an imaginary conversation with the man she loves (Rex Harrison) but is furious with, all while holding a framed photo of him. She barrages him with every insult imaginable, calling him a "bad-tempered, obstinate, ill-mannered brute." Despite Merle's chewing into this material with brio previously unseen in her work, some reviewers again complained that Technicolor was unflattering to her complexion, which might be the reason why she would not make another film in color until 1945.

Nineteen thirty-eight was the same year that Merle began to see Alexander Korda as more than just her boss. She didn't perceive their age difference—she turned twenty-six that year, he was forty-four—as a deterrent. Rather, his years had given him a sageness she appreciated. The two were also bound by a fealty to their careers; unlike David Niven, who saw Merle's ascent in Hollywood as an occasion for insecurity, Alexander respected Merle's ambition. He, like Merle, had begun his life in poverty, so he enjoyed splurging on clothing, restaurants, and jewelry, extravagances she coveted. He began to love small quirks about her, like the way her nose crinkled rather like tissue paper when she laughed. Merle took the initiative to ask him out to dinner, chasing the life she now realized she wanted.

★

IN THE SPRING OF 1938, dejected by the raggedness of the British film industry after *Over the Moon*, Merle headed back to Hollywood, again ready to deliver on the promise of her burgeoning American career. But when she returned, not even her dear Dalmatians, Entwhistle and Trubshawe, took to her. When she carried them to her old Santa Monica beach house, they became unruly: pouncing on tables, jumping into the pool, somehow even managing to climb to the garage roof. She decided to part with them, returning them to the kennel and allowing the highest bidder to have them. Merle was at least reunited with Norma. Their friendship resumed as though little time had passed, and Norma assisted Merle in reacclimating to Hollywood life, gathering photographers to take new publicity stills of Merle. But Merle's absence from the American screen since *Beloved Enemy* had been more damaging than she'd anticipated. When she went to a film preview with Norma that same season, Merle found that the crowd wanted everyone's autograph but hers. Filmgoers had forgotten her face.

★

SOON ENOUGH, MERLE WAS starting to regret signing the unique contract that divided her allegiances between America and Britain. Reporters characterized her as a woman without a country. "I am a split personality because half of me is owned by Alexander Korda and the other half by Sam Goldwyn," she complained to one. She felt she had begun to lose touch with her essence. "I'm an actress without an accent of my own, and the longer I work in pictures the more difficult it gets to adjust myself," she told another journalist—a quip flush with subtext, considering all that Merle had done to erase her origins in South Asia, how deep her shame about her "chee-chee" accent once ran.

With Merle's return to Hollywood, too, came her realization that she had been idiotically naive about practical matters—namely, her money. She acknowledged that she was careless with her finances, perhaps the result of her impoverished childhood before she suddenly began drawing sums beyond her comprehension. She must have been "the world's worst businesswoman," she later joked to the media. Dizzied by the legalese in her contracts, she usually didn't even bother to scrutinize them. Merle knew that moviegoers assumed actresses like her were swimming in cash, but, in truth, she was barely making much money. She paid national taxes in both America and England, alongside property taxes on her London home, medical bills from the accident, and agents' fees. Goldwyn's previous oath to make her a millionaire seemed like a real pipe dream. Anxious for money, Merle once again flexed her litigious muscles and sued the driver of the car that collided with her chauffeur's vehicle back in England; the mess of a three-day trial that year resulted in her chauffeur owing her thousands of pounds after the judge found him, too, to be negligent. Yet, as a further testament to Merle's lack of financial aptitude, her taste for luxury remained undiminished: She clomped around Hollywood in fur coats of skunk, ermine, and fox—a princess of ostentation. She had not outgrown her tendency to live beyond her means, even as she'd done as an earnest teenager in Calcutta overspending on perfume for her friend Phyllis Beaumont.

Back in Hollywood, Merle became determined to recoup her status as a rising star. She threw herself into radio performances where she'd reenact scenes from Hollywood movies, reminding listeners around the nation of the talent lost the previous year. Meanwhile, Sam Goldwyn was determined not to give up on Merle, though he also knew that she could not yet carry a movie on her own after *Beloved Enemy*'s whimper at the box office. He began searching for a movie that would team her with Gary Cooper, a lanky skyscraper of a man from Montana who had cemented himself as a dependable box-office draw. Though Goldwyn had a fantastical epic called *Graustark* slated for the two of them, he abruptly canceled the project the day before shooting. Instead, he opted for a contingency plan: a trifle called *The Cowboy and the Lady*, in which Merle would play a presidential candidate's pampered daughter who goes rogue and falls for a sturdy cowpoke, all while keeping her real identity a secret from him. Here was, again, a chance for Merle to play a distorted echo of her own life in which she went to great lengths to conceal her class roots.

If Merle had been expecting a smooth operation in Hollywood after the disarray of British films, she certainly didn't find it on the set of this movie. The script went through a string of reworks, directors stepped in and out due to Goldwyn's surliness, while the budget climbed to an extraordinarily steep $1.5 million. Merle had been away from the sweat of the California sun for so long that she collapsed from heat prostration while shooting. Filmed in black-and-white, the movie represented Merle at the apex of her beauty, her brown skin aglow. But it put her back behind Gregg Toland's camera, which prized realism over fantasy, thus exposing her to censure. Critics sniveled that the lighting "handicapped" her. Merle herself saw this film as a throwaway, but she handled its flimsy material with professionalism, a grenade of charisma in a part that did not call for much else. The sole—albeit major—deficiency in her role came, once again, with her inability to attempt an American accent, a persistent problem since *These Three*, bespeaking her lack of formal acting training. Her apprehension about even trying to sound the part would limit Merle's ascendance in Hollywood and prevent her from essaying a wider gallery of roles. Braving an accent when her entire acting career, thus far, had been predicated on suppression of her own innate accent could easily have confirmed the suspicions about her South Asian origins. Merle had to do all she could to avoid landing in hot water.

The year of *The Cowboy and the Lady*'s release, 1938, also saw the appearance of another Goldwyn title, *The Adventures of Marco Polo*, starring a purportedly Norwegian-born actress named Sigrid Gurie—whose career was severely hampered when the press learned that she was, in fact, just a girl born in Brooklyn, nowhere near Scandinavia, forcing Goldwyn to drop her. Given the racial element to her ruse, Merle would have met a far worse fate than Gurie if someone had spilled that she was an Anglo-Indian from Calcutta. Even with Gary

Cooper's name attached, *The Cowboy and the Lady* operated at a loss at the box office, stirring Goldwyn's doubts about Merle's longevity. Just as Merle found herself in a rut, though, Goldwyn was eyeing a vehicle that he was firmly optimistic would course-correct her trajectory once and for all.

Chapter 8
I *Am* Heathcliff!

(1938–1940)

Promotional poster for Wuthering Heights *(1939).*

CATHERINE EARNSHAW IS ONE OF ENGLISH LITERATURE'S great creations: the temperamental, high-class heroine of Emily Brontë's 1847 novel *Wuthering Heights* who falls for Heathcliff, a man below her social station in eighteenth-century England, and who tries, in vain, to sublimate this animal attraction. Heathcliff's ethnic provenance is ambiguous, but some refer to him as a "Lascar," slang for

South Asian. Catherine—or Cathy, as the other characters call her—is unmistakably white. William Wyler, Merle's director on *These Three*, had been eager to mount an adaptation of Brontë's book after reading a script by Charles MacArthur and Ben Hecht that had been floating around Hollywood. Bette Davis—whom Wyler had recently directed to her second Academy Award for Best Actress for *Jezebel* (1938), in which she played a Southern belle, and who was under contract to Warner Brothers—read the script and adored it, envisioning herself in the role of the doomed Cathy. But Samuel Goldwyn, hearing murmurs of the interest in this hot property, muscled in and bought the rights, with Wyler attached to direct, asking Wyler whether Merle could play Cathy. Goldwyn had his reservations about the film, finding the adaptation—which would end with Cathy's death—too glum, despite the love story at its core. Yet it was clear that this film would also provide a rich opportunity for its leading actress. Merle, still settling back into Hollywood after her longer-than-expected stay in England, was in need of a film that could reestablish her as a dominant talent. The film's script would position Cathy as a porcelain beauty while describing the man she loves as "a dark-skinned, saturnine looking figure." These words resembled the way journalists had once written about Merle before Goldwyn began to degrease her. With this role, Merle had an even greater chance than the one she had in *The Dark Angel* to shed the skin of the "ethnic other" and become a Hollywood star of lasting import, which Goldwyn had begun to question after *The Cowboy and the Lady*.

Though Goldwyn was adamant in his refusal to have anyone else as Cathy, others on the project were skeptical. After initially acquiescing to Goldwyn's request to have Merle in the part, Wyler started to feel she was miscast, privately preferring Katharine Hepburn, whose sparkplug personality was more apt for the woman of wild abandon Brontë had conceived on the page. But Goldwyn's word was final. The crew then set its sights on Laurence Olivier, Merle's *Divorce of Lady X* costar, to play Heathcliff. The only caveat was that the team would need to help him overcome his fear of Hollywood and give American cinema a second shot after his earlier disappointment opposite Greta Garbo. Olivier's insecurity about his acting abilities on screen could manifest as snootiness; he found the medium beneath him. Though Merle was in favor of Olivier playing Heathcliff, given their strife-free experience on their earlier film together, she had no idea how little respect he had for her as an actress. As Olivier considered the offer, he was holding out the false hope that Cathy could instead be played by his life's great love, the actress Vivien Leigh.

With the eyes of a lynx and a Cheshire's smirk, Leigh had a background much like Merle's, though one that would prove to be more palatable to American audiences in the long run. Leigh had been born in the Bengali town of Darjeeling two years after Merle. Her father was white, while her mother was of obscure—likely Armenian, though possibly Parsi or Bengali—heritage; this admixture gave Leigh a pearly complexion. (In fact, Merle's offscreen biography more closely resembled that of Leigh's mother, who was often circumspect about her heritage.) American publicity mavens would later fudge the details and say Leigh was French and Irish, but that was the extent of any revision. Her coloring—unlike that of Merle, whose tan-prone skin could ignite speculation about her heritage after a minute too long under the sun—allowed Leigh to blend into Hollywood's bevy of white beauties far more easily than Merle.

Leigh began her career in films earlier in the 1930s as another charge of Alexander Korda, who'd been swayed by her formidable beauty on the London stage and regarded her with a similarly parental outlook as he did Merle, seeing her as another pile of putty whom he could sculpt into a star. Korda even shared Leigh in a contract with the producer David O. Selznick (whom Merle had sued acrimoniously in 1936), an echo of Korda's arrangement with Goldwyn over Merle. Leigh and Merle also had an American agent in common, Myron Selznick (David's brother). But Leigh's skimpy filmography—quota pictures and the occasional Korda title—did not inspire confidence in Goldwyn. Despite Olivier's pleas to have Leigh play Cathy, Goldwyn offered Leigh the ancillary role of Isabella, thinking that part was the best Leigh would get as someone more or less unknown in America. Perceiving this as an insult, Leigh rejected the role. Instead, she engaged in a vigorous—and successful—campaign, not unlike Merle's very own for *The Dark Angel* years earlier, for the coveted part of the capricious Southern belle Scarlett O'Hara in a planned adaptation of Margaret Mitchell's 1936 novel *Gone with the Wind*. In short order, that role would immortalize her as a Hollywood star, writing her into history.

Olivier accepted the role of Heathcliff, despite not getting his way with Vivien Leigh as his leading lady. Merle began work on *Wuthering Heights* in the fall of 1938 with a begrudgingly compliant director and a grumpy costar. She understood the colossal weight of the assignment before her, sensing that audiences would remember her more vividly in tragic parts, not the lollipops like *The Divorce of Lady X*. But troubles mounted quickly, almost comically: Olivier, afflicted with a nasty case of athlete's foot, was hobbling around on crutches during those first few days, though he took his craft so seriously that he also caked himself in grubby makeup, darkening his skin and essentially adopting brownface to get in character. Every aspect of this scenario horrified Goldwyn. "This actor has to be the ugliest in pictures," he yelled, strolling onto the set. "He'll ruin me."

Merle soon came to learn what a brute Olivier could be. He lorded his extensive stage experience over her, weakening her confidence despite her comparatively more robust filmography, while he also consistently crowed over the fact that she wasn't Vivien Leigh. He called Merle "a little pick-up by Korda," who had come to town from Britain and sometimes visited the set. Wyler, continuing his trend of offering scattershot directorial cues, paid more attention to Olivier, whose growing pains in adapting to this new medium of film were far more challenging than anyone anticipated. The tension between Merle and Olivier reached a head during one of their romantic scenes, when they found themselves so close to one another that their breath seemed to commingle. "You had a drop of spittle come flying across in your goddamned passion," she complained to him. "You spat, and it hit me."

"Oh, Merle, I beg your pardon, but these things do happen between actors," Olivier barked back, as if the art were a foreign language to her. A retake followed. Merle found it plainly unsatisfactory, thinking it was the worst take she'd ever seen in all her years of screen acting— and she told Olivier as much. This reproach seemed to unlock a new dimension to Olivier's temper and condescension: "Why you amateur little bitch, what's a little spit for Chrissake between actors?" He proceeded to call her a "bloody little idiot," reducing Merle to tears. He continued his tirade while Merle ran off, crying. Olivier made offhand remarks, too, about her pockmarked face, the result of a mild bout of smallpox she'd had in India. Even Wyler, whom Merle essentially saw as a negligent parent to her at this point in the filming process, had to step in, asking Olivier to apologize. Olivier churlishly tried. "Over with your tantrum, dear?" he asked Merle. For her, such an attempt at an apology rang insincere.

Alexander Korda stood by Merle as she dealt with these taunts. (At that time, he had also faced humbling experiences of his own: London Films more or less ceased to exist due to its tattered financials, and Korda would now be making films under an entirely new company name, Alexander Korda Film Productions.)

By the end of 1938, Merle realized that she had fallen in love with him, though she wasn't yet sure what that would bode for her pact with Goldwyn. Their coupling did indeed stir friction with Goldwyn, who would, via his publicity team, feed the press bogus stories about Merle's alleged marriage to David Niven, who was playing the supporting role of her husband in the film. Merle had moved on from David at this point, now fully attuned to her feelings for Alexander. But it was he who found this gesture from Goldwyn to be crude, even hurtful, seemingly a veiled comment on how odd their relationship looked— painting Alexander as some jowly sack of a man, Merle his young trophy. Merle knew this to be untrue in her heart, but for Alexander, that insecure suspicion that Merle saw him as a stepping stool as she had Joseph Schenck—an older man she could use to get ahead—would linger in the back of his mind. Whatever the case, Merle's allegiances in both life and work were shifting toward Alexander, whom it seemed obvious she would marry.

Compounding the stress of Wyler's invisible directorial hand and Olivier's fetid temper were the physical aggravations of Merle's *Wuthering Heights* role. Her corset stays kept breaking, stabbing her in the back; she could barely eat meals out of fear that she wouldn't be able to fit into her dresses. The costume department cinched her so tight that she struggled to recite her lines audibly enough for a microphone to register her voice, which was compressed in her diaphragm. She sprained her ankle when winds toppled her portable dressing room. She injured her foot yet again while climbing over a wall for a scene. She caught a cold after a three-hour sequence where she had to sit on a drafty soundstage in a tub, its suds stirred by a contraption that resembled an eggbeater. The demands of her part became especially unbearable when Wyler forced her to walk over and over again toward winds fanned by propellers. Spumes of water ran through the blades and lashed her face; Merle shivered so much that she began to choke, then vomit. A hospital stay followed as she wrestled with a fever, her absence losing the production thousands of dollars. Upon her return, Wyler was still dissatisfied with the shot, so he ordered her to try again, rigging heaters to the fans so the water hitting her would be warmer. Filming Cathy's death—Merle's final scene in the movie— had also been a source of torment, lasting for four days. She couldn't die properly without sneezing, while Wyler's instructions to her were sparse, other than telling her to generate "a little bit more" tears in her left eye. This film had become an endurance test.

Despite all these elements colluding against her, Merle surprised everyone with the depths she plumbed in this role, and even today one can clearly see how this film represented a progression in her skill. In one pivotal scene, when Cathy realized the gravity of her bond with Heathcliff, she proclaimed, "I *am* Heathcliff!" The sequence, accompanied by a dramatic strike of lightning, might have invited a thunderous declaration from a stage-reared actor inclined toward broadness, but Merle was a child of cinema. Her interpretation of Cathy was thus decidedly interior, akin to a private storm; Merle resisted the temptation to play to the cheap seats with such a line, her delivery piercingly direct. But one can also see, in this scene, how Cathy's plight was much like Merle's, too. Cathy's affinity toward Heathcliff represents a part of herself—dark, dirty, unwanted—that she cannot express to the outside world, not unlike Merle's lifelong offscreen struggle to accept who she was and where she came from. Merle's work in this film becomes richer, and infinitely more moving, with this subtext in mind. The symmetries between character and actress may explain why the performance retains such a unique power and today still stands as Merle's claim to fame.

Merle was disappointed, then, to hear reports that her role didn't stand out during the previews for the film in early 1939, ahead of its April release. The crew then recut the film to put greater emphasis on her, considering this was ostensibly her star vehicle. Despite the rearrangements that led to praise for Merle's work (with some writers saying it was the best she'd ever done in a film), critics were more enamored of Olivier's pyrotechnics—which, to be fair, were highly effective—than her restrained acting. Today, though, one can understand that the conflict of approaches between the two actors gives the film its anxious pulse. If one were to fault Merle's performance for lacking intensity (as a few critics did), well, that was the point: Cathy's tensile composure made her the perfect foil to Olivier's showboating Heathcliff. Yet the polite but muted critical reception to Merle in the film, coupled with an upstream swim at the box office (the movie didn't turn a profit until 1963, too tragic to have wide appeal in its initial run, as Goldwyn feared), cast further doubt on Merle's star power. Privately, Goldwyn took a look at the money—or lack thereof—she was generating for him and started to lose faith in her.

★

MERLE WAS NO DOLT: After *Wuthering* Heights, she, too, was sensing that she'd blown her chance to be the great star Goldwyn wanted. With the film behind her, Merle was free to return to England to be with Alexander in April 1939. The two of them began to gallivant around town in public, fueling more rumors of their coupling. The grief of Charlotte's death—plus her cascade of career setbacks—had fully altered Merle's perception of him. They could be partners in art and life; he could give her security, both emotional and financial. Any gossip about what, exactly, was going on between them ended in early June 1939, when the two of them traipsed over to the town of Antibes, in the South of France, and wed. The bare-bones ceremony, a mere exchange of words, was far from the lavish occasion that Merle had once dreamed about, yet Alexander consoled her with a showpiece necklace that reportedly had once been worn by Marie Antoinette. He would continue to bathe her in such jewels, catering to her tastes; another present he would give her was a necklace, commissioned from Cartier, made of twenty-nine graduated cabochon emeralds on a chain of round-cut diamonds. That number became the prize of the magnificent jewelry collection she amassed later in life.

Upon arriving back in England three days later, Merle learned she and Alexander would be moving into a spacious London house with enough room for his entire family. She would now be living among his brothers, their wives, even the little Korda boys, including her nephew-by-marriage Michael, who was then five years old. Their early married life made Merle realize that they were incompatible in key ways: She did not smoke, ate sparely, and usually went to bed early, while her husband was a cigar-chomping insomniac with the appetite of a gourmand. Being with the Korda clan was also lonely for Merle. Their frequent swanky gatherings bored her silly, with cocktail hour making her feel out of place. She preferred to sneak up to the children's room, curl up in bed with them, and read them stories; around these kids, she could become her true self, the kind and sincere woman she was. She could abandon any hoity-toity pretensions she adopted for her own protection around the grown-ups. After all, Merle was certainly aware that Alexander's brothers resented her ascendance in his life, feeling she'd siphoned his attention away from them. Most distressed was his former wife, María Corda, the woman who'd spotted Merle at the canteen earlier in that decade and remained in her ex-husband's orbit. She started referring to Merle as "that black bitch," saying she "is like Boris Karloff, but in *vooman!*" Whispers about the secret Merle carried with her—that she was a poor brown girl named Queenie who'd been born in Bombay—spread like savage gossip throughout the family, even reaching the ears of the children. Merle began to carry herself with an air of arrogance, swanning around in her extravagant jewelry and asserting her right to luxury. Her posture was a defense mechanism against those who had always seen her as subordinate, against people who wanted to keep her down.

MERLE WAS AT HER husband's offices that day in September 1939 when she heard that Britain was entering the war. Her reaction was instant, irrepressible: She began to cry. From then on, gas-mask drills became a daily occurrence, rattling her. The sound of air-raid alarms sent her into a panic. Upon hearing this news, Alexander decided to shift his creative energies toward supporting Britain's war efforts, a project in which he involved Merle. He began *The Lion Has Wings*, a docudrama that he shot in under two weeks, with actual footage of British combat machinery interpolated by dramatic scenes of British soldiers heeding the combat call while their wives remained on the home front. Alexander constructed this film as a chest-thumping paean to the glories of the Royal Air Force, or RAF, and the unrepentant evils of Nazism. Merle would star in these fictional interstices as a Red Cross nurse married to an RAF officer, watching her husband go to war. The film gave her a substantial monologue about a woman's sacrifices during the war, which she portrayed movingly, admiring how, for centuries, Britain's women had "given their lovers, husbands, sons" to the cause.

For Merle, the war's outbreak gave her a chance to express her patriotism toward Britain, confirming her fidelity to the Empire in its stand against the horrors of Nazism. In her spare time, she knitted socks for soldiers, though she worried this was not enough. "But lots of times at night, while lying awake in bed, I think of the many things I would do to Hitler if I could just get my hands on him," she told the *New York Times* that year.

Worried for Merle's safety in Britain during the war, Alexander shuttled her off to America that fall. Wanting to feel a sense of familiarity in Hollywood, Merle started residing in an English-style mansion in Bel Air that recalled the feel of London, its L-shaped lounge flanked by lawns and a garden that overlooked the sea; she arranged to ship her furniture from England to California. In her solitude, Merle began to sort through her true feelings for her husband, trying to tell herself that their relationship was predicated on something deeper—truer—than a business negotiation. With great pride, she would flash the jewels he bought for her, such as three diamond roses taken from a tiara that she wore around Hollywood as clips in her lapel, her wealth a status symbol as her star was on the wane. She would alternate between calling him "my husband" and "Mr. Korda" to the press, the latter a sign of the reverential rather than romantic attitude she had toward him.

Merle had arrived back in Hollywood with a plan: She would ask Sam Goldwyn to cancel her contract. Alexander Korda now was the object of her professional (as well as personal) devotion. In Merle's time away from Hollywood, Goldwyn had also come to the conclusion that her contract had run its course, given Merle's inability to draw steady box-office numbers. The two of them met, and, just as Goldwyn raised the possibility of releasing her from her contract, Merle beat him to the punch: She requested to be relieved of her duties, not even asking for a settlement. Thus came the closure of a vital chapter in Merle's Hollywood career. Though Merle was free of bitterness, no longer having the protection of Goldwyn would mean that she would have to work much harder to maintain her status as a lead actress in Hollywood; she also threw away one buffer against any threat of exposure regarding her racial heritage, a secret that Goldwyn had worked untiringly to keep airtight.

In Hollywood that year, brownface as it applied to South Asian characters remained common, particularly in epics that used the subcontinent as their background. *Gunga Din* (1939) featured the white actor Sam Jaffe as an Indian water boy who sacrificed his life for three British soldiers. Not all these films relegated South Asian characters to stereotypical roles: *The Rains Came* (1939) starred the white actor Tyrone Power as a turbaned and tanned Indian doctor in a forbidden romance with a British noblewoman (Myrna Loy). Both films attracted hefty box-office sums, evidence of American moviegoers' expansive enthusiasm for racial mimicry. *Gunga Din* and *The Rains Came* were also significant titles released in what would amount to a banner year of Hollywood's Golden Age. The American box office was in the pink of health in 1939; World War II had just begun to loom over public sentiment, making diversions like the Technicolor *Wizard of Oz* appealing to the masses. By the time the magisterial epic *Gone with the Wind* came out late that year to high raves and equally high box-office receipts, the war had already started in Europe; it was as if that cinematic parable of the American Civil War was foretelling what was about to happen to America again. In the musical chairs of Hollywood's female stardom, *Gone with the Wind* established Vivien Leigh as a force on par with Bette Davis. Leigh thus leapfrogged past Merle's ascending position in a time when so few foreign talents, aside from Marlene Dietrich or Greta Garbo, managed to make a lasting impression on American moviegoers.

Though she was now without Sam Goldwyn, Merle thankfully found a lifeline from one of the Big Five, Warner Brothers, who took immediate interest in her that October after she and Goldwyn parted ways. Warner Brothers offered her a contract, wanting to turn her into the next Bette Davis, who had been one of the studio's front-rank stars. But Merle soon realized that her new bosses would not give her the same loving treatment she'd enjoyed from Goldwyn. Her first project for the studio would be a picture that Davis had turned down, *'Til We Meet Again*, a remake of the earlier 1932 American film *One Way Passage*. Merle would play a woman dying of a heart ailment who falls in love with a criminal on a cruise ship. She gave a performance of unusual spiritual depth. The film would become one of her career's sunken treasures, displaying just how effective her emotive capacities had become after the dramatic tests that *Wuthering Heights* had put her through. What helped her dig deep into her character's condition was the fact that Merle herself fell ill with a vicious throat infection while making the film. This woman's reality was Merle's own. "Now, I want to live so much," she'd defiantly state in one stirring scene when she speaks of the happiness that this man's love has given her amid her literal death sentence; she would end the monologue in tears. Critics sat up and took notice, writing that Merle made one "feel the tragedy hovering over her head" through her expressive performance.

Whatever stability of psyche Merle had achieved from that experience totally collapsed when nominations for Academy Awards rolled around in early 1940. Merle's name wasn't on a list that included virtually everyone else from *Wuthering Heights*: Laurence Olivier was up for Best Actor, Geraldine Fitzgerald—who'd received Vivien Leigh's sloppy seconds as Isabella and worked wonders with the part—for Best Supporting Actress. The film vied for Outstanding Production (precursor to Best Picture), William Wyler for Best Director. But voters slighted Merle, implying that Goldwyn's prior efforts to validate her had, indeed, been for naught. She was no longer the industry's shiny new toy. That year of 1939 had yielded an unusually lush bumper crop of leading female performances: Beyond Leigh hypnotizing critics and audiences in *Gone with the Wind*, Bette Davis was playing a socialite with a brain tumor in *Dark Victory*, while Greta Garbo was toying with comedy in *Ninotchka*. The snub was a clear rejection of Merle, who had worked herself sick for the part of Cathy. One of Merle's contemporaries, Spencer Tracy, consoled her by saying that the Academy Awards had lost all meaning after she was snubbed. Though it would take time for this reality to bear out, the oversight was a sign that the peak of Merle Oberon's career was over.

Chapter 9
My Dearest Joy
(1940–1942)

*Indian-born Sabu, star of Anglo-American cinema, meeting Shirley
Temple with Alexander Korda and Merle Oberon beside him.*

*I*N EARLY 1940, MERLE WAS MISERABLE. WARNER BROTHERS
had arranged for her to make more films after *'Til We Meet Again*, but
the illness she'd picked up while shooting the film threw a wrench
into those plans, unexpectedly leading to one of the most trying peri-
ods of her life. Her treatment involved an injection of sulfa drugs. This

triggered such a severe allergic reaction that Merle's skin, already vulnerable due to forced bleaching treatments (or what papers obliquely referred to as "a make-up infection"), became a scarred site of terror. This was far from ideal for a woman whose mug had routinely been on ads for Lux Toilet Soap and Woodbury Face Powder extolling her unblemished complexion, and whose beauty had been regarded—perhaps unfairly, given her considerable talent—as the primary reason for her celebrity. Makeup became anathema to her, with doctors warning her against its use. Otherwise, she would never be able to act again. Because of her sickness, Merle's film career lost any momentum it had gained after she'd signed her contract with Warner Brothers. She tried all she could to reverse the damage, such as subjecting herself to chemical peels, but nothing stuck. She barely wanted to step outside; all she could do was stay in a dark, candlelit room. Merle grew to hate the look of her face so much that she thought, quite seriously, that she might end her own life.

In the doldrums of her depression, Merle began to reevaluate what mattered to her. She would think of the woman she used to be. The more time that had passed since Charlotte's death, the more India began to fade in Merle's mind. Yet triggers to those memories, locked in her homeland, seemed to be everywhere. She hated how little it rained in California; rain reminded her of India, for she had grown up around Calcutta's mean monsoons. It had been so long since she'd been back there, so long since she'd spoken with Charlotte, that she was starting to forget Hindustani. A panacea to Merle's melancholia came soon enough when Alexander decided to move to Hollywood, where he felt he could contribute meaningfully to Britain's combat efforts by making Hollywood films that would, in turn, incite America to join the war. As a result, he would transplant his productions, one of the most notable being a film called *Jungle Book*, with another Indian-born star he'd been nurturing.

Like his compatriot Merle, the Muslim teenager Sabu worked under the guidance of Alexander Korda, but there was a key difference in the way their boss marketed them: Korda made no effort to conceal

Sabu's obvious South Asian heritage, as he did with Merle. In fact, that very identity was central to Sabu's appeal, for Sabu's public persona relied on certain assumptions moviegoers in America and Britain had of India: that its people were primitive and lacking in worldly sophistication. Sabu had become an unlikely star of British cinema during the late 1930s when he was barely out of his preteens, enchanting audiences in such colonial fantasias as Robert J. Flaherty and Zoltán Korda's *Elephant Boy* (1937), in which he starred as an Indian mahout, or elephant driver. Osmond Borradaile—a cinematographer who had assisted with lighting Merle on *The Private Life of Henry VIII* earlier in his career—had come across eleven-year-old Sabu in 1935, while in Mysore, South India. An orphan with no cinema experience, Sabu had a brushfire-bright smile that Korda's crew rightly felt would translate well to the medium. Korda's company then decided to structure *Elephant Boy* around Sabu's personality, feeding him his lines phonetically, as he knew no English. After shooting some footage in India, Korda's team then transferred Sabu to England, where he went to school and began to dress in proper British suits. He, like Merle, even posed in photographs that depicted him washing his face with soap, a visual representation of the civilizing project his handlers had undertaken in bringing him to the British Empire's cradle and despoiling him. Sabu became a token of imperial possibility and correction, even if British reviewers wrote about him with a tinge of racism, with one calling him "a brown frog of a boy."

In his homeland, meanwhile, critics tended to pillory Sabu as a stooge to the imperial cause, with India's leading film magazine, *Filmindia*, referring to him as "Korda's chief instrument of anti-India publicity." One of Sabu's films for Korda, 1938's *The Drum*—in which he played an Indian prince colluding with his benevolent British oppressors to topple his evil uncle—incited such agitation in British India that it was banned in many parts of the country. But the voltage of Sabu's charisma was difficult to deny; his presence, often in adventure films set in British India, provided a dose of reality to scenarios that teetered into the realm of artifice with their raft of white actors in brownface.

If it seemed, then, that the only prominent South Asian roles were available to white actors during the 1930s, Sabu disrupted this pattern before he had reached adulthood, even though the parts he played were rooted in stereotype. His success carried over to America in 1942 with *Jungle Book*, in which Sabu would leap through verdant foliage in a crimson-colored loincloth. One may wonder how Sabu managed to capture the imagination of moviegoers in Indophobic, Hays Code–era America, where logic suggests his stardom should surely have been improbable; the Immigration Act of 1917 and the 1923 ruling against Bhagat Singh Thind's bid for citizenship continued to cast a long shadow. But Sabu's youthful presence proved more charming than threatening to the sensibilities of audiences. He was not, in other words, the dusky peril made flesh. As Sabu's star was rising, he was often seen in public with his head enveloped in a turban (while otherwise wearing suit jackets and slacks), which had become a favored fashion item for the white elite. Despite the abiding prejudice toward South Asians in America, the nation managed to develop a sartorial fetish for the turban. "Turbans do things for you," shouted an advertisement for the department store Sears in 1940. The same apparel that had marked South Asian immigrants as vectors of danger at the start of the twentieth century had now become co-opted by the white majority as a status symbol.

Merle, too, posed for a portrait in *Vogue* with her head swaddled in a turban just months before that Sears ad appeared. Seen today, this image might carry great symbolic weight, an instance of Merle claiming one of the most visible emblems of her homeland. But the photo was less a gesture of aesthetic kinship with her South Asian roots than a studied alignment with white womanhood, a role that Hollywood asked Merle to perform. Though Merle still had to furtively sheathe her South Asian heritage from the public eye, she would bond with Sabu when she gathered the courage to show her face at cocktail parties in early 1940. He would teach her how to wrap turbans around her head, reconnecting with the homeland she'd left behind.

★

MERLE'S SORRY SKIN CONDITION prevented her from taking on any new films until the summer of 1940, by which point her symptoms started to calm and she regained enough strength to face the glare of the studio lights again. From then on, she would begin to use soap containing sulfur, whose properties allowed her to wash off makeup needed for shoots more easily, thereby preventing her skin from further lacerations. In Merle's time away from films that year, American viewers had been growing more fatigued by cinematic fantasies that had little obvious relevance to the global goings-on, especially as America inched closer to entry into World War II. Audiences ached to see stars who played gutsy, independent women grappling with the imminent realities of what it meant to survive in this grimmer world, adjustments to which Merle would have to adapt. She decided to stretch her limbs back into comedy, albeit one in which she would play a modern woman: *That Uncertain Feeling* was a United Artists title that Korda had negotiated for her outside of her Warner Brothers contract, with an impressive salary of nearly $100,000. She'd star as a woman living on Manhattan's Park Avenue who suffers from a perennial case of the hiccups, a physical manifestation of her unhappiness with her marriage. Berlin-born Ernst Lubitsch, its director, was a master of such comedies. He even managed to revitalize the personae of Merle's contemporaries, such as the oft-sullen Greta Garbo, with 1939's sidesplitting *Ninotchka*. Lubitsch had a peculiar manner of working, and Merle would sometimes stare at him in amusement as he paced around the set, a self-contained hurricane muttering to himself, or when he enacted her role (which was part of his method when working with his players). She could feel herself wanting to become a better actress under his erratic tutelage. Though Merle had previously starred in such comedies as *The Divorce of Lady X* and *Over the Moon*, this film called for more subtlety than those peppy parts. She would have to be less reliant on dialogue than on detailed gesture, throwing her husband (Melvyn Douglas) vinegary glances to convey her displeasure. There were also slapstick elements: Scenes required Merle to faint onto the hard sound-stage floor repeatedly, until she was covered with bruises. "If I wore a sarong in this picture, they'd have to give me 10 days to heal up," she joked to a reporter.

Despite Merle's gossamer touch—and critics' conclusion that she retained her customary "sparkle"—the film was a wash at the box office, yet another blow to her fast-falling position in the Hollywood firmament. After finishing *That Uncertain Feeling*, Merle, as if compensating for lost time, opted out of a vacation and instead bounced immediately into another comedy, *Affectionately Yours* from Warner Brothers, in early 1941. Merle played, yet again, a woman ensnared in an unfulfilling marriage—this time to a war correspondent (Dennis Morgan)—who tries to obtain a divorce, despite the two of them still obviously loving one another. Merle's role was physically punishing: Her character was carried out of a car as if she were a sandbag, kicking and screaming in a man's arms; she plunged into a body of water inadvertently. Merle's complexion trouble, which she'd kept at bay, resurfaced during the shoot. She wore so much makeup to conceal the craters in her face that the film's cameraman, Tony Gaudio, would shine a four-foot soft spotlight on her, minimizing any noise.

The level of duress on Merle might explain the lackluster quality of her performance. In a film surrounded by players who sounded like New Englanders, Merle, with her patrician British twang, seemed resolutely out of place, creating stylistic cacophony with her screen partners. Her presence threw the film off its American tilt, according to some reviewers upon its release in May 1941. "What Miss Oberon has for us is the Oriental princess look, the touch of jade and jasmine," one critic wrote. "Here she is the orchid wasted in a field of corn, pure corn." After *Affectionately Yours*, Merle promptly aborted her special contract with Warner Brothers, who realized that they obviously didn't have another Bette Davis on their hands. Without a steward like Goldwyn to help pasteurize her image, Merle found herself adrift in Hollywood, too foreign to retain the position she had briefly occupied mere years earlier. Her difference from the normative—white—female star had rarely been more obvious.

★

"I ENTERED THE ROOM as one enters in a dream, walking on air," she would say with her bell-chime voice while dancing up the staircase into the ballroom, the cream-puff ruffles of her dress brushing against her skin. The room seems to be suspended in time. Men strum violins; women play harps. A chorus begins to sing. Couples waltz slowly, and she is swept up in the movement. "Do you remember the graceful way people walked on those mirror-like floors? Thousands of mirrors on the walls. The chandeliers hanging from the ceiling like enormous magnolias." This entrancing early scene set an elegiac tone that suffused the entirety of *Lydia*, Merle's next film, which began shooting in spring 1941. It would tell the story of a wizened Boston spinster looking back on her youth and the four men she loved but couldn't commit to, a circumstance she reflects upon in old age with regret. This role gave Merle the chance to play, in essence, several women threaded together on the same soul. She could have the bratty demeanor of a preteen girl in some scenes and the composure of a mature woman in others, and she would play this role's many colors with equal vigor.

The film was a gift to her from her husband, who had been hunting for a Hollywood role for Merle that would demonstrate her full capabilities. He enlisted the French director Julien Duvivier to helm this vehicle, but the Hays Office sterilized its ending by demanding that the narrative punish the free-spirited Lydia for her loose morality by dooming her to a life spent alone. As the script conceived her, Lydia was fundamentally inscrutable; it was a testament to Merle's talent that she was able to give Lydia's romantic quandaries specificity. "You all knew me so well, and even love me," she would tell her past suitors. "And yet you never knew me at all. It wasn't I you loved, but an imposter, an illusion that got stuck in your Boston heads." In another especially notable sequence, one of the men, Bob (George Reeves), tries to rape her, only for her to fight back and escape. Lydia was a survivor, like the woman who played her, drifting through life and its attendant challenges with her spirits unbruised. "I never really acted until now," Merle would say while making the film, which would become one of her favorites in her entire oeuvre. "I just said those words and let it go at that. Korda makes me give out."

Alexander Korda may have been a boon for Merle's art, but it was becoming increasingly clear that, despite the equivalence on which their marriage was ostensibly predicated, there was an irreconcilable chasm between the two of them. His hair had gone gray; his once-sharp features had become too gooey with meat for her liking. Being married to her boss had put Merle in a unique position to exert a degree of creative control in an otherwise-repressive star system, one engineered to limit the power of actresses. But she realized this came with downsides, for she had trouble shaking the feeling that this marriage was an extension of a business arrangement. Independent in spirit, Merle was so much more than her husband's creation. She was the agent of her own fate: It was she who had charmed Ike Edwards enough so she could escape Calcutta, she who had elbowed her way to a screen test, she who had survived Hollywood even when it was determined not to give her a chance. Given her growing disillusionment, Merle worked through her second wedding anniversary, despite Alexander's desire to celebrate. He had greater plans for them, dreaming of mounting an adaptation of Leo Tolstoy's late-nineteenth-century novel *War and Peace*, in which she'd star as Natasha. But *Lydia* would be the last film they would make together.

★

UPON ITS RELEASE LATER in 1941, *Lydia* did not perform at the box office as well as Alexander and his crew had expected. Merle saw it as an acting achievement on par with *Wuthering Heights*. There was a poignancy to this performance that Merle's critics—many of whom complained about her quavering and craggy voice in old age (the elderly Lydia was the kind of woman who'd exclaim "Blow me down!" periodically)—could not completely see. Indeed, the great tragedy of this stage in Merle's career is that she was, aside from the misstep of *Affectionately Yours*, giving some of the finest performances of her life, having honed the raw talent she displayed in her work under Sam Goldwyn in the previous decade. Yet the critical establishment had moved past her now that she was no longer attached to Goldwyn, and the patina of novelty that had made her so attractive to tastemakers in the 1930s had worn off.

Though Hollywood was in very sturdy shape at this point—collated studio profits garnered by the Big Five and the Little Three rose from $19.4 million in 1940 to $35 million in 1941—Merle was not a beneficiary of the upturn. She would later claim that *Lydia* got lost in a wartime shuffle. American movie screens were, indeed, about to be pollinated by morale-arousing war pictures following America's entry into the conflict that year (an artistic swivel that would, a year later, largely be dictated by the country's Office of War Information, a body that instructed studios to shift their energies over to war-related films). Thoughts of the war galloped through Merle's head with increasing frequency. She considered adopting a refugee kid in need, though she, unaware of her teenage sterilization at this point, still had dreams of having a biological family of her own. "My husband does not think this a particularly good time to bring children into the world," she would tell a columnist. "But what I say is, that by the time our children arrive at the age of understanding we will have made life a thing worth having again." That's what the fight was for, she reasoned.

After *Lydia*'s completion, and with the war on her mind, Merle began to question the point of acting. She offered herself pro bono to a panoply of stars joining *Forever and a Day*, a sprawling Hollywood propaganda film made throughout 1941 (and eventually released in early 1943) that traced life in a British hotel over the course of generations through episodic tableaux. Merle's story, set in 1917 during World War I, would dominate the final stretch of the film. Her role of a plain English secretary who falls in love with an American was no challenge to her competence, and she fluently captured the fear of living through a war and trying to find happiness within it. In the wider industry, though, most of Merle's female peers were starting to take sabbaticals to focus on wartime resistance efforts, including but not limited to fundraising, while male stars of the era would be marching off to battle themselves, thus resulting in a shortage of romantic leading men. The nation's turn to war also led to a minor upheaval in female stardom. Of Merle's contemporaries, two—her best friend, Norma Shearer, and Greta Garbo—had retired by the early 1940s, clearing the way for new talents to seize American hearts. Greer Garson, seven years Merle's senior and from Britain, would become one of the most vital embodiments of wartime female courage. MGM had been carefully positioning her as the successor to Norma, classy and dignified. Films in which Garson starred, such as 1942's wartime drama *Mrs. Miniver* (which ran the table at the Oscars, including netting Garson a Best Actress trophy), in which she was a British housewife during World War II, established her screen persona as that of the selfless Earth Mother. Moviegoers also responded with great enthusiasm to the Swedish actress Ingrid Bergman devoting herself to the anti-Nazi cause in *Casablanca*, released nationally in 1943.

After filming for *Forever and a Day* wrapped, Merle decided to follow the example set by some of her female colleagues and temporarily leave her career in movies behind for this higher social purpose. She made regular radio appearances on behalf of the United Service Organizations (the USO) and the British War Relief Society (BWRS), two groups with war-shortening aims. She also earnestly abstained from sugar, reasoning that soldiers needed it more. ("The thought of what we are giving up will sweeten our tea and coffee," she, shimmering with sincerity, told a reporter, "and give spice to our whole existence.") Some of her radio appearances even involved working with Sabu, with whom she would reenact some of Rudyard Kipling's stories, almost as if they were taking a trip back home. Sabu also would later fight in the war on behalf of America. His eagerness to serve his country granted him citizenship just before his twentieth birthday in early January of 1944, expediting his naturalization—along with that of many other noncitizens who wanted to enlist on behalf of the United

States—during a time when South Asian immigrants could not otherwise secure such a status.

It was through her wartime work in New York that Merle met Richard Hillary, a Royal Air Force pilot—in a twist of kismet, born in her fabricated birthplace of Australia—who was eight years younger than Merle. He'd come to America to broadcast under the Ministry of Information, a British governmental outfit that had begun during World War I, and Merle, so skin-starved without her husband beside her as she was traveling in late 1941, saw in Hillary a temporary source of comfort. Having suffered severe burns after a plane accident, Hillary's reconstructed face still carried the whisper of that trauma. Yet he also retained a virility that would have been far unlike the namby-pamby manner of Alexander, a homebody who was now edging toward fifty. The affair with Hillary, which lasted into the following year, was a joyful distraction and little more for both parties; she'd "raised scarcely a ripple on the surface of my existence," Hillary would later write in a letter to a friend. But the fluffy romance gave Merle the feeling of what life had been like before she'd settled down with the man who wrote her checks.

Beyond the occasional jaunt to New York, Merle's radio commitments also had her bolting to Canada; she could earn up to $5,000 for a single broadcast. Her constant motion, however, nearly compromised her US immigration status. In 1941, on her return to New York from a trip to Toronto to broadcast for the Canadian government (part of broader British War Relief), Merle was summoned by Ellis Island officials for questioning because she hadn't secured a proper reentry permit. She hadn't known she needed one. In a time when immigration law targeting South Asians remained strict, the incident could have put Merle in a compromising position, opening her up to a potentially ruinous degree of public humiliation had authorities learned she was a South Asian born in British India.

Merle became ill with exhaustion because of the stress of this matter, so much so that she couldn't attend her scheduled hearing at Ellis Island. Instead, an immigration official came to her hotel room to grill her about her absentmindedness. She begged him to let her make a belated application for a reentry permit. Her celebrity eventually insulated her: The case became so public that the city's then-mayor, Fiorello La Guardia, took pity on her for what he saw as an honest mistake; he contacted the US State Department and arranged for her to stay in the country without penalty, sparing her any shame or embarrassment that would have accompanied the revelation that she was a mixed-race South Asian from Bombay. To return the favor of La Guardia's goodwill, Merle vowed she would do anything she could to support America against the war—to show her fidelity to this country where she'd made a life for herself.

IT WAS AFTER THIS close call with immigration authorities that Merle received a letter from Constance Joyce, the mother she didn't know she still had on this planet. Back in Bombay, Constance Joyce was hard up for cash; she was wondering whether Merle, this big star abroad, could send her some money. She'd had a difficult life in the years she had spent apart from her daughter. Hers was a riches-to-rags story: Though Constance Joyce had seemingly found material salvation in the arms of a wealthy Goan man during Merle's youth, the two of them separated, sending her back to straitened circumstances. Constance Joyce was disabled, too, in one leg and one arm. Work was not easy for her to find, despite the fact that she was a learned, well-read woman: She would busy her mind with crossword puzzles, lose herself in the poetry of Wordsworth. After the break from her husband, she had to do needlework, selling as much as she could to provide for her kids. She had four children after Merle and was possessive of them all, especially Harry, the fourth of five, all while living what was in effect a secret life, much like her firstborn daughter was doing. She told her kids that Merle was her half sister, sustaining the charade she'd lived for years, while watching Merle's movies on the Bombay screens whenever she could. Doing so was the closest she could get to her daughter. When her husband's family was keen on taking the

youngest of her children following her divorce and changing his surname from hers to his father's, she could feel control slipping away,
much as she had when she lost Queenie. And Constance Joyce wanted
to be British; she prized fair skin and observed British tradition carefully, including having plum pudding on holidays. The daughter was
living the mother's dream.

"My dearest Joy," Merle opened her response to this woman's plea
in the one letter between them that survives today. She explained that
she'd been so busy with war relief that she'd "given up films since July
last to do this work—so I haven't been too flushed—therefore haven't
sent any money—when I return to Los Angeles I will try and arrange
to send you something every month." She made good on the promise.
What was chump change for Merle would help Constance Joyce put
her other kids—Merle's siblings—through Jesuit school (along with
the help of subsidies Constance Joyce relied on), and Constance Joyce
would carry gratitude with her in the following years. As she closed
out the letter with her signature, Merle tempered this transactional
message with a sign of affection—for her past, for the woman who was
her only remaining link to it, for the mother who could not claim her
daughter as her own: *Love, Queenie.*

Chapter 10

I Wasn't Born Heroic

(1942–1945)

Newly knighted Sir Alexander Korda leaving Buckingham Palace with his wife, Merle Oberon, now Lady Korda, on September 23, 1942.

MERLE'S BOREDOM WITH HER MARRIAGE TO ALEXANDER Korda intensified as they spent more time in their respective wartime silos. While he continued to make films in Hollywood, she fundraised and entertained troops in a dozen cities across America as part of the Hollywood Victory Caravan, a traveling railway show, mobbed by men in uniform who wanted her autograph. Merle was averaging about twenty-one shows a week for six weeks, totaling 126 shows, in front of seventy-five thousand American and English soldiers. This work made her realize the symbolic duty she carried as a movie star. "I began to appreciate more than ever before how tremendous is the responsibility which we of the films have toward all of these people," she told one reporter. "They look to us as fulfillment of certain ideals. In our pictures they see realization of things they dream about." This was the unspoken contract she had with her audience: to embody a fantasy, no matter how discordant it was with her own reality.

Despite the increasingly obvious incongruence between wife and husband, Alexander would still festoon Merle with gifts; for Valentine's Day in 1942, he gave her a heart-shaped ring of diamonds kissed with three rubies. But he was fully aware of her infidelity, and bitterness began to fester within him. Merle valued her independence, including an active social life, while he seemed to have given up on fun. When Merle tried to remind her husband how much she loved him, he responded with resentment: "Yes, oh yes. Just as you would love a father." Their marriage got the shot in the arm she was looking for in June of that year, when, much to Alexander's surprise, the British government bestowed the honor of knighthood upon him, among the highest titles a subject of the Empire could receive. Since the conferral turned him into a Sir, Merle would, from that point forward, be known as Lady Korda. She wasted no time in giddily extracting the benefits of the title: The day after she received notification of his imminent knighthood, Merle called up Romanoff's, a Beverly Hills restaurant, to book a reservation under the name "Lady Korda," flaunting her newfound social capital. There were no legal obligations accompanying the title, only symbolic ones, but her transformation from Queenie Thompson to Lady Korda in the span of a decade reflected how completely and totally she had risen above the conditions of her upbringing—beginnings that the world had taught her to regard with shame. This Anglo-Indian girl had striven for assimilation because it seemed like the only way to survive. Now, she was one of the Empire's most prominent emissaries.

Had Merle's racial background been public knowledge, it would not necessarily have precluded her from accepting her title, as she was not the first South Asian to receive such recognition. The Bengali poet Rabindranath Tagore, for example, was famously knighted by the British government in 1915, only for him to renounce the title out of principled objection to their killings of peaceful protesters during 1919's Jallianwala Bagh massacre in the Indian city of Amritsar. Back home in British India, the recognition Merle received may have been a cause for celebration among those Anglo-Indians, like Constance Joyce, who worshiped British culture, or who saw the war in Europe as an opportunity to align themselves more fervently with British loyalism. Where they had once been parched for stable employment, many Anglo-Indians—sensing impending alienation with the mushrooming Indian independence movement—now had the chance to dedicate themselves to the British cause as soldiers or nurses. With ever-louder calls for India's severance from British rule came the question of where Anglo-Indians would even belong when Britain inevitably lost its claim to the subcontinent.

Dressed all in black with a flurry of fur, Merle accompanied her husband to the investiture ceremony at Buckingham Palace that September. Then, tightening her hands into fists to stop them from trembling, she watched him glide across the red-carpeted marble floor and kneel before the King of England while a band blared "God Save the King." She had helped him rehearse for this procession for hours, and she was now standing with other wives of knights-to-be. But the chill of animosity soon came from some in the British aristocracy who resented that a common girl who had begun her film career as an extra was now a Lady. Upon returning to Hollywood after the ceremony, then, Merle vowed to resume her acting career and only star in films that would reflect her allegiance to the Allied war effort. Merle cameoed in a pageant of stars, 1943's *Stage Door Canteen*, a flag-waver set in New York that followed women volunteering at a social club where American and Allied servicemen could fraternize and be enter-tained by celebrities. Merle would appear as herself, in only one scene, to deliver a rousing speech before a crowd, thanking Chinese soldiers who were fighting on behalf of the Allies.

Increasingly, Merle's screen image became bound with her offscreen jingoistic leanings. That same year, a recut version of *The Battle* from 1934, the film that costumed her in yellowface, was thrown into Amer-ican theaters under the new title *Hara-Kiri*, an unusual revival for the time that nonetheless demonstrates how pungent anti-Japanese sen-timent was within America. This new edit of the film opened with a text overlay declaring that the Japanese were "shy and arrogant, sick with envy and greed," while it ended with a voiceover from a stento-rian narrator decrying the moral bankruptcy of "the Jap."

Merle, now a freelancer untethered to any studio, soon found a more substantial leading role with *First Comes Courage* that year. She would play a Norwegian spy, Nicole Larsen, who poses as a Nazi ally, a disguise she wears so persuasively—she even marries a Nazi major, their wedding altar decorated with Nazi flags and swastikas—that her compatriots impugn her as a traitor. She feels she is carrying on this ruse for a worthy cause. As she had proven three years ear-lier with *'Til We Meet Again*, Merle excelled in such roles of women who are tormented by a secret but manage to maintain the outward posture of bravery, their backbones undamaged. *First Comes Courage* gave Merle the chance to deliver a mid-movie monologue in which Nicole recounted her radicalization, explaining that the sight of blood on a street years earlier had exposed her to the sadism of the Nazis. "All the terror and the suffering—it was a hideous nightmare I came back to," she'd say, her voice freighted with horror. "It was so hideous and frightening at first I thought of running away. I'm afraid I wasn't born heroic."

Intended as a resolutely feminist film, *First Comes Courage* was ini-tially helmed by Dorothy Arzner, one of the few high-profile female directors working in Hollywood at the time. Merle observed the way the studio, Columbia (one of the Little Three), steamrolled over Arzner after she contracted pneumonia and replaced her with the male director Charles Vidor, an experience that virtually forced Arzner out of the industry. Making the movie wasn't easy for Merle, either. Though the film was in black-and-white—a practice that the industry was still phasing out (Merle herself hadn't acted in color since *Over the Moon*, four years earlier)—Merle was reminded, yet again, of the industry's wanton hostility toward South Asian performers when the crew put her under strict orders to minimize her time in the sun, fearing she would become too dark for the camera. But she couldn't help it. She was thirty-two, still young, but the older she grew, the more challenging it became to veil the nose that columnists had long complained was hooklike, the copper skin. When she spent too much time in the sun in Palm Springs, the crew delayed shooting for a week so her skin might fade.

The film's muffled reception amongst critics and audiences suggested that limiting herself to war movies might not be the most sustainable path forward for Merle after all. America was still in the process of diversifying its cinematic diet beyond films on the war; an oversaturation of war-related titles may have played a part in the response. Merle then shifted her focus to new narrative territory: In the summer of 1943, Twentieth Century–Fox asked her to play a cabaret performer targeted by Jack the Ripper, a serial killer in nineteenth-century London, in *The Lodger*. This film had the potential to snap Merle out of any artistic abeyance, for it involved scenes where she'd dance the Parisian trot, a cousin of the can-can, pushing muscles she hadn't worked in years while cupcaked in frilly costumes. On the first day of the shoot, she heard the soft drum of knuckles knock on the door to her portable dressing room, followed by the sight of a willowy man she hadn't met before. He stared at her in awe, she back at him, before he muttered to himself: "I have never seen such beauty."

★

COLUMNISTS THOUGHT THAT LUCIEN BALLARD was handsome enough to be a movie star himself. He grew up in Oklahoma and was part-Cherokee, so he may have understood the particulars of Merle's predicament better than her husband could have. Lucien took public pride in his Cherokee roots. Unlike Alexander, he had no noble airs about him; he came across as a man of the soil. He was a few years Merle's senior—records indicate his birth year was actually 1904, rather than 1908, as some sources would state—not eighteen years, as Alexander was. Merle didn't think news photographs captured how gorgeous he was. And the minute she stepped before Lucien's camera, Merle came to understand that he would placate her vanity, with an approach that diverged from Gregg Toland's harsh realism during her Goldwyn years. As the ultimate gesture of tribute to Merle, Lucien mounted a special kind of key light (a light meant to illuminate the subject of a scene, such as a performer) on a camera to give her skin an iridescent glow. That light would blur the reality of her life—the facial scars from her car accident, the pockmarks dappling her cheeks from her sulfa allergy, the lingering damage from the forced bleaching of her skin. It would also help secure her within whiteness at a point when time was caramelizing her complexion. Lucien would come to call this device the Obie—in Merle Oberon's honor—which would endure within the industry, thus making it one of the most significant hallmarks of Merle's legacy.

Under Lucien's light, Merle became the precise realization of what *The Lodger*'s antagonist so despised: He was a murderer who harbored a pathological and hyperspecific hatred of actresses, whom he called "powdered and painted to look beautiful." Aside from a whoosh of the leg during dance sequences that made her resemble a loose-limbed flamingo, Merle barely got the chance to act in this role (she was "hopelessly miscast," one reviewer lamented). But Lucien's flattery helped reignite Merle's love for her craft. With her husband back in London for work, Merle began dating Lucien through late 1943 as she kept signing film contracts. She accepted an offer to play the lead in a pulpy thriller that would become *Dark Waters*, from United Artists, along with the role of the writer George Sand in Columbia's *A Song to Remember*, a fictional biopic of the Polish musician Frédéric Chopin. In 1943,

Merle also decided to put down deeper roots in Hollywood by purchasing another home: a Malibu ranch where the nearest telephone was ten miles away, while a telegram would take a full twenty-four hours to crawl its way over to her. Alexander, sensing that the marriage was dissolving, rushed to Hollywood in early 1944 to mend what was irreparable. By that point, Merle had made her needs clear to him: She wanted a divorce.

MAKING A LAST-DITCH EFFORT to salvage his marriage, Alexander promised to help Merle find a director for *Dark Waters*, whose script, he feared, was rancid bunk. The eventual director, André de Toth, who signed on at Alexander's insistence (de Toth had assisted in directing *Jungle Book*, starring Sabu), read the screenplay and agreed, declaring it "the biggest piece of shit I have ever seen"; he ordered rewrites immediately. Alexander had become pathetic in his desperation, feeling Merle sliding away from him. "But I made Merle Oberon," he would tell de Toth, territorially but earnestly. "She is my creation." At this point, Merle had outgrown her Pygmalion.

The story for *Dark Waters* concerned a girl named Leslie Calvin who has survived a deadly maritime accident that claimed her wealthy parents. She then finds herself hornswoggled by a band of imposters masquerading as her extended family members, a scheme masterminded by a killer who wants a clump of her inheritance; they lure her to the family plantation in the Louisiana bayou, where she tries to outsmart her captives while losing her sanity. The film, which began shooting in May 1944, today stands out as one of the stronger in Merle's filmography, despite Alexander's and de Toth's early reservations. De Toth imbued the film with a hallucinatory quality; the film seldom collapsed into garish melodrama, even if the narrative proceedings may have justified such a treatment. Merle calibrated her work accordingly, bringing to life a tightly wound woman wracked with survivor's guilt. The film's gripping climax would take her to the bayou where she would hide beneath a tangle of water lilies. "If the audience suffers as much as I do the picture will be a huge success," Merle joked to a reporter about the film, which would, indeed, become one of that year's sleeper hits, the closest thing she had had to a box-office success in years.

Merle's commitment to the role was evident from the opening scene, in which she, bedraggled in her hospital bed, utters the script's first lines with convincing delirium. "Did you ever go to a funeral where the minister forgot the service?" she'd ask on screen. "Did you? When the man next to you died and they threw him overboard, and all you thought was, 'There'll be more water to drink,' and didn't even care that he was dead?" While shooting, Merle attacked her first swing at this scene as if her career had prepared her for this moment: She did not seem to have the self-conscious affectation of a movie star slumming it in a haggard role. The sequence was meant to strip Merle of her usual glamour, saddling her with eyebags reminiscent of her dying moments in *Wuthering Heights;* her cheeks were gaunt and hollow, her lips parched, her hair stringy. She kept her face still with control, her eyes glazed with terror. The crew applauded, marveling at how Merle had completely subsumed herself in this character. Even Merle recognized how well she'd done, almost as if she had lived the lines rather than merely reciting them.

But then she asked de Toth for one more take. And then another. Maybe one more. She must have ordered forty takes, crushing her director's patience. He didn't understand what was going on until he noticed Lucien Ballard—ever-present on set even though he wasn't even the film's cinematographer—standing behind him in a doorway. Lucien would nod to Merle when he felt she'd gotten the most flattering possible shot, so she had been tilting her head to and fro until she gained his approval. Merle had an apprehension that she wouldn't look perfect enough on camera, an anxiety that Lucien stoked. She was toeing that thin line between vanity and self-consciousness. Though Merle wasn't quite cognizant of it, the pressure on her was making her question her instincts as an actor, and she was falling into a trap of letting Lucien exercise power over her. But she was so taken with him that her mind was settled on him, and she became the cruelest version of herself when dealing with her husband, who would beg to stay with her on phone calls; he would even send her bundles of posies. Merle was unmoved, budging only to delay their divorce until the war's end. In the ultimate show of viciousness, she began negotiating with gossip columnists for the exclusive rights to the report of their separation. Merle realized that she would be forfeiting the social cachet that accompanied her Lady Korda title, and that she would slide down the industry's ranks when she eventually took the step of marrying a lowly cameraman (and a mixed-race one at that); the Hollywood elite had already begun to see her as persona non grata for dating while married. But in Merle's calculation, Lucien was worth the risk. He nicknamed her "Mamma," while she called him "Baby." He was the picture of youth, a renegade: He proposed to her on a hunting trip by shooting off a gun near her ear, a portent of what was to come. This man was far more dangerous than she realized.

Chapter 11

I Ruled My Own Life

(1945–1948)

*Lucien Ballard, Merle Oberon's second husband,
with Merle aboard RMS Queen Mary in 1947, the first year
the ship returned to peacetime service after World War II.*

Once Merle separated from Alexander, she moved around the world with a freedom she hadn't known in years. She appreciated Lucien's healthy disconnect from his art: Whereas Alexander had found it impossible to decouple work and love, Lucien saw Hollywood as a mere factory. Visitors to Merle's homes were few now, for anyone who had flocked to her in the years when she was a titled woman had all but vanished with the drop in her social status. The loyal Norma Shearer, disregarding the conventions of the industry (especially now that she had retired from films), was one of the exceptions, sneaking away to see how happy her friend Merle was.

Merle soon began filming *A Song to Remember*, the Chopin biopic that would be released in 1945. She would be photographed in color, a format she hadn't ventured into since critics had winced at her appearance in *Over the Moon* six years earlier; even the script's character description referred to her as "dark-complexioned." Merle would play the eccentric real-life figure George Sand, a staunchly feminist nineteenth-century French female writer who dressed as a man, a choice she made to weather a perilously sexist society. This role was in a different key than the two previous films Merle had done, both thrillers, and the script took abundant creative liberties with Chopin's life. But Merle's performance was not among the problems in *A Song to Remember*. She would waddle through the film's early scenes in a top hat while swiveling a cane. Her steely disposition would conceal, barely, a fear that the world would not take her seriously if she were to present herself as a woman—fear she sublimates beneath rage. She would keep a cool temperature throughout the film until an arresting monologue near the end, wherein Sand seethes with titanic fury about the nature of her public performance. "I ruled my own life," she'd say, practically spitting each line—explaining that she had taken a man's name as her pen name, wore pants instead of dresses, played the rules of a game she didn't design, and lived on her own moral terms. In doing so, she accomplished precisely what she intended with her life: She survived in a world that otherwise saw her as a second-class citizen.

Merle chomped into the scenery with hammy gusto, but the approach was warranted: Beneath the showboating was a basic truth. Sand, like Merle herself, was a woman whose performance of deception may have caused ridicule, but she did not know any other way to get by. Whatever emotional price she had to pay for this gambit was worthwhile. There was, as Sand had said, the reward to remember. It was as if Merle were narrating the story of her life. This startling moment of vulnerability, in a performance justly celebrated as Merle's finest since *Wuthering Heights*, provoked widespread acclaim: Audiences recognized the power of that monologue, with reports of applause thundering through theaters; even her old boss Samuel Goldwyn called her to express his admiration. The film was an unequivocal box-office success for Merle after what had mostly been slow burners, like *Dark Waters*, or outright disappointments. But working on the film drained Merle, perhaps because it forced her to cut deep into the marrow of her being. She felt it was the hardest role she'd ever played. "I had to pull up strength from my boots," Merle would later say of this performance, thereafter hesitating to attempt such a role. But, for a moment, the character and the actress had become one.

★

AFTER THE EMOTIONAL NUDITY of *A Song to Remember*, Merle retreated into the comfort of roles that asked very little of her talent. She metabolized a childhood fantasy she'd had back in India of playing a princess in the Technicolor epic *Night in Paradise* (filmed in 1945 and dumped into theaters a year later) as a Persian royal in antiquity, lounging in a swan-shaped bathtub filled with milk. Hers was the kind of "exotic" role that would have sent Samuel Goldwyn straight to the hospital. The film torpedoed at the box office and was a critical bust. After that, *This Love of Ours*, a black-and-white drama, fell more squarely within Merle's wheelhouse. It was a weepy about a woman who struggles to reconnect with her daughter after abandoning her family, and it gave her the chance to collaborate again with her beau, Lucien, whom she had come to trust so deeply that she felt no need to study her face in the film's rushes. The two of them forged an oath to work as a package deal from then on, meaning that Merle would decline any assignments that came her way unless they involved him.

Around the time Merle began filming *This Love of Ours* in early June of 1945, World War II was nearing its end with Germany's surrender, and Merle would begin the bureaucratically cumbersome process of officially divorcing Alexander Korda. She expedited matters by going to the Mexican border town of Juárez—a locale favored by the Hollywood elite who wanted to avoid the copious paperwork and legal proceedings involved in American divorces— and finalized the divorce that month, just after their sixth wedding anniversary. She then turned her attention to tying the knot with Lucien, though the two of them buried themselves in their work so completely that they were unable to sneak away from the studio while making *This Love of Ours* to have a formal marriage ceremony. They arranged instead for a proxy wedding, again in Juárez, with two Mexican stand-ins in their place while they remained in California. (Miscegenation was still outlawed at this time in California, and even though Lucien was technically classified as mixed-race, a marriage outside of American borders would have had the added benefit of inoculating Merle from scrutiny about her own origins.) Merle naively believed that her proxy ceremony wouldn't attract any publicity until she was in the middle of shooting when newspapermen started calling her, asking about her wedding. Privacy was impossible in this town.

Once Merle and Lucien had made their marriage official that summer, she began trying, in earnest, to have a child. She was feeling time's heavy pressure at this point, telling reporters she was thirty at the time of her marriage, even though she was thirty-four. Yet, growing desperate, she seemed to be fighting a biological impossibility, unable to conceive. It was on a quasi-honeymoon on the East Coast in the fall of 1945—by which point *This Love of Ours* had opened in theaters and was shrugged off by reviewers, while the war had officially ended— that Merle and Lucien decided to visit a gynecologist in New York. She wanted to see whether this doctor could resolve whatever issue had been inhibiting her from achieving pregnancy. During this visit, Merle finally came to understand the extent of what Charlotte had forced her

to endure as a teenager when she effectively ordered Merle's sterilization. The New York doctor tried to rectify the situation, transplanting
one ovary directly into Merle's uterine wall—specifically onto the site
where the fallopian tubes would have connected to the uterus. But
this, in fact, made matters worse for Merle, all but destroying any further possibility of her becoming pregnant. Frantic to reverse a disaster
that this doctor had compounded through his intervention, Merle and
Lucien then went to the Boston offices of the pioneering gynecologist
Dr. John Rock, famed for his ability to work reproductive miracles.
Because of Rock's stature, the visit was covered with great fanfare by
the press, though few knew the particulars of Merle's troubles. She
informed Dr. Rock of the operation she'd undergone early in life at
the instructions of Charlotte. Merle was hoping that he'd be able to
correct the New York doctor's attempt to override her teenage procedure by performing what is known as tuboplasty. But, as he began,
he found that Merle had almost no tubal tissue with which he could
work, and his efforts didn't take. He delivered the news to Merle with
great regret: There was nothing he could do. She would never be able
to conceive.

MERLE ENDED HER "HONEYMOON" by maintaining the surface
stance that their well-publicized visit to Dr. Rock's office had gone
just fine. She began bracing herself for questions from Hollywood folk
who would ask her when she'd have her baby. She and Lucien delayed
their return by taking a cross-country car trip. He was equally disappointed in her inability to conceive, and this shook their young marriage's foundation so badly that it would not regain its strength. They
would stop along different spots in America where autograph-seekers
both young and old besieged her. She indulged their requests while she
was bottling up one of the great heartbreaks of her life.

"Please have a baby so I can use the item on my next radio show!"
one radio columnist squawked to Merle once she arrived back in
California. She tried to reorient herself from this psychological free

fall with work, sliding into Universal's *Temptation* (1946), playing a London socialite living in nineteenth-century Egypt and plotting to kill her husband, an Egyptologist. But Merle, having endured such a rather painful setback, wasn't herself on set, and she became hideously tetchy. One day, she found herself flubbing her lines—a rarity for an actress who prided herself on memorizing pages of dialogue before the cameras began rolling—and took out her ire on the crew, irrationally raking them over the coals for some perceived offense. She would complain about the strangle of her corsets, even stopping midway through a love scene, vanishing into her dressing room, and returning sans constriction. "How our grandmothers ever got their necking done I'll never know," she grumbled. Despite the issues, Merle's carefully modulated portrayal of selfishness, with her sedate exterior masking a viperous impulse, was so strong that a few industry commentators thought she'd be under Oscar consideration for it, a full eleven years after her first nomination. But critics found the film surrounding her to be "rheumatic," as one wrote, and box-office receipts were unimpressive.

American filmgoing was enjoying a pleasant postwar boom that peaked in 1946, the year of *Temptation*'s release. According to some estimates, studio profits crested at a record $122 million. Servicemen had returned from the war, while millions of women had exited the workforce. Weekly theater admissions were close to one hundred million that year, well over half the population. But the reverie would be short-lived: In the years that followed, those same couples were going to marry, have kids, and pollinate the suburbs. A new technology called television was presenting itself as a viable alternative to the movie theater, providing entertainment without the hassle of having to leave one's home. The very enterprise of studio filmmaking itself was also coming under threat. The Justice Department began to crack down on the Big Five and the monopoly they held over theaters for violating antitrust laws, a probe that would intensify in subsequent years. In short, studio moviemaking in America was drawing its last gasp that year.

It was within this landscape that Merle—grieving the loss of biological motherhood's possibility while preparing to eulogize a dying film culture—considered curbing her film career and settling into a bucolic life with Lucien, despite their ever-present troubles. Her Malibu paradise, which she began calling her Shangri-La, was secluded enough from Hollywood that she could decompress from the industry's noise, spending her days wielding a shovel as she crushed her feet into the grime of the garden. (She and Lucien also had a ranch in Valley Center, in San Diego County, where the land and cattle yielded walnuts and butter.) As Merle found herself reevaluating her life's priorities, she made an announcement to the press that might today seem surprising, given her conscious efforts to bury her past: After seventeen years away, she wanted to visit India. She was circumspect with journalists about her reasoning, understandably so, considering her ongoing commitment to her Tasmanian origin story. Merle simply wanted to go back to India, the columnist Sheilah Graham wrote, because she "thinks she'll enjoy it better now."

THE VERY MONTH THAT Merle expressed a desire to go back to her birth country—which she had once regarded as a site of provincial limitations—saw America, at long last, slacken its immigration policies toward South Asians. In July 1946, President Harry Truman signed the Luce-Celler Act, which significantly undermined the Immigration Act of 1917 and effectively rebuked the 1923 Supreme Court ruling against Bhagat Singh Thind. Now, one hundred Indians—residents of what today includes Bangladesh, India, and Pakistan—were permitted entry to America per year through a national-origins quota. Prior to this point, only white immigrants born in British India—say, British or French nationals—were allowed to immigrate to the United States and become naturalized citizens. At that point, as many as three thousand nonwhite Indian nationals were in America trying to live in secrecy, Merle among them. Even though she could have obtained American citizenship by this time, she likely didn't pursue it because any press surrounding this process, in a community that tracked her every gesture, would have revealed her secrets.

This swirl of changes, evidence of a much softer attitude toward South Asians than Merle had ever known in America, might explain why she may have been motivated, briefly, to return to her home country. The passage of the Luce-Celler Act was also a strategic move by the United States to support the growing Indian independence effort, which would eventually come to fruition in the summer of 1947. Independence would initiate a brutal Partition after British aggressors diced the British Raj into India and Pakistan (the latter comprising present-day Pakistan and Bangladesh). Anglo-Indians residing there would confront the existential question of where home was. Tens of thousands of Anglo-Indians would flee the subcontinent in the years after 1947, just as Merle had done nearly two decades earlier; some Anglo-Indians who stayed behind—like Constance Joyce—would find themselves feeling as though they belonged to a disenfranchised class, struggling to find basic material stability while living in exile within these hastily defined borders. The sociopolitical agitations may have informed Merle's months-long dithering about her plan to return to her birth country.

Merle soon found a convenient professional excuse to forgo the visit to India: The same year that India unfastened itself from British rule, Merle received a contract from RKO Radio, a ballast of the atrophying studio system and one of the Big Five. That contract would have been a security blanket after years of freelancing in an industry on life support. She signed on for a role in *Night Song* (1947), again with Ballard as cinematographer, to play a socialite who falls for a blind pianist and, to win him over, feigns blindness herself. The film made it clear that Merle had ceased pushing herself artistically. But RKO continued to tempt her with scripts, leading her to stay put in America. She and Lucien would work together again on a drama called *Berlin Express*, RKO's next project. A slick noir, it would be the first American movie filmed on location in postwar Frankfurt and Berlin, and Merle would play a French secretary who helps thwart a brewing underground

Nazi conspiracy. The film couldn't have been a less adequate vehicle for Merle, who traveled to Europe to film the movie in the summer of 1947. Accent work was never her strong suit—note that she hadn't attempted to suppress her manicured Mayfair intonations when playing American women in *These Three* or *Lydia*—yet, here, she took a swing at a French accent, with disastrous results. Even her friend Hedda Hopper had no hesitation in pointing out Merle's sonic inadequacies, saying that Merle "forgets her accent more than she remembers it." Other viewers said Merle should sue Lucien for libel because of his shoddy way of lighting her, a sharp reversal of his earlier paeans to her beauty with the Obie. Critics were shocked, saying she'd never looked worse. They wondered whether Lucien had sabotaged her. Maybe he was even trying to spite her.

The loose seams in Merle's marriage became ever more apparent on set. She began to nurse a crush on her leading man, the burly Robert Ryan, and Ryan reciprocated. Her fights with Lucien subsequently became intense, to the point where she bore the brunt of his anger. On the sea journey back to America, the two of them quarreled ceaselessly until, at one point, he reportedly struck her. The alleged assault was, by most accounts, brutal: Merle returned to Hollywood with a mouth full of chipped teeth, requiring her to sport a wire on her battered jaw. The obvious injury got everyone talking, a humiliation. Merle, valuing her privacy, was roundabout regarding the cause of these bruises. When onlookers asked her what happened, she told them that she had slipped in the shower.

★

MERLE SPENT THE MONTHS after making *Berlin Express* trying to keep the peace with Lucien. Though her contract with RKO demanded she make one movie annually for the next five years, Hollywood's boom times had ended. Profits from studios were at a historic low, having dipped from $122 million in 1946 to $89 million the following year, a downward trajectory that continued into 1948. Making matters worse, the Supreme Court, in May 1948, handed down a series of decisions that effectively killed the Hollywood studio system that had shepherded Merle's career. One of those rulings deregulated the domination that majors like Paramount had over movie theaters that allowed them to block-book—that is, to sell a bundle of its titles to movie theaters all at once. Another ruling targeted theater chains that had first dibs on certain studios' films and thus disenfranchised independent theaters. These decisions were hammers to the scaffolding of the studio system, which would continue to slouch toward extinction in subsequent years.

Work began to matter less to Merle as she and Lucien vacationed through Europe together in early 1948. While in England, they visited the very first flat where she had lived with Charlotte, when she was just barely an extra. Merle found that it had been bombed out during the war and was about to be razed. That piece of her own history, evidence of the girl she'd once been, had disappeared. The sadness continued once she and Lucien reached Italy in the summer of 1948 to mark their third wedding anniversary. They fought constantly. Merle became frustrated that her rugged husband lacked sophistication in the elite settings she'd been used to, especially when married to Alexander—circles where she still felt comfortable. She had gone to great lengths to groom herself as a high-society lady despite her lower-class upbringing. Lucien represented a side of Merle's nature— her beginnings as an outsider looking in—that she wanted to abandon. The tension between them climaxed when they boarded a yacht in Capri, in Italy, for a short cruise, an excursion that would alter the course of her life.

Chapter 12

To Belong to This Country

(1948–1953)

The last photograph of Merle Oberon with Count Giorgio Cini,
taken on August 31, 1949, in Cannes, France.

WHEN MERLE LOCKED EYES WITH COUNT GIORGIO CINI, she felt she belonged to him. The son of a rich industrialist and a former silent-film actress, Giorgio—the yacht's owner—was a total catch in Merle's eyes, a tall man possessed of wealth, the perfume of gallantry, and sensitive looks reminiscent of the Italian actor Rudolph Valentino. He was twenty-nine when they met, she thirty-seven, and in some ways he had not outgrown his youth. He was a proud playboy who, despite having an aristocratic wife, womanized with the abandon of a bachelor. The chemistry between them was so obvious that Lucien, realizing he was losing Merle, exited the boat puffing with jealousy. The ugliness of Lucien's character prompted Merle to treat their imminent separation as if it were the dissolution of a professional contract, just as she had done when sharing hints of her Alexander split with gossip columnists. Together, she and Lucien went to Rome, where Merle cabled Hedda Hopper on the morning of August 5 with the news of her intent: She and Lucien were separating due to the simple matter of "incompatibility."

From that point forward, her affair with Giorgio began in full view of the public, feeding Lucien's rage. The next morning, he caught Merle and Giorgio together in bed at the Excelsior, a Roman hotel owned by Giorgio's family, barreling into the room and shattering glass in fury. Alexander, her ex-husband, just happened to be staying at the same hotel; he was still desperately in love with Merle, and she even asked him for advice on how to escape the danger of her situation. He did what he could to guide her, wishing she could flock back to him instead. But Merle had already glued her gaze on this much younger man. Giorgio had Lucien kicked out of the hotel before he and Merle checked out that evening and went to the Grand Hotel in Venice. Lucien, however, trailed them there with a gun. Seeking refuge, Merle and Giorgio climbed down from a balcony and hopped aboard his nearby yacht, finding safety.

★

THAT FALL, MERLE RETURNED to America, flying separately from Lucien. She sifted through the terms of her divorce and her contract with RKO, the latter an increasing afterthought as her personal life seemed so alive with possibility. RKO was now commandeered by the industrialist and aviator Howard Hughes, a louche who represented the conservative guard in Hollywood. At this point, the Red Scare was infecting Hollywood, with the industry sniffing out suspected Communists in its ranks while the studio system continued to corrode. Interpersonally, however, Hughes was unusually gracious to Merle. His soft spot for her led to his relaxing her contract, telling her she'd receive her agreed-upon fee of $250,000 for a pair of films, even if he couldn't find two acceptable projects for her. She hoped this would be the case, as she yearned to return to Europe to be with Giorgio.

Streaming beneath Merle's single-minded fixation on Giorgio, however, was a disquietude that she would express to her longtime friend Norma Shearer. Despite the divergences in their lives over the previous decade since Norma's retirement, the two women hadn't lost the love they had for one another. Merle told Norma that she wasn't sure how Giorgio's aristocratic Venetian family would react if they were married; his father, who had been a member of the Senate under Benito Mussolini, saw the older and twice-married Merle as damaged goods. She also told Norma that she felt her career had slipped away from her after the momentary firecracker of *A Song to Remember*. Merle now expected to give up her career for Giorgio. His mother, Lyda Borelli, was an actress who had been second in talent only to Eleanora Duse (a name synonymous with thespian excellence), but Borelli sunsetted her career after her marriage, an example Merle planned to follow.

After some tussling with Lucien, Merle relinquished ownership of Shangri-La, her beloved Malibu home, to him. Merle's divorce, obtained in Juárez, finally came through in February of 1949, and Lucien vanished from her life soon thereafter. He would go on to carve out a steady career of his own as a cinematographer. She didn't waste time, immediately jetting to Paris that month to meet with Giorgio, who made Merle flutter with nervousness, electrifying her insecurities: She wanted to impress this younger man so much that she would change her dress six times before meeting with him for dinner, making sure she fit his imagined ideal. No matter how hard she tried, she never felt beautiful enough for him. This pursuit of perfection had consequences that would reverberate for years. Merle and Giorgio would argue

often. One April day in Paris, her hotel neighbors heard a violent scuffle coming from her room. When Merle emerged with a broken nose,
though, she just told everyone she'd skidded on a bar of soap in the
bathroom, slamming her face against a faucet. Her excuse resembled
what she'd said after her alleged fight with Lucien months earlier had
left her with a broken jaw. Gazing at this new injury, Merle panicked
at the sight of herself, worried that her nose would never look normal
again. She sought out a plastic surgeon, thus beginning the first of
many revisions to her face that Merle, now in her late thirties, would
undergo. The surgery would also take care of lingering scars from her
sulfa-induced allergy attack, whose imprints had become more prominent with age. From then on, Merle would devote herself to plastic
surgery to survive the ageist glare of the public eye. Later in her life,
comedians would crack jokes at her expense about the immobility of
her face, unaware that her preoccupation with cosmetic surgery began
as an attempt to correct a very serious, and cruel, injury.

Despite sliding into a relationship with the same augurs of doom that
had marked her marriage to Lucien, Merle was still dazzled by visions
of a life with Giorgio. Soon enough, his family even came around to
Merle's charms. Venice began to buzz about Merle's romance to such a
degree that Italian theaters began to revive the silent movies that Giorgio's mother had made decades earlier, a testament to Merle's power to
generate publicity globally. Merle and Giorgio went to Europe's plushest resorts, its most luxurious restaurants.

In August 1949, they would find themselves vacationing in Cannes,
on the Riviera. They agreed that, once their trip ended, she would see
him off at a nearby airfield from which he would leave for Venice in a
twin-engine plane. The night before his planned flight, the duo went
to a seance. A spiritualist read Giorgio's palm and, with a funereal
voice, asked him to step into another room with him, without Merle.
The man's instructions to Giorgio were clear: Do not board that plane.
The spiritualist came back into the room and glanced at Merle, muttering, in Italian that was imperceptible to her ears, that the stink of
death was floating around her. In private, the spiritualist found Merle

to be a confounding presence, with green eyes that "look like those of a dolphin," as he would later write of her. He regarded her as a sort of brown temptress, a woman whose "charm does not come from her physical appearance, but instead is something mysterious that emanates from her soul. It is likely for this reason that many people say she has Asian origins."

Even as Giorgio ignored the forecast of this Cassandra, Merle had a bad feeling about the flight. "Couldn't you take a train?" she asked. After eating lunch with him the next day at an airport restaurant, she stood on the airfield bathed in sun as she watched his plane climb into the air. It was nearly out of her eyesight before the pilot rubbernecked back toward her; Giorgio had wanted to wave good-bye to her, he'd told her just before taking off, and here he was, as promised, swinging a handkerchief in the sky. She watched him blowing her kisses, before lowering her eyes in relief. But then she heard the choke of the engine. She gazed upward to see the plane struggling to gain altitude, dipping and scraping against the topmost branches of the nearby trees before plunging to the ground in flames. Giorgio's seatbelts ruptured, ejecting his body, but only the handkerchief with which he was waving to her floated to the ground. He died at that very moment. Merle stood there for a beat, her face locked in disbelief, before her knees buckled and she fainted. People rushed over to take care of her. "My life is finished," she yowled after coming to, unable to see her future without Giorgio. "There's no point in going on."

★

IN THE WAKE OF Giorgio's death, Merle became a carcass of herself. As she had earlier in the decade when hobbled by her skin infection, she contemplated suicide. She feared people would blame her for his death, and her reputation in Hollywood became that of a femme fatale. She flickered in and out of consciousness while on opiates, wondering whether she might have to go to a sanatorium to recover. The world around her seemed to scream with Munchian agony. She could think of nothing but Giorgio, this man who'd exited her life as quickly as he had entered it. Merle insisted that the medium who had had that foreboding sense of Giorgio's imminent death stay in the next room at her Cannes hotel; she wanted to consult him so she could talk to Giorgio, and he would summon Giorgio nightly. Ultimately staying in Europe for over a year, Merle otherwise remained under medical care, seeing few people. Alexander Korda, still in love, visited her in Cannes and begged her to remarry him. She still considered him, at best, a friend, though one she held in high esteem. Norma arrived, too, though she and Merle would begin to drift apart as Merle sank farther into her grief. She became a recluse from Hollywood, barely speaking to much of anyone. With the downturn in her film career, Merle was fast becoming famous more for her private life than for her acting, with story-hungry papers salivating over her pathetic troubles. They began to print canards about Merle being strapped for cash. The fact that Merle hadn't made any movies since *Berlin Express*, a middling title, didn't help mute rumors about her financial woes.

But by the end of the year, Merle realized she couldn't wallow in the debris of her grief for the rest of her life, and perhaps work might indeed shake her out of her torpor. She made peace with the fact that romance would no longer be in the cards for her. Committing herself to her art would be the next best option for fulfillment. With RKO remaining rather undemanding with her contract, Merle forced herself out of her seclusion at the close of 1949 to begin filming *Pardon My French*, an independent film, in the South of France. The film reunited her with Bernard Vorhaus, who had drooled over her lecherously when he directed her in 1934's *The Broken Melody*, the low-budget production she made before she got to Hollywood. When Merle arrived on location, though, Vorhaus felt she wasn't well enough to start working. She was quiet and calm, but not all there. He delayed shooting until early the following year in the hopes that she'd be of sounder mind and body by then.

On paper, this role—in a film that was being made simultaneously in English and French (Merle had a dubbing coach for the latter; her studies at La Martinière in Calcutta had included French)—was a walkthrough of her greatest hits: She'd play a Boston schoolmarm (reminiscent of her role in *Lydia* a decade earlier) named Elizabeth Rockwell who inherits a French castle from her grandfather (recalling *Over the Moon*), only to find that a swarm of grubby squatters has overtaken it. She pouts at the prospect of having to share space with these derelicts, many of whom are children. She has the humorlessness of a basilisk—one character even calls her a "cold, inhibited spinster" and adds that she's unattractive—before she gradually falls in love with one of the residents, a widower named Paul (Paul Henreid). The film was a comedy, a welcome change from what Merle felt was a sameness to her string of roles in the late 1940s. The waterworks were kept to a minimum, to Merle's relief. "If I had once started crying, I might never have stopped," she said to a journalist, cracking a rare smile.

The crew did everything it could to make her life as easy as possible, building a chalet dressing room for her away from the set where she could spend her lunch hour alone, with ten minutes of eating and fifty minutes of rest. A doctor ordered her to have her dinner at 6 p.m. after shooting each day, lights out at 9 p.m. Even so, Merle was still somewhat irritable while making the film. Vorhaus borrowed a few kids who were playing in a nearby street, their faces smudged with grime, and put them in a scene. Merle was supposed to kiss one on the cheek; she demanded the crew scrub the poor child's face with alcohol, despite knowing quite well what it meant to be destitute. Working on this film over the course of twelve weeks didn't cheer up Merle in the way she was hoping, though she was raking in a lot of cash for it—a third of its reported $300,000 budget. She was second-billed behind Henreid (who had been in *Casablanca*), a sign of how much her star had sunk in the estimation of the industry. Vorhaus could tell she was sad, so he helped arrange another film for her, *Affair in Monte Carlo*, as a pity picture; produced by the Associated British Picture Corporation, it would be directed by Victor Saville, who'd given her that work as an extra all those decades ago when she was working at the Café de Paris.

In the downtime between the two films, Merle fell back on old habits: Only able to think of Giorgio, she started attending seances again, constantly trying to communicate with him. This obsession drove a wedge between her and Norma, her best friend.

Overworked and fatigued, Merle subsequently crumbled into another nervous breakdown in April 1950, seeking shelter and care in a Swiss sanatorium. She became ever more concerned about her face, pursuing further facial procedures in Biarritz, on France's Basque coast. (The paranoia would, unfortunately, turn out to be warranted: One of the many unfavorable reviews of *Pardon My French* commented that the camera was "ungracious" to Merle.) She would wander alone through the Biarritz spas like a banshee; she gained weight, which provoked judgment from the Hollywood set. Merle was terrified of having to face the press again, though her RKO contract was still a matter of practical concern. She thought of selling all her Hollywood holdings and just settling down in Europe—she longed to stay near the site of Giorgio's crash. Merle hated that newspapers were printing stories about her visits to seances. Even when she was far from Hollywood, its prying eyes seemed to trail her everywhere. In quite the turnaround from an early life when she felt so friendless, now she wanted people to mind their own business, to leave her alone. But she had signed up for a life in which that was not an option.

*

In December of 1950, beckoned by her obligation to RKO, Merle limped back to America with all the enthusiasm of a child being dragged to the dentist's chair. At the start of 1951, she found herself back on the studio lot, where Howard Hughes had mercy on her. She owed the studio two pictures, but Hughes was so lax that he told her that if she didn't get an assignment, she could just go back to France. As she waited, Merle settled back into her Bel Air home, kept pristine by her maid as though she'd never left. Yet not even that sort of devotion could restore her mood. She had become a transparently fragile thing. Journalists asked her whether she was happy. "Well," she could only respond, "I'm living."

A reason to enjoy life, rather than just sluggishly glide through it, surfaced that March when Merle became involved with an all-American doctor named Rex L. Ross. Freshly divorced, he was everything she wanted in a man, just like Giorgio in her head: Moneyed, handsome, tall, and—this was important—totally smitten with her. Merle's romance with Rex would, without warning, become the first serious one she'd had since Giorgio's death. Merle knew that she had been refusing to let herself find happiness. But Rex helped her hoist herself out of this emotional ague. They danced Viennese waltzes together on Sunday nights at the Macayo, a restaurant in Santa Monica; she began hosting dinner parties with him. They spent so much time together that she suddenly didn't feel like returning to Europe to make *Affair in Monte Carlo*, a picture she now regretted she'd contracted. An ambivalence toward the industry was starting to brew within her. The day before she flew to Europe late that summer, she told a journalist that she was going to retire from movies after this forthcoming shoot, finding that the quality of her offers—along with the films themselves—had regressed. "Why are pictures so bad these days?" she said. "I've asked people and nobody seems to know. I'm always being pushed into something that's wrong or not carefully thought out for me. It was different when I was with Samuel Goldwyn, of course." Merle had her reasons for feeling that Hollywood movies—at least the movies she knew—were on the decline. The consumption habits of Americans were changing; moviegoing as a social activity had become less hallowed a hobby than crowding in front of a television, which was undergoing an explosion in household usage over the first half of the 1950s. Though the studio system was, to be clear, a structure that had strangled Merle—crafting her image and forcing her to follow its rigid rules—it was also all she had ever been familiar with. Now, actors of Merle's generation found themselves forsaken. Peers of hers who were once cushioned by that very system saw their contracts being terminated by studios who, scared silly by television's competition, no longer saw the value of such agreements if it meant hemorrhaging money.

While Merle was in Europe to shoot *Affair in Monte Carlo*, she fought her feelings of misery about being away from Rex by pouring out her soul to him in passionate missives, convinced she had landed her one true love. "Millions of people love + die without even realizing their dreams," she wrote him that October. "I'm terribly grateful I've found you." In the film—shot in Technicolor between England and the French Riviera—Merle brought plaintive longing to the part of a widow who falls in love with a young gambler, against her better judgment. Critics were displeased with the film, with some feeling that Merle "seems more maternal than passion-dominated," as if those two traits were oppositional.

Merle, forty-two at the time of this film's release, was caught in that creaky middle ground between the sprightly leading lady and the sage character actress. She was a senior citizen in Hollywood's vicious eyes, and the industry had no idea where to slot her. The wartime star Betty Grable, plus newer entrants such as Doris Day, both sunflower blondes, were thought to be the bankable actresses of that era—primarily, though not exclusively, in comedies or musicals—as was the brunette Susan Hayward, who excelled in dramatic heavies. Not all these women were significantly younger than Merle, but they had gotten their start in the industry after she had. In a time when the tastes of both audiences and gatekeepers changed on a whim, Merle was old hat. Some of Merle's contemporaries in the industry back in the 1930s had managed to survive or reinvent themselves in that fair-weather period. Bette Davis received the role of her career as an actress idolized by a fawning (and sniping) starlet in Joseph L. Mankiewicz's *All About Eve* (1950), giving voice to the anxieties of a generation of stars who worried that their positions might be overtaken by girls who were younger, dewier, and hungrier. Vivien Leigh offered a stirring portrait of fading sanity as an aging Southern belle in Elia Kazan's *A Streetcar Named Desire* (1951). Even women like Gloria Swanson, who was rarely in direct competition with Merle because of a career recession with the advent of the talkies, had scored the lead role in *Sunset Boulevard* (1950), in which the fifty-one-year-old actress played a delusional diva of the silent screen trying to cling to her past grandeur. Such roles were scarce for women in a certain age bracket. These actresses also had a key advantage that Merle didn't: reputations as respected performers. Critical esteem for Merle had taken a steady backslide over the previous decade; the roles at her disposal were limited without the legitimacy that Goldwyn or even Korda gave her, while her poor choice of parts during her marriage to Lucien Ballard further thwarted her. The fact that she had been married to a cinematographer, a peasant in the status-driven view of the industry, further damaged Merle's standing. It was no surprise that the roles thinned out. For Merle, that RKO contract may have been the closest thing she had to an anchor in a time of unmooring.

IN JANUARY OF 1952, when Merle joined several other stars in the RKO stable for a trip to Punta del Este, Uruguay, for a film festival, she made a somewhat striking decision: On her travel visa, she labeled her birth country as India. One can only imagine why she would be compelled to do so, even if Merle herself may not have been able to parse her own motivations. America was starting to open its arms to South Asian culture, Hollywood included. On a visit to Bombay for the International Film Festival of India that same month, the Hollywood filmmaker Frank Capra was enraptured by the beauty of the actress Madhubala, already a star in India's burgeoning Hindi-language cinema known as Bollywood. He offered to launch her in Hollywood, only for her father to decline on her behalf, saying she did not know how to eat with forks and knives. This publicity, though, led to photo spreads that year in *Theatre Arts*, an American magazine, proclaiming her to be "The Biggest Star in the World—and she's not in Beverly Hills," showing the growing enthusiasm for talents who came from the very part of the world Merle could not celebrate as her homeland.

The interest in South Asian performers also permeated the wider entertainment world. A singer who went by the name Korla Pandit became a durable presence on California television in the 1950s, alleging he was the mixed-race son of an Indian father and a French mother; he would express his ethnic pride by ensconcing his head in a turban. In truth, Pandit was John Roland Redd, a Black man from Columbia, Missouri, who, trying to escape the discrimination of the Jim Crow era that still limited opportunities for African Americans, would glide up the racial hierarchy and pass as South Asian, a fact that would not emerge until after his death in the new millennium. In the years that followed passage of the Luce-Celler Act, there was currency to be mined in the adoption of a South Asian cultural costume—even safety for those like Redd, who sought out a life that would otherwise be unavailable to him by dint of his race.

Now that it had been years since the Luce-Celler Act had finally allowed India-born South Asians like Merle to become naturalized citizens, Merle announced to the press she'd take the leap of applying for American citizenship, even if most of the public may not have realized how fraught that pursuit had been just a short time earlier. "I have come to the happy conclusion that I want something more than just an American film career," she proudly announced to Louella Parsons in February 1953. "I want to belong to this country, so I have asked my attorney, Greg Bautzer, to make the necessary application on my behalf to the Department of Naturalization." But she did not follow through on this declaration. To obtain citizenship, she needed a birth or baptismal certificate, which would reveal all she'd been forced to hide. Having lived in a cloud of fiction for so long, Merle got cold feet.

Chapter 13

Like a Virus

(1953–1956)

Poster for The Price of Fear (1956), Merle's final theatrically
released film before her third marriage.

As the husk of the Hollywood studio system contin-
ued to desiccate, Merle still more or less disregarded her contract with
RKO. She began to consider acting on television, a medium she'd initially viewed with a snob's skepticism. Since the start of the 1950s, television had slowly been gaining newfound respectability; actors of her

generation, who had once turned their backs on it, now saw financial opportunities. Networks churned out one-off teleplays with factory-like efficiency; these low-lift commitments offered ample money to stars on the decline. Merle's old boyfriend David Niven, for example, began participating routinely in live television dramas after he began to worry that his film career had petered out. In 1952, he even corralled a few of his friends to start a TV production company, Four Star Playhouse, to make dramatic productions for CBS in which actors in his age bracket could rely on consistent work. Television was an especially logical destination for actresses who found themselves flayed for succumbing to the supposed ravages of time. Women like Lucille Ball, who had achieved a mild degree of success on film incommensurate with their talent, were enjoying fame on television through sitcom work.

Merle came to regard television as a way to stretch herself. She took on a handful of projects tied to Four Star Playhouse, making her television debut in February 1953 with "Sound Off, My Love," a teleplay with a twisty, nonsensical-sounding plot crammed into a mere half hour: She played a woman who suddenly loses her hearing and tries to keep this secret from her husband out of pride, only for her to learn that her husband is not only having an affair but also attempting to kill her. This role put to good use Merle's previous work in thrillers such as *The Lodger* and *Dark Waters*, and she could sufficiently wring truth from the inherent absurdities of the story. But critics lambasted the "transparent idiocy" of the script. More television offers came that year—Merle drew $4,000 checks for appearances on the TV series *Four Star Playhouse*—and the medium became a lifeline for her. She bristled when she learned, after the fact, that Alexander Korda had married a young woman, Alexandra Boycun, in June 1953. Though Merle had steadfastly ignored all of his pleas to remarry in the previous years, she was stung by his choice of a girl more than a decade her junior. When the three of them ended up in the same hotel on a visit to London not long after their wedding, Merle promptly and quietly checked out.

While abroad, Merle was starting to fear that Rex Ross would not be able to offer her the companionship she wanted. She continued to send him long letters attesting to her love for him, yet he seemed ill-equipped to offer her adequate emotional support. "I want love + closeness + companionship," she would write to him in June, the month of Alexander's wedding. "Maybe I'll find it one day." But Rex's California medical practice kept him busy; he also had a son on whom he doted. "I think you are one of those people who want to walk alone," she wrote to him in another letter a few days later. "You don't need the closeness of another spirit."

Merle now found herself wanting a happy marriage over an acting career, for Hollywood had become a dead zone for her. Her more fruitful film acting opportunities that year were outside America: Merle traveled to Spain in September to make *All Is Possible in Granada*, a film in which she played a representative of an American oil company who finds love in Andalusia. The film was never released stateside, much less reviewed there, despite its premiere at the prestigious Cannes Film Festival. Gossip columns chided her for gaining weight during her time in Spain, saying, "She'll have to go over the Panama Canal instead of through it" on her way back to America.

But by the time she had wrapped the shoot for *All Is Possible in Granada* in January of 1954, Merle set her sights on returning to Hollywood. There, to the industry's surprise, she managed to snag two high-profile feature-film roles—a near-miracle at a time when most her age were fighting for scraps on film. In March, she accepted an offer for a supporting part in the musical *Deep in My Heart*, an elephantine MGM biopic of the composer Sigmund Romberg. She would take on the dignified role of the actress and librettist Dorothy Donnelly, a classy doyenne of the Broadway stage who would succumb to pneumonia. In this film, Merle would project a sageness that her previous performances lacked. Though some reviewers would pick up on the grace of her performance, the film—at more than two hours, one of the longest in Merle's filmography—was a tough sit for audiences. A plummier role arose in May, when Merle agreed to play in *Désirée*, a Twentieth Century Fox epic about the Emperor Napoleon in which she would be the Empress Josephine. Merle would be starring opposite the flashy and rebellious upstart Marlon Brando, an actor thirteen years her junior. Brando had blazed to screen fame opposite Vivien Leigh in *A Streetcar Named Desire*, where the interplay of his more modern kineticism against Leigh's grande-dame posturing gave the film its soul. That performance of his was an announcement: American cinema had found a bracing new presence who might be able to infuse rickety studio jalopies with blood and passion. One of the first film performers associated with the Method school of acting, Brando took a naturalistic approach to his work: His characters seemed to burst from within, incongruous with the passé Golden Age style that Merle had perfected in her two decades of screen acting.

The prospect of working with Brando intimidated Merle. She had heard stories about his aggression, even unkindness, toward actresses of her age. So it surprised her when she came on set and found that Brando was, in fact, a fount of generosity. He told her how much he'd loved her screen work; he even asked for her advice on how to inhabit his character. (She told him to stop chewing gum, for starters.) They spent so much time together that Merle's accent tattooed itself on Brando's. Brando had just lost his mother; though it had been years since Charlotte's death, Merle knew his pain, and she would comfort him in her dressing room. *Désirée* was a sumptuous production shot in CinemaScope, a widescreen technology that studios had latched onto to entice television viewers back to the cinema. The role of Josephine was appropriately glamorous for a woman of Merle's social stature. Her taste for jewelry rivaled Merle's own in real life; the script described Merle's character as "sultry and theatrical" with all those glittering rocks, concluding, simply, that "Josephine is Something." The character bore other meaningful parallels to Merle's own story: Josephine, like the woman who would bring her to life more than a century later, had gone to great lengths to conceal her birthplace, which was in the Caribbean. In a tragic reflection of Merle's life, Josephine's marriage to

Bonaparte would also fizzle out because of her inability to bear children with him.

Brando could tell that Merle was insecure about how she, now forty-three, looked on camera. "You're the best thing in the picture," he'd tell her. By this point, Merle's ardor for Ross had cooled considerably as he began dating other women. Merle followed suit, inviting Brando to dinner parties at her home. Their mutual respect blossomed into a brief romance. Though he viewed her, greedily, as a trophy—to friends, he'd express his boyish disbelief that he'd slept with a Tasmanian aristocrat, unaware of Merle's secret—Merle found her pillow talk with Brando taking an unusually honest turn on some nights. She told him she felt she was on borrowed time. "The only roles open to me in the future will be that of a rich old lady involved with a much younger man," she said to him, fearful of what lay ahead. Now, playing the haughty wife of Bonaparte, Merle got to put these inchoate feelings of self-pity somewhere. Though Merle's character in *Désirée* disappeared just around the film's one-hour mark, this was the closest she'd get to a Swanson-in-*Sunset-Boulevard* role. Merle seemed to be well aware of it, milking her few scenes for all their worth; she found unexpected depth in a woman who felt powerless against time, limning this part with a tragic undercurrent that she could only have brought to it at this phase of her life. "She's only eighteen, you know? That Marie-Louise . . . that Austrian princess he's marrying," she said in her final scene, her grief for a lost husband capsizing into hysteria. Regrettably for everyone involved, critics were unmoved by her Josephine. Some even levied the ultimate insult against her: "Miss Merle Oberon, on the other hand, portrays a singularly unattractive Josephine," wrote one reviewer. "Frankly, she looks more like Mr. Brando's mother than his mistress and wife." To them, the woman once famed for her beauty had become a droopy hag.

For Merle, jabs at her age began to come routinely, no matter the medium. Throughout 1954, Merle also continued her work with television, starring, for example, as a secretary in "The Man Who Came to Dinner," a comedy that netted her a $12,500 paycheck. Reviewers, taking potshots at her age, said she "suffered brutally from time's inroads." (Many of her teleplays would become lost to time due to the practices of the era in which initial broadcasts were taped over, or "wiped."*) She made dutiful appearances on game shows, too, such as *What's My Line?*, in which a group of blindfolded panelists would try to guess the identities of celebrity contestants. She seemed good-humored but shy, affecting the demeanor of a New England spinster to baffle contestants. Yet there was a glint of sadness in her eyes, too, as if she felt her era had passed. As 1954 went on and Merle soldiered through her film and television projects, her attitude toward acting began to shift. "All I want to do," she said to Hedda Hopper one day that year, "is to enjoy myself quickly before I die." Merle wasn't crazy to speak in such fatalistic terms: Both *Deep in My Heart* and *Désirée* were released at the tail end of 1954, the same year that the studio system as Merle knew it collapsed for good. MGM, the studio that had released *Deep in My Heart*, broke off from Loew's Theaters, which had been its reliable theatrical platform.

But there were also intimations of more positive change. Due to considerable pressure from figures such as Merle's former boss Samuel Goldwyn to keep pace with the times, a slight revision of the Hays Code came in 1954, bringing with it permission to depict interracial romance "within the careful limits of good taste." The terminology was vague enough for filmmakers to interpret it freely. By this point in Hollywood, actresses of color were also managing to break through the pollution of racism that had once prevented them from receiving institutional recognition. Merle's few champions in the critical realm thought that she herself might contend for an Oscar nomination for either one of her American film performances in 1954, albeit in the

---

* "Sound Off, My Love," "Love at Sea," "The Frightened Woman," and "Cavalcade" are the sole surviving telefilms of hers as of this writing. "Allison, Ltd." (1953) for the *Ford Television Theatre*, "The Journey" (1953) for the *Playhouse of Stars*, "Second Sight" (1955) for the *Ford Television Theatre*, and "The Bracelet" (1955) for *The Loretta Young Show* are among Merle's television works that are now lost. They are listed in the filmography at the end of this book.

Best Supporting Actress category. The nomination did not materialize, but the Academy Awards for that film year did take a major step
forward in the Best Actress category, where Merle had made her mark
nearly two decades earlier: The Black actress Dorothy Dandridge,
with her flutelike singing voice and the grace of a dove, was a nominee for Best Actress in a Leading Role for *Carmen Jones* (1954). Here was
a role for a Black performer in which Dandridge played a woman of
great confidence, a signal of change for a demographic who had long
had to settle for parts defined by subservience. Dandridge would say
that her heart "swelled with pride at the thought of what this means
to me as an actress and for the significance the nomination has." She
would publicly celebrate her achievement, and its symbolism, in a way
Merle couldn't nineteen years earlier.

Beyond Hollywood, some of the vitriol against immigrants from
South Asia that had been so normative when Merle first arrived in
town was abating. Saris came into fashion, even featured in *Harper's Bazaar* spreads in 1954, and Merle began to adopt the trend: That
same year, at industry gatherings, she would shimmer in pink silk
saris with flowing shoulder stoles. This was one of the few ways she
could work through her connection to her racial identity as America's
tolerance for South Asians grew, even if she still couldn't tell the world
the truth.

★

THOUGH TELEVISION WORK—WHICH MERLE continued throughout 1955 with a number of different teleplays—provided a modicum of
consistency for Merle, she wasn't yet ready to call it quits on film acting. This despite every indication that the industry had little time for
her. She would watch, dispirited, as crowds flocked to new box-office
stars like Marilyn Monroe—so blonde, so young, and so white—all
while ignoring Merle. Fans were no longer asking to kiss Merle's cheek
or obtain her autograph. In October of that year, Merle signed on for
what would become Universal's *The Price of Fear*, her final Hollywood
film for some years. Merle played a ruthless careerist named Jessica

Warren, who is seen in the film's first few minutes cruising down the street, drunk, when she fatally strikes a man walking his dog and flees the scene. After parts that had felt so narrow in moral terms, here, Merle thought, was an opportunity to spin gold out of an unsympathetic role. Gliding through the film with Sphinxlike poise as she tried to evade justice, Merle had enough innate pathos not to make this woman completely repellent. But the production company, Universal-International, cut some of her role and substituted narration, much to her annoyance, for she felt she was most charming in those sequences. Thus, it was no surprise when critics dinged her for failing to salvage her already-unappealing role, and the film cratered with audiences. By the time of *The Price of Fear*'s release in 1956, it seemed obvious that the curtains on her film career had closed. She began that year with a contract to host a twenty-six-episode television series, *Assignment Foreign Legion*, shooting in Europe and North Africa. She would even act in a few of those segments herself as a newspaperwoman investigating the lives of men in the French Foreign Legion.

But just weeks after the project was announced, Merle learned of the death in London of Alexander Korda, her first husband. He was sixty-two when a heart attack claimed him in late January of 1956. Grief, a state that Merle had managed to avoid since Giorgio Cini's 1949 death, locked its grip on Merle. She sobbed before reporters, unable to muster up any words. Alexander was one of the very few people who knew her to her core, rather than the version of herself she paraded before the world. He represented a part of her history she would no longer be able to access. Though she had kept him at a polite distance since their divorce more than a decade earlier, he had continued to love Merle long after their separation, even if he had tried to heed Merle's wishes that they not remarry. In a motion of scorn that may have been motivated by her rejection of him, he eliminated her from his will, while allotting a sizable chunk to his first and third wives.

Merle finally sloughed off the loss of her mentor and father figure as she began work on *Assignment Foreign Legion* (which, like much of Merle's television work, is now entirely lost). "Acting is like a virus," she explained to the *Los Angeles Times* in April. "You have to get it out of your system. I guess I'll never get it out of mine." Each episode cost a pretty penny at an average of $26,000, centering on stories about French Army officers whose wives cheated on them, for example, or about Frenchmen accused (and exonerated) of being Nazi informers. Merle dove into the task with innocent studiousness. She'd ask journalists who interviewed her how they did their jobs so she could mimic their vocation convincingly. Although some of the material was preposterous—in one sequence, she had to pretend to run miles carrying a seven-pound typewriter in sweltering heat, asking anyone she passed where the cable office was—the work threw Merle back into the memory of her days as a receptionist clacking away at a typewriter for Halley Brothers in Calcutta. Being away from the movies as she signed on for *Assignment Foreign Legion* worked miracles for Merle's self-image, for she was no longer hobbled by the insecurities that had nagged at her during the making of *Désirée*. The show did not expose her to the typical oafish criticism about her wrinkles that came her way when she starred in films. Merle realized she was no longer the same Anglo-Indian wallflower who'd arrived in England in 1929 wishing she could be a cerulean-eyed blonde on a candy box. "When one is very young it is sometimes painful to be different, but it helps to remember the story of the ugly duckling," she told one reporter. "Then you appreciate your individuality." She was unique, and she liked it that way—liked that jutting, crooked tooth of hers and her large forehead, aspects of her beauty that she had once struggled to accept.

The cultural climate around Merle may also have given her ample reason to begin being kinder to herself. The year that she filmed *Assignment Foreign Legion*, 1956, saw a revision of the Hays Code that got rid of the rule on miscegenation completely, deleting that opaque language about "good taste" from the 1954 clause. One of the dictums that had made passing for white an imperative for Merle over two decades earlier had now come to an end. Likewise, the shifts in public sentiment that followed Indian independence back in 1947 led to a scattering of South Asian–origin actors trying to stake their claim in Hollywood. Among the more visible of those figures was Anna Kashfi, who married Merle's *Désirée* costar Marlon Brando in 1957. Born in 1934 in British India, Kashfi had skin as dark as Merle's at this time, a trait that Kashfi chose to brandish, often swathing herself in saris. Kashfi faced cruel accusations that she was just a white woman leaning into a new cultural fashion by claiming to be Anglo-Indian, perhaps because the industry was so unaccustomed to seeing women of her kind own their identities so openly. Even her parents, in the Welsh city of Cardiff, publicly repudiated the pride she expressed in her heritage. The truth, revealed in a 2019 biography of her, was that Kashfi's parents were Anglo-Indian, and they belonged to Merle's generation: They came of age in an India in which they, like Merle, lived under such oppression that they saw salvation in moving to Britain and reinventing themselves through assimilation into whiteness. In the post-Partition period when Kashfi began her modeling and acting career, her mixed heritage was less a defect than an asset. Kashfi's big-screen debut came with an ancillary role as a "Hindu girl" in the Spencer Tracy and Robert Wagner vehicle *The Mountain* (1956).

Yet opportunities remained dire for other South Asian actors. Actual South Asian performers like Kashfi, whose acting career would be destroyed by a scandal surrounding her racial origins (and also eclipsed in public memory by her fractious marriage to Brando), would primarily find themselves cast in roles of other races, and rarely at the narrative heart of films. Leading roles for South Asian performers remained scarce, while the practice of brownface failed to die out in American cinema, despite those years of reduced social intolerance against South Asians. The same year Kashfi made her Hollywood debut, George Cukor's *Bhowani Junction* (1956) appeared, featuring both Ava Gardner and Bill Travers in brownface as Anglo-Indians. Gardner's brownface makeup was faint rather than cartoonish. (Although Gardner was generally accepted by moviegoers of that era to be white, her racial heritage would be a source of occasional debate, even with murmurs of alleged Black ancestry.) She would play Victoria Jones, an

Anglo-Indian woman who serves in the Indian Army just as British control over the region is declining in 1947. The film would explore the condition of Anglo-Indians who were pulled among allegiances to different groups—South Asian, British, Anglo-Indian—unsure of where they ultimately belonged. "And who are we?" Gardner's character, trembling with angst, shouts to her brown mother in one scene. "I'll tell you! *Chee-chees! Eight-annas! Blackie-whites!*" These were the same invectives hurled at Merle back in India. Despite the characteristic fire and verve of her work, Gardner was totally miscast in this role, rattling off these lines as a New Englander might; a layer of reality was missing. In another universe, one can imagine an Anglo-Indian performer like Merle making a meal of this part. But that was not the Hollywood she knew.

Chapter 14

Being Mrs. Pagliai

(1956–1965)

Merle Oberon with her third husband, Bruno Pagliai,
in Rome in December 1957.

MERLE COULDN'T UNDERSTAND WHY THIS MAN WAS HOV-
ering over her table. It was a night in December 1956 when she was in
Mexico City to celebrate the opening of the hotelier Conrad Hilton's
latest four-hundred-room palace, the Continental Hilton Hotel. She
shimmied around each festivity with her incandescent emeralds and

diamonds, having insured each of her necklaces individually for the trip. This stranger kept saying he'd rather be sitting with her than some "Minister of Whatever-It-Was." It took him a few more tries before Merle finally got the hint.

There were symmetries between Merle and this stranger, Bruno Pagliai. He'd had multiple marriages, like Merle. He was also self-made. Italian by birth, he had emigrated to the United States in his teens, clerking at the Bank of Italy—a company that would become the Bank of America—and working his way up to become the magnate of a steel-and-aluminum empire in Mexico. His was a lucrative trade; his fortunes were said to be beyond $50 million. Now a Mexican citizen, Bruno had a massive French and Italian Renaissance art collection. His Mexico City mansion was just a little smaller than the White House, while another of his homes, south of Mexico City in Cuernavaca, had once been a section of the bastion of Hernán Cortés's palace. Though Bruno was not as classically handsome as her more recent paramours, such as Giorgio Cini and Rex Ross, Merle found him charming, clever, and—unlike Lucien Ballard—sophisticated. With Bruno, Merle had a chance to become a society lady, the life she'd run away from years earlier with Alexander, when she was still invested in her acting. That lifestyle was a far more attractive prospect to her now that she wanted stability. Bruno told Merle he'd met her a decade earlier, but that she hadn't even noticed him, though he gladly would have dropped everything and followed her had that not been the case. Things were different now. By this point, Merle had begun to fear that she was too old to fall in love again. Merle's anxiety that she would never have the chance to marry once more may have contributed to her decision, ultimately, not to tell Bruno about her South Asian heritage.

After that December meeting, Bruno promptly invited Merle to his New Year's Eve celebration in Mexico City. When she returned to Hollywood at the start of 1957, Merle fêted him as a guest of honor at a seventy-person dinner party at her home. Despite the speed with which Merle and Bruno were engaging in their courtship, Merle's friends didn't detect much cause for alarm. Hedda Hopper, for example, would throw cocktail parties for them on those weekends when Bruno visited Hollywood, encouraging their relationship. It came as little surprise, then, when Merle called her friends in the gossip world to break the news at the start of February, barely two months after she and Bruno had reconnected: She was engaged.

The obscenity of this man's affluence became clear to Merle when he gave her a 25-karat, teardrop diamond ring for their engagement, a gift that rivaled Alexander's emeralds for her. Whenever the ring became too heavy for her dainty finger, she would wear it on a chain dangling from her neck. In March came the announcement of what would be Merle's final acting commitment before marriage: a television special in which she played the Dutch spy Mata Hari, whose public persona involved a reversal of Merle's own. Mata Hari had adopted the affectations of a South Asian temple dancer in her costume of espionage. The episode, now lost, focused on Mata Hari's psychological state hours before her execution, when a sympathetic French officer would enter her cell and tempt her with the false possibility of escape. Merle made it explicitly clear that her career would no longer be a priority moving forward, though. "My marriage will come first," she told a journalist. "I'll work only when I have the inclination." This was a privilege she could now happily afford.

That summer of 1957, she and Bruno married quietly in a fourth-century church in Rome—like her earlier marriages, well outside American soil, thereby shielding her from any questions about her origins—a far less slapdash affair than her previous ceremony with Alexander in Antibes or the proxy arrangement with Lucien. Right after the wedding, she and Bruno flew to Nice to begin their honeymoon on a month-long yacht cruise through the Greek islands, parrying requests from reporters. "I didn't quit the movies to be bothered by interviews," she told them.

Once she and Bruno settled into married life in Mexico, Merle had the sudden urge to domesticate herself. "My career is being Mrs. Pagliai, and running my husband's homes," she told Louella Parsons that December. Within the first few years of their marriage, Merle would personalize Bruno's Mexico City white-brick wonderland with her own touches, installing a pool fountain and bedecking the mansion's interiors with the art of El Greco and François Boucher. Her leisure time would be devoted to painting and playing canasta. Merle's new life would also require her to host lavish parties. The year of their wedding, she and Bruno held a grand New Year's Eve bash in his Cuernavaca home, while Bruno ushered her into his social circle, which included Mexico's ex-President Miguel Alemán. Having finally settled down into the comfortable existence she had long desired, Merle decided that this was, at long last, the right time for her to do what she'd yearned to do for years: adopt children.

★

THE BABIES HAD BOTH been orphaned in an earthquake in Italy. Some said the boy, whom they called Bruno Jr., even looked a bit like Merle herself, with his tufts of black hair. Francesca didn't look like either Merle or Bruno, with her granola hair and sweet, oblong face. Merle treasured the children to the point that, when she first adopted them in 1959, she had an irrational paranoia that someone would take them from her. She would become wary of neglecting them, tending to them in a way that Charlotte just couldn't do when Merle had been little Queenie in Calcutta. "When they are with me, they are completely all I do," she would later insist to a reporter. "Nothing else."

Even as she was rearing her children, though, Merle would maintain an active social life, hosting soirées with Bruno at her longtime Bel Air home, where she curated and pruned her guest lists with exacting discretion. When the socialite and actress Zsa Zsa Gabor arrived with a man who wasn't on the guest list for a Halloween dinner in 1959, Merle told them that there was only room at the table for Gabor, not her escort, though they both were free to enter and have cocktails. Insulted, Gabor decided to leave the party, along with her date, afterward complaining to the press about Merle's diva-style behavior. "If Miss Gabor wants to make headlines, she'll have to make them alone," Merle told the press of this fracas. "I have no comment." Merle would sometimes have her children present at these gatherings, and she would integrate them into her public life. As Bruno Jr. and Francesca grew older, Merle would pose with them in *Vogue* spreads.

Though Merle generally did her best to inoculate her children from the horrors of the world, it was impossible for her to shield them from some realities. Through the late 1950s, Merle, inching closer to fifty, began to accept that her body couldn't withstand Mexico City's elevation, which, at more than seven thousand feet, would activate her heart murmur, a health condition that began to claw at her body. This necessitated the occasional use of an oxygen tank, a sight that scared the children. Merle would tell her kids the same stories of her life that the world knew, such as the way she cheated death in 1937 after a car crash. Despite her honesty on such matters, though, Merle would never speak much about her own childhood, even as she saw her kids through theirs. They, too, knew her only as a woman from Tasmania; they would continue to believe that until the day she died. At this juncture in her life, Merle had obtained all she wanted: fame, wealth, and, finally, children. Why risk forfeiting such security? Though Bruno Jr. would die a few years after she did, in a car crash at the age of twenty-five, Merle did not consider that she would be leaving daughter Francesca with questions for which she would never have answers, ones she would yearn for long after her mother was gone: What had it been like to grow up in India? And to become a movie star after that?

★

BACK IN INDIA, MERLE'S own mother, Constance Joyce, was growing ever more eager to rekindle relations with her daughter, to let her know how often she still thought about Merle. She grew so desperate for connection that she wrote a letter to the gossip columnist Sheilah Graham, stating that she was Merle's sister; Graham reprinted part of the letter in her syndicated column in July 1960, unbeknownst to Merle. Constance Joyce may have had every reason to express enmity toward the woman who refused to claim her publicly, yet even Graham was struck by the kind tone, unusual for these sorts of letters she received from family members of celebrities. The letter was filled with nothing but affection. Constance Joyce expressed gratitude to Merle for having "educated all four of her children," as Graham paraphrased it, the implication being that the trickles of money that Merle had sent back home were enough to give her siblings a life. "If you happen to meet her, kindly convey my love to her," Constance Joyce wrote to Graham. "Tons of it."

★

IN THOSE EARLY YEARS of motherhood, Merle split her time between Mexico and California. She sold her Bel Air home and, by September 1960, bought another in Beverly Hills. She began to call it the Selby House, honoring Charlotte Selby, her grandmother, who had raised her. The portals would swing open and a white-jacketed houseboy would greet you when you pulled on the sixteenth-century carved door. Inside was a palace decorated with pre-Columbian artifacts, paintings by Botticelli, even a desk that once belonged to British royalty. Merle's old friend Anna Lee from her days as an extra in London, now an established Hollywood actress in her own right, would sometimes visit her there, remembering that Queenie and the woman dressed in a sari didn't even have a bathroom of their own. Now, Merle had all the bathrooms she could want.

Throughout 1960, Merle began letting her hair grow down to her waist. Her inky tresses reflected the fashion of the era, while also being reminiscent of hairstyles from South Asia. She began to carry herself with undisturbed confidence, as if she were coming into her own; at some dinner parties, she would prance around in revealing negligees, a daring sartorial move for the time. ("Guess the old gal has to get attention somehow," one columnist oinked.) After decades of being a workhorse before the camera, Merle now slipped into another role entirely—that of the international socialite and hostess—which kept her in the spotlight. As a corollary to this lifestyle, she became a permanent fixture on lists of the world's best-dressed women. Having access to pools of wealth, thanks to her husband, sometimes made her terrifically, brazenly careless with her luxuries. On a trip to New York in late 1961, she left a $15,000 sable coat at a restaurant where she had lunched, unaware that she'd even abandoned it until she received a call from management. (She sent her chauffeur to retrieve it.)

Meanwhile, Merle still managed to keep alive a major artery to Hollywood; throughout 1961, for instance, she talked to Louella Parsons every day. But she hesitated to step before the camera again. When William Wyler, her *These Three* and *Wuthering Heights* director, asked her to play the demon child's grandmother in a more faithful adaptation of Lillian Hellman's *The Children's Hour*—now with the initial lesbian plotline gently restored (thereby undoing its sanitized revision in *These Three*)—she declined. "Actresses should retire after a certain age and let the public keep its pleasant memories of their youth," Merle had told Louella Parsons shortly after becoming a mother. Playing a grandmother would certainly destroy that pristine image Merle wanted to preserve. Her costar from that earlier film, Miriam Hopkins, would also be making an appearance in the film as another character. Merle may have been throwing away a worthwhile opportunity, for the actress who played the part in her stead, Fay Bainter, received an Academy Award nomination for it. But Merle would likely have had other grounds for indecision, given what *The Children's Hour* represented about changing industry mores. In the time Merle had been out of the film circuit, Hollywood had been moving away from the moral stringency that had run rampant during the peak of her career decades earlier. Though the Hays Code was still nominally in effect, its application had relaxed to the point that major studio films had marginal room for liberal provocation like the kind that Hellman had woven into the text of *The Children's Hour*, while films like Alfred Hitchcock's *Psycho* (1960) enraptured filmgoers with their blatant psychosexual themes. Merle represented a more conservative era in American cinema that was slowly receding into the background.

That said, more hospitable racial representation, at least for South Asians, failed to accompany these positive developments. While Anna Kashfi's acting career had concluded by the early part of the 1960s due to the misplaced uproar over her alleged lies about her racial roots, a few other South Asian names entered the scene, though they were minor players (through no fault of their own). The Indian actress Simi Garewal played an Indian princess in 1962's *Tarzan Goes to India*, an extravaganza released by MGM, before defecting to Bollywood. Otherwise, the racial ambiguity of South Asian actresses was often their primary locus of appeal: The Sri Lankan beauty queen Maureen Hingert, a contract player with both Universal and Twentieth Century Fox, was a Native American woman in Wallace MacDonald's Western epic *Gunmen from Laredo* (1959), as was the half-white, half-Indian Kamala Devi in Arnold Laven's *Geronimo* (1962), in the same genre.

Despite conditions having barely changed for South Asian actresses like Merle, she felt the ache to act returning in full force at the end of 1961, around the time *The Children's Hour* came out. Merle had begun to realize how hard Bruno worked—seeing her very little and confining her to the role of housewife. She became, quite frankly, rather bored. In December, Merle announced to Louella Parsons that she would be staging a comeback by starring in an independent movie eventually called *Of Love and Desire*, shot rather conveniently in her Mexico homes. Going this route would give her more control over her image than accepting the screen role of a grandmother. This was also likely Merle's way of circumventing the lack of parts then available to an actress of her age and complexion. Production lasted a few weeks. Cables were strewn across the rugs of her handsome houses; extras flooded every room. A hundred of them showed up for the first day of shooting, and little Bruno Jr. complained that there were men in his bedroom.

Of Love and Desire was a minefield of absurdities with an element of incest. Merle would play a nymphomaniac whose half brother has a sick crush on her; the film would end in a chase scene after her half brother confesses his love to her and she runs away in disgust. Merle recited the suggestive dialogue with tart charm. "I might look like Champagne, but, deep down, I'm Scotch and soda," she'd tell one conquest in the movie. The film's racy thematic preoccupations may have been a signal to the public that Merle hadn't calcified into some strait-laced fossil. Yet Merle felt that, beneath this film's veneer of vulgarity, there was a basic purity. "Styles have changed in movies and you have to keep up with them," she explained to a reporter after she finished filming in 1962. "Our picture isn't lurid or in bad taste; it is the story of a woman with a problem: She likes men too much." Merle relished the experience of acting again after so long, so much that a peculiar grief overcame her after the shoot wrapped. She'd forgotten how much fun making movies was, how lonely a life without them could be.

MERLE MAY HAVE BEEN ignoring signs that she had a stinker on her hands. *Of Love and Desire* had trouble finding a distributor in the United States when Merle was shopping it around in late 1962, and she almost took it straight to the graveyard of television. It wasn't until the following April that Twentieth Century Fox mercifully bought it, which may have been a mistake: The press had a field day clobbering this "nasty, overwhelmingly stupid little melodrama" that might have seemed cutting-edge thirty years earlier. Some journalists suggested that Merle looked as if she had been photographed through gauzy lino-leum; others felt that the sight of her pirouetting around in a bikini was so unbecoming that it polluted the memory of her beauty—fulfilling Merle's precise fear about returning to movies. Even moviegoers wrote into gossip columnists' inboxes, saying the film was "embar-rassing and pitiful."

Merle tried her best not to take these reactions as personal affronts, but the real test came when she read the words of Bosley Crowther, who, reviewing the film for the *New York Times*, pummeled her as "sadly worn." Merle thought it beneath her to protest poor reviews, but, in this case, she'd make an exception. "I feel that artists must be good sports about bad reviews, as long as they stick to the perfor-mance," she said of Crowther to the press. "But personal slashing is unfair and cruel, like shooting at a sitting duck." She fired off an angry telegram to him. Shortly thereafter, in October of 1963, she saw him at the New York premiere of the theatrical revival of *Wuthering Heights*, where she reacted horrifically to his stab at an apology. Merle assured him she meant every word of her written retort, flouting any rules about industry propriety in the name of self-defense. She was a star, damn it; she expected people to treat her as such.

It's understandable why Merle's attempts at asserting her sexuality on the screen may not have played well with either critics or audiences at the time. Merle was fifty-two when the film was released. By that point, stars in her age bracket, such as Bette Davis and Joan Crawford, had graduated—some might say succumbed—to horror territory with films like *Whatever Happened to Baby Jane?* (1962), in which they played two jowly sisters who delight in tormenting one another; that same year, Katharine Hepburn had played a family matriarch, and a recovering morphine addict, in *Long Day's Journey Into Night*, one of the few roles of substance for women in Merle's generation. (At the 1963 Academy Awards ceremony, both Davis and Hepburn received well-earned Best Actress nominations for their performances.) The 1963 box-office queens, meanwhile, included Doris Day (whose stardom survived the 1950s), blonde ingenues like the shining Sandra Dee (barely out of her teens), and a spellbinding girl with violet eyes named Elizabeth Taylor—all of them younger than Merle.

In that youth-infatuated moviegoing climate, the chatter over Merle's looks in *Of Love and Desire* put a match to her dormant insecurities. She began to fuss over the lines under her eyes and over her brows, once again beholden to the punishing beauty standards of American cinema. Merle took her self-maintenance seriously. Despite her social life being in full swing (in 1963, she began overseeing construction of what would become a fourth home, this time in Acapulco), Merle still disliked smoking, and she didn't drink much. She swam daily and went to bed early. "The only time I stay up late is to dance," she told one journalist, as if she were back at Firpo's again with Phyllis Beaumont.

Audience inquiries about Merle in the months after *Of Love and Desire*'s release also took on a racial component. Readers would write to newspapers with questions about Merle's origins, as if the cracks in the Tasmanian façade had become too glaring to ignore. "Can you tell me how old she really is, her real name, and where she comes from?" one asked the columnist Walter Scott (a pen name for the journalist Lloyd Shearer), sensing that Merle wasn't what she seemed. The complexion that black-and-white cinema had dulled was now becoming impossible to hide with age and constant sun, and the questions resembled those that had puddled around Merle nearly thirty years earlier, when she first migrated to Hollywood. Journalists in that era also had no hesitation in remarking on the striking resemblance between Merle and India's Gayatri Devi, the Maharani of Jaipur. But the curiosity about Merle's provenance may also have been motivated by the fact that America's long-enshrined incivility toward South Asian immigration was further subsiding. This was evident two years after *Of Love and Desire*'s release with the 1965 passage of the landmark Immigration and Nationality Act (better known as the Hart-Celler Act). Approved amid the heat of the racially progressive civil rights movement, the law effectively dismantled the quotas that had curbed South Asian immigration to America, ushering in a fresh wave of immigrants from the region, with a preferential system that favored educated professionals and facilitated family reunification. Alongside this was the entry of South Asian—and specifically Indian—aesthetics into the bloodstream of the counterculture, especially given the association of the Indian musician Ravi Shankar with the Beatles. South Asian fashion remained in vogue; that decade, Merle herself even posed in advertisements for the designer Oleg Cassini, draped in a sari-inspired "Singh dress" of cranberry and lemon silk. Americans would thus regard South Asian culture with a sense of intrigue, yet, tempering this appreciation was the long-held belief from earlier decades that its people might never be able to integrate within America's greater racial fabric.

At the start of 1965, the same year that America would pass the Hart-Celler Act, Merle boarded an inaugural Qantas Airways flight from Mexico to Sydney, where she was greeted by the press for what they assumed was a homecoming visit to Australia. But she became understandably shifty when asked about her attachment to the country. "Both my parents were English," she said, facing reporters, "and they just happened to be visiting Tasmania as tourists when I was born. As soon as I was well enough to travel, my parents took me to India where I lived until I was 14." Anyone paying close attention would have known that Merle was fudging the details; in earlier versions of her studio-concocted story, it was her widowed mother who had taken her to India from Tasmania. But she banked on no one noticing the inconsistencies. The tale she spun in this episode seems, today, quite noteworthy an instance of Merle trying to cut off firm ties to Australia and instead admit that she had spent her early life in India. This was as close to the truth as her comfort would allow.

Chapter 15

The Last of the
Great Faces

(1965–1971)

*Merle Oberon with her two adopted children, Bruno Jr.
and Francesca Pagliai, at Ghalal, her showplace home
in Acapulco, in 1968.*

TOWNSPEOPLE CALLED IT ACAPULCO'S TAJ MAHAL. THE
resemblance wasn't a mistake: Merle had designed Ghalal, her home
hidden on a rocky road in Acapulco, intentionally to recall what
one journalist characterized as her "fond memories" of India. You

could easily miss spotting the gates to this five-house compound—named for the phrase *to love* in the Indigenous language of Tzotzil—that Merle added to her growing portfolio of homes in October 1965. Its guest rooms—one green, the other pink, both with balconies—allowed Merle and Bruno to host visits from the jet set, starting with Henry Ford II and his wife Cristina in November, followed by the singer and actor Frank Sinatra the next month. She put a Ming dynasty canopied bed, carved from teak wood, in a bedroom of her very own (Bruno had an individual one, too, less evidence of marital strife than their propensity for grand living); her walk-in closet was essentially the size of a chapel, leading to a marble bathroom with a sunken tub. Outside were manmade lagoons for pet ducks; lemon and mango trees; macaws, parakeets, and parrots squealing in the garden. She and Bruno had a private patch of beach where she played with the children. The braided perfumes of tuberose and blooming jasmine would waft into the living room. She and their guests dined outdoors, where camouflaged speakers would blast music against the scream of a waterfall. Fifty-four at the time of the home's completion, Merle was photographed extensively at Ghalal, appearing in such publications as the November *Vogue* as she posed elegantly on the rim of her swimming pool, draped in white and hair streaming down.

Throughout 1965, Merle had done her best to maintain her ties to the film world before moving into Ghalal. She'd gone to the Academy Awards that year (the last year it would be televised in black-and-white) as a presenter, looking like a clam pearl with a looped diamond tiara in her hair. That stunning appearance revived interest in Merle, and she was soon entertaining the solicitations of producers, despite the momentary mess created by *Of Love and Desire*. She indulged the opportunity to play herself, flaunting $500,000 worth of her own jewelry, in a short cameo at the end of the dramatic film *The Oscar*, about the travails of an incorrigibly selfish actor. It was released the year after Ghalal was completed. She even revisited the *I, Claudius* debacle of 1937 for a British Broadcasting Corporation documentary, *The Epic That Never Was*, which examined the implosion of the film after the BBC came across discarded cans of reels from the movie. But Merle wanted to make another movie that would give her the chance to really act. By 1965, feeling the pinch of ageist pressure, she began to lie more promiscuously about her age, claiming to journalists that she was fifteen when she made *The Private Life of Henry VIII*. (She was twenty-one.) She also would announce that she saw herself as part of a shrinking generation. "I'm the last of the great faces," she proudly and nostalgically told a reporter that same year, unsure of whether film studios had room for a woman of her stature.

Despite Merle's stubborn determination to remain aligned with Hollywood, she was gaining a reputation as a socialite first and artist second, made evident when *Town & Country* magazine listed her among the world's greatest hostesses that year. The citation horrified her. Now, having Ghalal, another showpiece home, would only fuel these perceptions. Though the Hollywood set certainly came to visit the Pagliais' Acapulco home—beyond Sinatra, there was also Douglas Fairbanks Jr., the son of her *Private Life of Don Juan* costar, who had met her when she was a hostess in London—their guests were not solely from the world of entertainment. Merle and Bruno received royalty such as Prince Philip, then the Duke of Edinburgh; they hosted politicians from across the political spectrum, including President Lyndon B. Johnson, a Democrat, and Clare Boothe Luce, a Republican, who, despite her conservatism, was a staunch critic of the British occupation of India and had been one of the coauthors of the Luce-Celler Act of 1946, which had opened a pathway to immigration and citizenship for South Asians like Merle.

But the chance for Merle to show the world she was more than a hostess, that she'd been a star in her day for a reason, came with an offer for *Hotel*, based on the 1965 novel by Arthur Hailey. The film's broad, whimsical canvas would track the intersecting lives of guests at a New Orleans hotel. Merle would play a countess reminiscent of Lady Macbeth trying to cover up her husband's involvement in a hit-and-run accident, a callback to *The Price of Fear* more than a decade earlier. On Merle's first day on set in July 1966, flowers and notes from well-wishers greeted her. The dressing rooms were just as she'd remembered them; the sound stages had that scent of bright light she had known so well for so many years. This had once been her life.

Refusing the cheap costume baubles the crew offered, and trailed by a gun-toting guard on set, Merle wore $350,000 worth of her own turquoise earrings and necklaces. Her outfits included a hyacinth-blue wool coat with a velvet collar and hat. Hers was a showy part, superficially speaking, but Merle approached it with imagination, wanting to play against the material rather than treating it as some spangly role. The crew bowed to Merle's veteran wisdom: When she was struggling with some dialogue she felt was unnatural for her character, the film's director, Richard Quine, acquiesced to her request to change it. "I see the Countess as a woman very much in love with her husband, but unable to communicate that love," Merle told a journalist about her role. "That happens so often in a marriage. I don't emphasize her ruthlessness and ambition the way the novel does." (She may also have been exorcising some of her frustrations with her offscreen marriage, given Bruno's work-related absences.) Indeed, in Merle's interpretation of the role, this royal became something more than a gorgon; she was a creature filled with longing for her dyspeptic husband. After he dies in a catastrophic elevator accident near the film's end, Merle's character unleashes a torrent of emotion: "Whatever happens, please don't let my husband's name be disgraced," she pleads with police detectives before she dissolves into tears.

Warner Brothers, the film's distributor, persuaded Merle to travel to Miami in January 1967 for *Hotel*'s world premiere. The night before, she stayed up until 2 a.m. watching *'Til We Meet Again*, with tears welling up as she wondered where that era had gone. When she sat down to view *Hotel* the next evening, she realized that a three-minute sequence she had been partial to had been deleted from the final cut. Merle hastily exited the theater, not even caring to feign decorum. "I'm sick," she shrieked, scurrying past photographers and repeating herself. "I'm sick." After the screening, she declined all press interviews for the film, ordering a limousine driver to take her back to her hotel, where she secluded herself. The next morning, she was a no-show at a press conference for the film; journalists who had scheduled interviews with her were told that she wasn't feeling well. This certainly wasn't the comeback she'd had in mind. In the months after *Hotel's* premiere, Merle weighed film offers, but she was holding out, in vain, for a meaty part rather than a glamour walk-through; most projects coming her way proposed she play a duchess or an empress. (Indeed, this typecasting was the price she had to pay for her socialite lifestyle; New York columnists would give her backhanded compliments by calling her the "Duchess" or "Queen" of Acapulco, dripping with derision.) People seemed to have forgotten that Merle was an actress. That July, when a reporter asked her whether she would be doing more film work, she answered bluntly: "They don't need me."

Hotel was a lemon at the box office, which is little shock in hindsight: The year of its release was one of tremendous turmoil and anxiety for America as well as its cinema. The artistic tension crested at the 1968 Academy Awards ceremony. Stodgy studio dinosaurs like *Doctor Dolittle*—an old-fashioned Twentieth Century Fox musical with a bulging budget that the box office soundly rejected—were nominated for Best Picture alongside the electrically violent *Bonnie & Clyde* and the sexually frank *The Graduate*. (The winner, *In the Heat of the Night*, a polished drama about race relations, based on a 1965 novel, represented a happy medium between these two antipodes.) The fifth nominee, *Guess Who's Coming to Dinner*, was a comedy about an interracial romance between a Black man (Sidney Poitier) and a white woman (Katharine Houghton), a rebuke of Code-era politics. It was released only months after the landmark Supreme Court decision *Loving v. Virginia* that, at long last, legalized miscegenation across the country. Then, too, younger American filmmakers had begun to absorb some of the cutting-edge aesthetic motions of European movies, taking cues from the French New Wave and Post-Neorealism Italian cinema. The popularity in America of more thematically challenging films from directors such as François Truffaut, Federico Fellini, and Jean-Luc Godard had called into question the purpose of the Hays Code.

Why did American cinema have to hold itself to such antiquatedly timid standards? The pressure exerted by distributors against censorship boards—along with groups on the right that wanted a more stratified system of film ratings to supplant the Code—resulted in the formal demolition of the Hays Code by 1968, a loosening of moral inflexibility that had previously hamstrung so much of American cinema. Gradually, popular American filmmaking became freer to show sex and gore, while the era that had made Merle a star had officially, unequivocally come to a close.

For South Asian performers like Merle, though, opportunities to act were still few. In the years that followed 1965's Hart-Celler Act, the influx of immigrants from South Asia, mostly students, changed the racial makeup of America. But American perceptions of the region were still lodged in amber: In 1967, Walt Disney Productions put out an animated adaptation of Rudyard Kipling's *The Jungle Book*, the same story that had made Sabu win over America decades earlier, proving not only how prone Hollywood was to recycling its narratives but also how much mileage certain images of the Indian subcontinent gained with Americans. Most other cinematic depictions of South Asians veered away from the stock roles of anticolonial rebels and grimy primitives that were present in the 1930s and 1940s. By the late 1960s, when South Asian characters did appear on screen, they were primarily sources of comic relief. It was the very year of the Hays Code's dissolution that the Blake Edwards film *The Party* appeared, starring the English comedic genius Peter Sellers donning greasepaint to play the klutzy Indian immigrant actor Hrundi V. Bakshi. He bumbles his way through an industry party where he does not know how to behave. This character was a riff on brownface caricatures that Sellers had played in British cinema earlier in the decade, particularly 1960's *The Millionairess* and 1962's *Road to Hong Kong*. Sellers also gave brownface a sonic dimension that was often missing from earlier spins: He would affect a voice that was the verbal equivalent of a head bob. With *The Party*, Edwards and Sellers offered the precise image of South

Asians that Americans may have craved. The film was a portrait of a foreigner incapable of integrating.

The discrimination that Merle had encountered decades earlier, when America had closed its borders to South Asian immigrants like her, had not disappeared; it had morphed. By 1968, Merle, with her unfading tan and penchant for wearing coral kurtas, would find herself fielding more questions from reporters about her heritage. Considering this hostile climate that still rendered South Asians in such stereotypical and unkind terms, Merle worked hard to continue to guard her secret. She began to revert to her old cover-up lines from 1934, when she first got to Hollywood. "Did you ever hear of an Eurasian [*sic*] with anything but black eyes? Or a half-caste Indian with curly hair?" she asked one reporter that year. "I'd be perfectly happy to be Oriental if I were." She may have been relying on her audience's ignorance. But this denial was taking its toll on her.

AFTER *HOTEL*, MERLE BOUNCED back into her hostess role. She'd throw six to eight Acapulco dinners a season, with no more than forty guests. Her soirées resembled those in Hollywood's heyday when she first broke on the shoals of that town in 1934, as if she were recreating a culture that she could no longer otherwise access. (The fact that Hollywood was unrecognizable to her was made obvious by the sorts of oddball roles sent her way—such as that for *The Killing of Sister George*, about a lesbian soap-opera performer, which seemed too risqué for her liking.) But the turn of the decade instilled a sense of spiritual fatigue within Merle. Her husband was usually away for work in Mexico City, and their kids were in school. By April 1971, Merle sold off her precious Selby House in Beverly Hills, reasoning that she just wasn't spending enough time there as in Acapulco. But even there, Ghalal began to seem like "a prison," she would tell a journalist. Her elegant parties made her feel lonely. To offset her ennui, she undertook philanthropic efforts. Wanting to improve the conditions of poverty-stricken children around her in Acapulco—whose straits were reminiscent of her own beginnings—she established, the same year she sold the Selby House, *Parque Infantil Merle Oberon* (now *Parque Merle Oberón*), a children's park in Acapulco forged in the vein of Disneyland, with a pool, a library, and an open-air theater. "I did a lot in this country," she told the *Los Angeles Times*. "I'd like to leave something here."

The start of the 1970s brought no meaningful changes to American film for an "Old Hollywood" actress like Merle. The country's filmmaking mood had shifted more toward testosterone since 1967, that watershed year for Hollywood when Merle had starred in *Hotel*. The movement known as "New Hollywood" was in full swing by this point, rejecting any thematic or aesthetic chastity. Despite the positive commotion of women's liberation, American cinema's masterworks in that moment tended toward the rough and virile, like 1971's *The French Connection* and *A Clockwork Orange* and 1972's *The Godfather*. Meanwhile, critical distaste for "the woman's picture"—the kind that had swaddled Merle through the 1940s (such as *'Til We Meet Again*)—was at a historic high. She had been swatting away scripts for Grand Guignol horror films like the ones her contemporaries Bette Davis and Joan Crawford had been plodding through for years, movies that surely would turn her into a saggy-skinned harridan. Merle told reporters she would have taken a job selling stockings before anyone would catch her starring in that slop. "I'd rather be a forgotten actress than become a freak on film," she told a journalist.

But the opportunity to rise above such grotesquerie came to sixty-year-old Merle in late 1971, when the critic, novelist, and screenwriter Gavin Lambert approached her with a script that belonged to that maligned woman's picture genre. Up to that time, Lambert's most notable screenplay had been for 1965's *Inside Daisy Clover* (based on his own novel of the same name), a film that suffered both critical and commercial drubbings. His new story—eventually called *Interval*—focused on the life of an Englishwoman vacationing on Mexico's Yucatán Peninsula after a grueling stay in a sanatorium. No longer institutionalized, Serena, as the film calls her, charms a flirtatious younger man. But Serena then self-sabotages her shot at happiness, wishing to bury the rotting skeleton in her memory's closet: She had been committed after murdering her cheating husband. Now unable to give herself over to love, Serena would die by suicide at the film's end. When Merle read this script, she saw a reflection of herself. Here, in Serena, was a woman who professed love for all living beings; in a scene that might sound preposterous on the page, she saw a snake and spoke to it as if it were a helpless human child. In another scene, she would buy a freshly caught fish from a fisherman before ordering him to toss it back into the water because she hated the thought of killing it. This was the vision of herself that Merle wanted to put forth: peace-loving and tasteful, with no intent to offend. She said yes to Gavin Lambert, believing she had lucked into the role of a lifetime.

Chapter 16

Where I Belong

(1971–1973)

Poster for Interval *(1973), Merle's comeback film costarring*
Robert Wolders, who became her fourth husband in 1975.

As Merle readied herself for her screen comeback, she began to take appropriate steps to assert her independence from Bruno. She pooled as much money as she could from what she later told a journalist were her "own miserable little savings," none of Bruno's, for the movie's financing. By the end of 1971, just months before the film was to begin shooting, Merle and Bruno decided to put her once-beloved Ghalal up for sale, a process that would stretch on for years. Now, *Interval* could be her focus.

One night at a Los Angeles dinner party, Merle found the actor who would play her leading man. She'd heard about a Dutch actor named Robert Wolders from a friend she'd been close to in her Acapulco years, Noël Coward, who told her about a fetching young performer he'd met at an arts festival in Italy. The son of an executive for the airline KLM and an actress, Robert was born in Rotterdam in 1936—exactly two and a half decades after Merle. He came of age during the Nazi occupation of that city before moving to America, settling in Rochester, New York, in 1959, and eventually studying theater at the American Academy of Dramatic Arts in New York. He would, with time, parlay his stage skills to the screen; a prominent role in the television Western *Laredo* in the mid-1960s and a movie contract with Universal followed. But he did not quite become the star that the studio was so carefully manufacturing, and his ascent was on the downslide by the early 1970s. Still, his princely looks—that face with its rugged bones but sugar-soft features—survived those career setbacks, and Noël recognized his potential. "He may have great promise, Merle, besides which, he struck me as an awfully nice boy," Noël told her. Merle realized that Noël was right: This pretty thing a quarter century her junior would be perfect to play the Lothario who captured Serena's heart. She had little idea how large a role he would come to play in her life.

Merle's inability to endure the intense heat of Yucatán, where they were filming, dictated that the shoot for *Interval* would have to begin in January 1972, before the weather became too overbearing. But trouble erupted at the onset of production, when the attached director, Vincente Minnelli—known primarily but not exclusively for musicals—dropped out. He cited his frustrations with the dysfunction on set, including the reported lack of a cameraman; he also had misgivings about Lambert's patchwork script. Daniel Mann, who had directed such foreign stars as the Italian actress Anna Magnani to Leading

Actress Oscars, stepped into Minnelli's chair. *Interval* was a high-stakes project, for Merle had the chance to reassert herself as an artist in a time when the culture had veered too far leftward for her comfort. In her years of living in a sheltered Mexican mansion largely secluded from America, her politics went full tilt toward conservatism. Women's liberation made her itch with unease; she thought it was "nonsense," as she told a reporter that year. "All that these movements manage to accomplish is to deprive women of their femininity and turn more men into homosexuals," she stated. Merle openly supported Richard Nixon's reelection in 1972, seeing in his right-wing ideals a proper vision for the country America should become. Her biases made her part of a fading breed of Hollywood stars: For every Golden Age actress with Republican beliefs there was a younger Joanne Woodward or Jane Fonda whose stances slanted proudly toward progressivism.

Merle's outlooks may have suited her silver-spoon existence in Acapulco, but they now put her at odds with the updated fashions of American movies and moviegoing. The year of *Interval*'s eventual release, 1973, was one in which American housewives would find themselves vomiting at the perversions of Bernardo Bertolucci's *Last Tango in Paris*, an Italian production from 1972 released in America early the following year. It featured Merle's *Désirée* costar, Marlon Brando, as a widower who, in grief's senseless fog, seeks out an anonymous sexual tryst with a younger woman played by Maria Schneider, who would later allege that Bertolucci and Brando had violated her on camera without her consent. Merle had no intention of seeing the film; the mere thought of it made her "shudder," she told a reporter. Films like these depressed her. "I don't really relate to what's on the screen at the moment," she said, glumly. Though Merle insisted upon a tragic ending for *Interval*, the film was otherwise free of the metallic cynicism that she perceived in such films. "I wanted to prove you could make a picture people would like to see that wasn't full of rape and murder," she would say to a journalist about *Interval*. The way Merle saw it, her film was a rejection of where the culture was headed with all its bloodshed; it would be a return to the purity of the era that had made her a star. And she believed, earnestly, that it was her greatest achievement on film.

★

OVER THE COURSE OF production, Merle found herself becoming enchanted by Robert. His demeanor was so respectful; it was almost as if someone who checked every requirement in her head materialized before her. Merle was gradually falling in love with him, and he with her, though it would take some time for her to act on her attraction. Her marriage to Bruno was breaking down by this point: He, as usual, remained in Mexico City while she was often alone, and she came to terms with the reality that he could not offer her the intimacy or companionship she so badly wanted and needed. For a time, Merle had felt she would never fall in love again, that she was too old for any man to love. Robert convinced her otherwise.

As filming continued, Merle became ever more fearful, concerned that the core of Lambert's script had been lost. So she decided to take matters into her own hands: She would produce the film, since she was unable to find anyone else willing to save this capsizing vehicle. Her involvement certainly was not superficial. In July 1972, she took a summer rental for an English cottage close to Beverly Hills. Every day for six weeks, she would pore over miles of film on a concrete floor, her back nearly giving out as she spliced a weepy score into the film. She taught herself how to work a Moviola, a contraption commonly used for editing. That Merle would produce, star in, and edit the film made her a unicorn, as few actresses of the era wore so many hats. (This was a decade before Barbra Streisand broke barriers to direct, produce, write, *and* star in *Yentl*.) Hollywood actresses such as Ida Lupino had directed their own films decades before, as had Barbara Loden and Elaine May earlier in the 1970s. But such instances of a woman feeling empowered enough to both produce and act were rare in mainstream terms, making Merle more of a pioneer than the industry may have been willing to acknowledge at the time, perhaps because the genre in which she was working had become so démodé.

Merle's nostalgia for the way things used to work in the industry certainly went deep. She would express regret that the Hollywood machine didn't run the way it once had, but she was doing her best to keep up with the times. The studio system made her feel "beautiful and secure," as she described it to the press. "Without security it is difficult for a woman to look or feel beautiful. She loses her sense of identity." She was well aware that the proverbial cards were stacked against her by virtue of her womanhood. Merle would tell journalists how often she wondered what life would've been like had she lived as a woman until the age of thirty-five and then as a man. But she tried to save herself from drowning in such laments. Instead, she funneled her frustrations about misogyny into proactivity. "For actresses who complain there aren't enough good roles for women I suggest they go out and make their own films," she remarked to a journalist glibly, as if doing so were easy enough. Merle had learned how to cut a film, how to set music to it; now, she had to learn how to market it. By September of 1972, she shopped the film to the distributor Joseph E. Levine of Embassy Pictures, an independent company, and he was an immediate fan.

Yet there were signs of trouble for this film Merle was plugging so indefatigably. It was a minor embarrassment when few of her former costars showed up at the two-day Mexico City premiere for the film in March of the following year, an event that commentators characterized as "a Hollywood Comeback without Hollywood." Merle had invited David Niven and Laurence Olivier, their relationships having been mended with time, hoping they'd help her celebrate her return. But the festivities were notable for their no-shows, making an already deadening process that much more tortuous for Merle. Relief coursed through her, at least, when she heard of the audience's post-screening reaction. Merle couldn't stop repeating every positive comment she heard to anyone who'd listen, even one from a thirteen-year-old friend of her son who said the movie made him think. She had given the entirety of herself to this project. "When this is all over— after the film opens in June in New York—I'm going into hiding," she joked, half seriously, to a journalist at the end of that two-day premiere, uneasy with the limelight's glare. "I've had enough of my privacy invaded."

★

AS INTERVAL LURCHED TOWARD its June opening in New York, Merle felt increasingly vulnerable. Her marriage's collapse came within full view of the public as she and Bruno agreed to separate just days after the Mexico City festivities; she asked for no settlement, only child support. Then, at the end of March, Merle lost her dear friend Noël, who succumbed to a heart attack one morning. With Noël gone, Merle could count on the fingers of a single hand the number of her true friends. She put on a brave face the day after Noël's death when she appeared in California to present a trophy at the Academy Awards, floating onto the stage in a strapless ivory gown, a cluster of diamonds and emeralds around her neck. Participating in the event further cemented her feeling that the film industry was moving in a direction where she wasn't entirely in lockstep: Upon the announcement of that year's Best Actor winner, Marlon Brando for *The Godfather*, the actress Sacheen Littlefeather, who claimed to be of Indigenous descent, accepted the award on his behalf as a protest gesture. She read his prewritten statement decrying the industry's maltreatment of Indigenous Americans. Merle was appalled at this perceived display of contempt against the sacred Academy Awards. "It's wrong to put down the Oscars, just as it's wrong to put down America," she fumed to the press.

Robert was one of the few true connections Merle had to the younger generation, from which she felt otherwise distant. Leaving Mexico, and Bruno's houses there, Merle soon relocated more permanently to an oceanfront Malibu beach home, where she and Robert would live. He cared for her so tenderly that she felt like a child in his presence. "I like to be looked after by a man," she said to a reporter for the *Boston Globe*. "I'm very feminine that way." But there were sides of herself that Merle was unwilling to share with him. As she had with

Bruno, Merle hid her Anglo-Indian identity from Robert, perhaps out of fear that she had too much to lose by being herself around the man with whom she had chosen to spend her august years. Her anxieties may have been unfounded, for he would, upon learning of her Anglo-Indian heritage after her death, claim that it only added to her allure. That is certainly how the world surrounding her had also begun to see it: There were even stray media mentions through the early 1970s about Merle's "half-Indian beauty," as a *Women's Wear Daily* article put it, and the "new type of beauty" she'd brought to the screen decades earlier with her "Eurasian heritage," per another piece in the *Cincinnati Enquirer*. These statements about her racial identity had crossed over from speculation into fact; anyone could see the truth when they looked at Merle's face.

By the 1970s, more immigrants from Merle's homeland had begun to arrive in America, and greater acceptance followed. The same year of *Interval*'s release, 1973, the actress and food writer Madhur Jaffrey brought out her cookbook *An Invitation to Indian Cooking*, whose success spoke to America's growing tolerance for, and interest in, aspects of South Asian culture, particularly its food. It was within this climate that Merle openly declared to journalists that she considered her comfort food to be curry, a dish that was then synonymous with Indian food to most Americans, and she even gave newspaper columnists her favorite recipe for it. (Merle's open adoration for curry would persist throughout the decade; when inviting friends for luncheons at her Malibu home, Merle would typically serve chicken curry.) As the world around her became more open, Merle had begun embracing her heritage in her own, quiet way. Beyond this, while gearing up to promote *Interval* that April, Merle, somewhat startlingly in contrast to previous decades, referred to herself as a "Javanese flower," a throwback to the charged descriptor reviewers had pinned to her four decades earlier.

Bullish about a full-throated acting comeback after *Interval*, Merle began to consider what might come next, and it was the most unexpected of roles that invited her serious contemplation: that of Kasturba,

Mahatma Gandhi's wife, in a biopic of the man that Joseph Levine himself was planning. Though the state of South Asian representation in Hollywood had not greatly improved since the release of *The Party* with Peter Sellers five years earlier, Merle saw a chance to begin a new chapter in her acting career with this role of an Indian woman. "It's not a very big part, but it means a new start—after 'Interval'—and right now that's most important to me," she said in May of 1973. "I feel I'm back again where I belong."

★

UNFORTUNATELY, MERLE HADN'T STEELED herself adequately for the brutal reception to *Interval* upon its New York premiere in June. There were press-screening reports of snickering at its melodramatic flourishes. Levine had cautioned her that the outside world might trash it, but she still held out hope that even the fiercest critics would recognize how personal the project was to her and thus maintain a level of politesse. But critics and trade publications seemed to find glee in their cruelty, torching the film as hackneyed and syrupy. Some compared it to a travelogue, others to a soap opera. The film's antiseptic approach to romance seemed hopelessly outmoded for the era, its score "as sweet as a $1 valentine." Writing that the film had an "aura of an empty perfume bottle," Howard Kissel of *Women's Wear Daily* wisecracked that the film "tries to be the kind of picture they don't make any more, and only succeeds in making you grateful they don't." The *Boston Globe*'s critic surmised that the script, so damp with sentimentality, must have been written on Kleenex.

And then there was the issue of Merle herself. Her involvement in producing this musty antique of a film was no cause for celebration to reviewers: It seemed less like a display of independence than an expression of Merle's narcissism, with critics by turns lampooning the film as "a vanity production" and "an ego trip." The opprobrium had a loud undercurrent of sexism. Some reviewers called into question her famed pulchritude, grimacing that Merle's efforts to outrun her age had turned her face into a monument she was trying to rescue from decay, with *preserved* being the operative word in several reviews. (Merle had frequent facelifts, cosmetic procedures that she didn't deny.) The more ruthless of the lot offered a forensic dissection of her looks. The *Boston Globe* observed that Merle's "polyethylene face nearly melts to her chin," comparing her to an undertaker's wife whose face had the finish of "a frosty ice cube." The *Washington Post* described her face as if it were a rotten piece of fruit: "She has the expressions and movements of a little old lady, but the expressions flicker over a taut, waxen, unreally smooth facial surface. In many shots Miss Oberon's upper lip looks deadened and her mouth puckers in a way that betrays her age." The *New York Times* wasn't much kinder, saying that time had eliminated Merle's expressive features: "There was never such a movie for observing its leading lady from the back of the head."

Merle, having come up in Hollywood during a period when looks were paramount, had worked hard to manicure her beauty with age, so the comments about her appearance in *Interval* surely were especially hurtful. Throughout the 1970s, she practiced yoga, swam in cold salt water, played tennis. She brushed her hair for an interminable forty-five minutes, and every morning she masked her face with the pale scum that formed overnight atop an oyster sprinkled with lemon juice. But beneath any presentation of self-assurance was an insecurity Merle could not quiet: She struggled to see herself as attractive, no matter how many people told her so. She told interviewers, while promoting *Interval*, that she felt that the accepted wisdom of her beauty was just a result of mass brainwashing. "I think they've been conditioned," she said to one reporter. "They've read it so often, they think it's a duty for them to respond, 'Oh, yes, isn't she beautiful?'" Hollywood, a town obsessed with youth and critical of those who tried to escape it, could only have aggravated her psychic turmoil.

Dutifully making the talk-show rounds—Johnny Carson, Mike Douglas—around the time of *Interval*'s release, Merle tried not to sulk in the surge of pans for this project that had meant so much to her. She would touch wood and tell interviewers to pray for the film's good fortunes, doing her best to inoculate herself from the reviews. Yet the response seemed to confirm her deepest fears about herself. "I feel the world has passed me by," she sighed to one reporter in late June. Box-office grosses weren't exactly dazzling, either, all while *Last Tango in Paris*—the movie whose mere premise (again, she refused to see it) Merle dreaded—dominated the New York screens. *Interval* vanished from the city's theaters after three weeks, despite the national press her comeback attracted. Merle ultimately lost money on it. The time wasn't quite opportune for the distinctly feminine *Interval*. In 1973, the industry propped up such idols of machismo as Clint Eastwood, Steve McQueen, and Burt Reynolds; the Brooklyn-bred Jewish actress Barbra Streisand was the only woman on the list of that year's ten most bankable stars, having headlined the romantic drama *The Way We Were* (1973). Streisand, with her striking and decidedly non-WASPy beauty, was far unlike the bubblegum blondes from previous eras, hinting that audiences had become bored with the mold of female stardom that had commanded earlier decades. Still, the mawkish trappings of a film like *Interval* had little place in the moviegoing mood of an era that leaned heavily toward masculinity.

There were, at the very least, intimations of positive industry developments at the Academy Awards, which were opening their ranks to performers of color. Two Black actresses, Diana Ross and Cicely Tyson, received Best Actress in a Leading Role nominations in early 1973 for their releases the previous year, *Lady Sings the Blues* and *Sounder*, respectively. As a sign of how regressive the thinking remained, though, prevailing wisdom suggested that the two Black nominees would effectively cancel out each other in final voting. (The white actress Liza Minnelli, daughter of Judy Garland and Vincente Minnelli, eventually won for *Cabaret*.) Whatever strides actresses of color had achieved, Merle was still living in the past, a fact that the retrograde *Interval* made plainly obvious. Try as she did, Merle seemed ill at ease with the dialogue in the film's early stages, and the scope of her technique did not allow her to rise above its purple phrases ("We're all caught in the same interval between being born and dying," she would say, absurdly). Nor could she muster much heat with Robert, making the central romance strangely pulseless. But Merle met the script's demands capably as her character's mental state became more fragile, giving emotional weight to otherwise-flimsy material. At its best, Merle's performance bore elements of some of her greatest work from the peak of her career in the 1930s. What resulted was an affecting portrait of a woman harvesting a painful secret. "Are you afraid of the past?" Robert's character would ask her in one scene. "Not at all," she would say in return, her voice hauntingly casual. "I'm bored with it. Most of it's not worth remembering."

IT WAS THE VERY year of *Interval*'s release, 1973, that Merle received a call at her California home from a man with a Bombay accent. His name was Captain Harry Selby, and he'd made a trip to the United States after serving in the Indian Navy. He asked for Merle Oberon. Merle panicked, pretending to be her maid and saying that Merle was out. She hung up promptly, not wanting to face this potential tie to her past. Harry was Constance Joyce's fourth child, and thus Merle's younger half brother. He'd heard stories about her from his mother, ever since she'd told him as a twelve-year-old boy that he had a supposed aunt who had become a great movie star. Constance Joyce begged him at least to contact Merle upon setting foot in America, so that he might have a better relationship with her than Constance Joyce herself was able to have. Harry managed to dig up Merle's number and dial it.

Over the years, Constance Joyce's health issues had become more unsalvageable. She thought of Merle constantly, talked about her all the time. Her eldest two children after Merle were living in England. Her youngest had been swiped from her by relatives after an acrimonious separation from her ex-husband. Harry was there for her, though. He had incredible compassion for his mother, knowing what she'd done just to provide for them when they were coming of age and she was a divorced single mother. He made it a point to provide her with all possible comforts, giving her half of his salary before asking her to move in with him, his wife, and their four kids in Bombay.

Constance Joyce would teach her children, and her grandchildren via Harry, always to aspire to something greater than the circumstances of their lives—to hobnob with people on social levels above theirs rather than mixing with their own. Her grandchildren were too young to have the proper context for such pressures, not knowing that Constance Joyce's own survival—of poverty, feelings of parental abandonment, and regret over having to place her firstborn in her own mother's arms—colored her grim perception of the world. She rarely talked about her roots in Sri Lanka, or her impecunious childhood in Bombay. The grandkids knew that Constance Joyce wanted to be British, and that she'd urged Harry to marry a British lady who fell for him in England. (Instead, he married a Jewish woman, making Constance Joyce furious, though she eventually warmed to her.) The grandchildren used to jokingly call her "Blondie." None of them— not Harry, not his children—knew the burden she carried. That she had to give up a child and keep that a secret was tragic enough. To then see that girl grow up and achieve stardom a world away was an unimaginable pain.

Merle's nieces and nephews—Constance Joyce's grandchildren— would sometimes notice that letters would arrive from California for her. They never opened those envelopes. They just knew that whatever was inside was transactional, curt, not some drawn-out missive. Constance Joyce would tell her grandchildren, as she told her son Harry, that Merle was her half sister. She always asked her grandchildren to talk to their friends about Merle, too, though they were too embarrassed to do so; to them, Merle was just some lady in a fantasy land. So when their friends came over, Constance Joyce would bring up the topic of Merle. "My half sister is a Hollywood actress," she'd exclaim. She'd regale visitors with stories of how Queenie, as she still sometimes called her, used to sit in front of the mirror for too long as a kid, combing her sooty hair instead of studying. She'd report having heard that all the boys in Calcutta were crazy about Merle because of her gorgeous figure. She wanted her grandchildren to speak Merle's story out loud, to say that she had been born in India. To keep Merle's connection to this family alive. To tell the truth.

Chapter 17
Local Girl Makes Good!
(1973–1978)

*Merle Oberon, wearing a dress made from a sari she purchased
in India, arrives with Robert Wolders at the American Film
Institute's 1976 tribute to director William Wyler.*

As INTERVAL SETTLED INTO A PUNCHLINE LATE INTO 1973,
the Kasturba Gandhi role—and the possibility of a public realignment
with her South Asian roots—faded from Merle's view. Had the film not
failed, maybe things would have turned out differently. Merle began
rethinking her lifestyle. After years of pomp, she turned to relative

frugality. That November, she auctioned off her costly antique furniture and set pieces—her crystal chandeliers, a black-and-gold-lacquer bureau-cabinet, a wooden carousel horse—seeing this ablution as one way to feel freer. She went on a January 1974 shopping spree and rejected big-ticket designer wardrobe items for corduroy slacks and solid-color T-shirts in navy and red, made in France. "I think it's disgraceful to spend a lot of money on clothes," she said—for what might have been the first time in her life—to a journalist.

With this came her sense that she wasn't long for this planet, so she decided to draft her will. All that Robert would receive, per his own request, was the Malibu beach house. She would ask that her extensive portfolio of jewels be auctioned off after her death, with half of that money going into trust funds for her two children and the other half going to the Motion Picture Country Home and Hospital, an organization that provided care for entertainment-industry talents.* Merle wanted a peaceful, spare life now. She and Robert spent the early months of 1974 drifting away from Hollywood on a round-the-world cruise. It was on that voyage that they docked in Bombay. Merle was at first fearful of disembarking, worried about who might recognize her and what that might make her confront about her past, especially in front of the man she wanted to marry. She even became ill. While there, though, she would buy a white sari that she brought back to Los Angeles, wanting to hold onto a memento from the place she once called home.

Merle poured her energies into her love for Robert, trying not to care about the fact that the press rendered their pairing as a sickness. He must've been just a gold-digging gigolo, journalists thought, and Merle, some deluded pensioner who was trying to recapture the glory that age had purloined from her. ("We sure hope he plays bridge!" one

---

* Despite the failure of *Interval*, acting still meant a great deal to Merle; on the grounds of the Motion Picture Country Home and Hospital would be a garden named after her. Norma Shearer would live out her final days at that home, in a room overlooking the garden named for her best friend, before her own death in 1983.

columnist honked.) She would call him Robin; she was his Merlie. And he gushed about her. "Regardless of the fact that she's the most beautiful creature you could possibly imagine, I love her because she has the wisdom of maturity and the body of a 25-year-old," Robert twinkled to the press about Merle. "He has given my life new meaning," Merle said of him. "Given me my youth back." Merle's regimen for self-maintenance did not relax with age, inviting parody: One columnist snorted that Merle's cause of death would be "from failing her terminal ambition to perfect, cosmetically or however, plastic adjustments included, the little league Mona Lisa smile standard in all her newspaper photos," while another said she'd croak due to "boredom lying in bed with 50 pounds of mashed cucumbers on her face." The actor Walter Matthau joked that she had so much silicone in her system that she "looks like she's been dead for 19, 22 years. . . ." The comedian Joan Rivers, never one to recoil from bluntness (or dalliances of her own with cosmetic surgery), bantered that her audience at gay clubs would beat her to the punch whenever she began her Merle bit: "I said, 'Merle Oberon' and they were ahead of me already with a silicone joke—'She sleeps on bubble paper.'"

Upon their return to California after the three-month decompression at sea, Merle, still unable to picture a life without any acting at all, wondered whether she might try her hand at the stage, perhaps by touring in the local summer stock. Robert encouraged her. Merle had always had a great fear of the theater; she thought that being put before the footlights would be akin to giving an oil painter a set of watercolors. When Robert heard that the screenwriter Tom Mankiewicz lived nearby, he asked Mankiewicz to scan his bookshelves for any plays that might suit Merle. Mankiewicz found one in George Bernard Shaw's *Candida* (1894), in which an older married woman would juggle the competing affections of her clergyman husband and a young poet. Merle read it that night, considered it, and appeared on Mankiewicz's patio the next day with a frank admission: "It's a great play and a great part, but frankly I don't have the talent," she told him. "I couldn't begin to play a character this complex, but thank you anyway for suggesting it."

Merle had lost faith in her acting ability; maybe those critics who felt that *Interval* illuminated the limitations of her talent had been right. The requests nevertheless continued from people who believed in her, even if she didn't see it herself: Later that same year, 1974, the writer and producer Leslie Stevens tried to convince Merle to reprise George Sand, the role for which she'd splayed her guts in 1945's *A Song to Remember*, for a theatrical production in which she would star opposite Robert. He argued that it could cap off her fine career. "We are not presenting a chunk of costume jewelry in Macy's window," Stevens wrote to her that November. "We are presenting Tiffany's finest diamond." But such flattery wasn't enough to temper Merle's skepticism. She declined. As Merle's acting career braked to a standstill, Robert's chugged along with guest spots on television shows, aided partially by the publicity created by his association with Merle. With her divorce from Bruno finalized by this point, Merle and Robert began planning for a scaled-down wedding with a tiny cadre of attendees. Finally, as summer stretched into autumn of 1974, the couple traveled to the Netherlands, where Robert's parents lived, with the intent to marry. But the plan to wed failed to materialize, because she needed to produce a birth certificate, and Robert still did not know that Merle had been born in Bombay.

★

MERLE'S HALF BROTHER HARRY, who had tried and failed in 1973 to reach the woman he believed was his aunt, was at a dinner party in the city of her birth when the news of her latest marriage hit Indian newspapers in early 1975. Just weeks shy of her sixty-fourth birthday, Merle had gotten married in Santa Monica, where, as if by bureaucratic miracle, she didn't need her birth certificate to obtain a marriage license. She and Robert wed with scant fanfare at a country club with her children present, alongside the judge and a witness. Harry's Bombay dinner-party hostess, an Australian woman, commented that Merle was the loveliest thing that had ever come out of her home country. Harry chimed in, assuring her that Merle wasn't Australian.

She was born in India, Harry said. Her name was Queenie Thompson. And she was his aunt.

Merle's rebuff of Harry just two years earlier had left him feeling rejected, and he gave up on trying to establish a connection after that. He wasn't keen on getting this family scandal exposed, despite knowing how much Constance Joyce had wanted him at least to try to build a relationship with Merle. By this point in Merle's life, though, the truth about her heritage had begun to leak out even more to the public. That March, when answering a reader's question about Merle after her marriage to Robert, the columnist Walter Scott responded that she was "partly Indian." (This would persist through the years: Later in the decade, Scott would tell a reader who asked, "Isn't she really Indian?" that Merle's mother was indeed "Anglo-Indian.") Unlike other gossip columnists from previous years—Louella Parsons and Hedda Hopper, Merle's friends who were now both deceased—Scott didn't hesitate to challenge the party line about Merle's background. Times had also changed; the cloud of discrimination that had surrounded her when she'd first arrived in America some four decades earlier, when immigration law both shaped and reflected a sentiment of hostility toward South Asians, had now somewhat cleared.

Merle's Anglo-Indian identity was certainly an open secret in the Indian press, too. That same decade, the Bengali newspaper journalist Sunanda Datta-Ray cited Merle as an example of an Anglo-Indian who had assimilated into Western life so completely that she had "carefully ironed out all trace of the past from [her] speech, mannerisms and even memories." But this was not exactly true: The memory of India was still alive within Merle. She asked the designer Luis Estevez, a friend from her Mexico years, to repurpose the white sari fabric she had bought in India into a dress resembling a caftan. He would preserve the soul of that garment—its fabric, its milky color, its silver embroidery—while rearranging its bones. She wore this stunning attire—a talisman from the country that had made her—to the American Film Institute's tribute to William Wyler in March 1976.

Yet Merle continued otherwise to inhabit the disguise of her Tasmanian origins that had been crafted for her by London Films in 1932, and Tasmania embraced her as one of its own: The Cabaret Room of the popular Wrest Point Hotel Casino in the Tasmanian capital of Hobart was christened the Oberon Theatre in her honor that decade. In the fall of 1978, the Australian government coaxed Merle to Sydney as a guest of honor, which would be followed by a visit to Tasmania for a Lord Mayor's reception honoring her. Robert, still clueless about the circumstances of Merle's birth, told her he wanted to see where she'd been born, so she accepted the invitations. Merle's fourth marriage, after all, had made her happier than any other; they were spending their days yachting off Catalina Island and using assumed names to check into hotels along the California coast. His persuasion would have made the Tasmania invite exceptionally difficult to ignore. Privately, though, Merle had no idea how she would handle herself. She worried about how ridiculous the truth about her birth in India would make her seem if it were to come out, and the accusations of being a liar that might ensue. But she felt unable to reverse years of a ruse she did not create. "It is very rewarding to be recognized as 'local girl makes good!'" Merle laughed to her Malibu friends just before departing for Tasmania.

THAT OCTOBER, MERLE NERVOUSLY glittered on the stage at the Sammy Awards, among Australia's most prominent film and television prizes, with her swan-white lace dress and teardrop pearls. She was a big get: The organizers of the event, held in Sydney, wanted an Australian legend for the occasion, and she was among the few available names who weren't pop stars. One presenter asked her if she, this false daughter of Tasmania, had any memories of this place she'd reportedly left when she was so young. "I'm sorry—none at all," Merle laughed brittlely, her voice growing reedy against the crowd's roaring peals of laughter. She would repeatedly field such questions in the span of those few days in Australia. "I've always read that you're an

Australian, but I gather the claim is a little tenuous," the talk-show host Mike Willesee told Merle. "Well, I'm very proud that they would claim me as an Australian, but I really was just born in Tasmania, and I've always said yes if they've asked me, 'Are you Australian?'" she told him, trying her best not to break character.

Countless legends had circulated about Merle in Tasmanian lore: that her mother was a Chinese chambermaid named Lottie Chintock in the town of Saint Helens and that her father was the married white hotel owner with whom Chintock fell in love. How Merle ended up in British India, these sagas claimed, was through adoption by an Indian silk merchant, or perhaps by the hotel owner's childless cousin who had been visiting from India. Or maybe it was a traveling troupe of actors with the surname O'Brien who had taken her. But these word-of-mouth anecdotes failed to stack up against the lack of documentation—chiefly, a birth record—supporting her Tasmanian provenance. As Tasmania prepared for her visit, no one could find any proof that she'd been born there at all.

Merle was overtaken by fits of crying the second she set foot on the island. Though she maintained her composure as the special guest who crowned the winner of the Miss Tasmania pageant on Friday the 13th, she was otherwise leery of any press attention; she granted only one interview to a radio journalist who unblinkingly bought her Tasmanian origin story. But she and Robert checked into the Wrest Point with instructions that no one speak to her. She barricaded herself in her room. Merle told Robert, utterly confused by her demands for privacy, to intercept any calls that came her way. When a driver came to take her to the town hall for the grand reception, Merle dragged herself out of her room. Unable to control herself, she snapped and went off script in a moment when Robert was out of earshot. "It's probably a bad time to bring up the fact that I wasn't actually born in Tasmania," she said as this stranger escorted her up the steps of the town hall. He asked her where she was born, and she decided to be honest with him. "I was actually born in India."

But it was a momentary lapse. Once Merle entered the reception room, her story continued to shapeshift. One attendee asked her about whether she'd really been born in Hobart; Merle responded that she'd been born on a ship passing by Tasmania. She then started to give a speech, looking rather like a woman under the influence. Some in the audience said they would have been concerned for her welfare if they were to walk by her on the street. Then Merle began to feel faint.* The trauma from years of anguish, spent hiding in shame, seemed to pour out of every crevice of her skin. The Lord Mayor's secretary fetched her a glass of water and assisted her from the room. For a few moments, Merle sat in silence. Then she collected herself before returning to the reception—ready, once again, to continue the most difficult performance she'd ever given in her life.

* Accounts differ about the severity of Merle's distress at the event. Some said she even passed out while giving her speech.

Chapter 18

It Has Haunted Me
Ever Since

(1978–1979)

Merle Oberon with Robert Wolders in 1979, the year of her death.

By the time Merle and Robert returned home from that disorienting Tasmania trip later in the fall of 1978, Merle's heart had all but given out. In November, she was rushed to Cedars-Sinai Hospital in Los Angeles for an emergency coronary bypass and replacement of her aortic valve, an operation that lasted seven and a half hours. The surgery left her with one of the greatest indignities imaginable: a scar running down the middle of her chest, making her feel more monstrous than ever. She would spend the early months of 1979 steadily recouping her stamina with walks along the Malibu beach. Merle didn't want to excuse herself from public life entirely, but her recovery was so protracted that she couldn't attend her daughter Francesca's wedding festivities in Mexico City later that spring. Instead, she would confine her minimal social activities to Los Angeles, joining fellow artists as she threw her support behind the Republican actor-turned-politician Ronald Reagan as he began another, ultimately successful run for president.

On the last Saturday in September of 1979, Merle took the stage of Santa Barbara's historic Arlington Theater before a crowd of nearly two thousand people who had come to see her career tribute. The American Film Institute had begun a classic Hollywood screening series across California. The space was nearly at capacity that evening as the audience watched clips from *The Private Life of Henry VIII, These Three, A Song to Remember*, and *Désirée*—covering three pivotal decades of Merle's filmography—before screening the highlight of her acting career, *Wuthering Heights*, in its entirety. A question-and-answer session conducted by Robert Osborne, then a journalist for the *Hollywood Reporter*, followed, and Merle, wearing a simple white gown, reminisced affectionately about her career. She recounted the misery she felt when she learned that her part in *The Private Life of Henry VIII* had been shredded to scraps, her sense of comfort under Samuel Goldwyn's wing, her experience of feeling somewhat abandoned by William Wyler during *Wuthering Heights* as he contorted in submission to Laurence Olivier.

"I feel well, *really* well for the first time in months," she told Osborne the day after her salute. Merle had recovered psychologically from her Tasmania visit, if not physically. But her spirits were soon injured when Wyler, stewing after reading Merle's remarks printed in the *Los Angeles Times* that following Tuesday, sent a scathing note to Merle. "Belated congratulations for surviving the 'suffering' you endured forty-one years ago," he wrote. He asked how and why she had become "so bitchy now" for dredging up such shopworn incidents. (Wyler even sent a copy of this particular letter to the *Los Angeles Times*, only to regret it so much that he asked the paper not to print his words. The paper obliged.) He also went so far as to draft a list of actors he had directed to an Academy Award—including Olivia de Havilland for *The Heiress* (1949), Audrey Hepburn for *Roman Holiday* (1953), Barbra Streisand for *Funny Girl* (1968)—while lamenting that he was sorry that Merle, so tragically unnominated for her *Wuthering Heights* turn, was not among them. Olivier's work in *Wuthering Heights*, he wrote in one of those letters, "has stood the test of time far better than Cathy—or Merle." He consigned Merle's performance, the crowning achievement of her filmography, to history's dustbin.

As Merle battled the demon that was her health, another threat to her legacy surfaced that year when her former nephew-by-marriage, Michael Korda, sent her an early copy of his family memoir, *Charmed Lives: A Family Romance* (1979), a group portrait of three brothers: Merle's first husband Alexander, Michael's father Vincent, and Zoltán. As Merle perused the text, she was startled to see he'd folded her real name and that bombshell of her Bombay birth, two Korda family secrets, into the galleys of his book. Merle didn't even let a day pass before she had a lawyer call Michael with the threat of a lawsuit. This worked: Michael disappeared Merle to a cameo player in the book. She wasn't satisfied with her minimized role in the book, either, but at least she was able to ensure that the record would preserve her memory as that "beautiful young Tasmanian-born actress," as the book called her, who had bewitched a Hungarian film producer in 1932 and became a star. By that point, America still remained a bit sluggish in its acceptance of South Asian performers, although a former pageant princess from India named Persis Khambatta would feature in *Star Trek: The Motion Picture* that year. Her striking looks and shaved head made her a sensation in America, so much so that she would present at the Academy Awards the following year. She was celebrated as the first Indian to present at the Academy Awards, even though Merle Oberon, Anglo-Indian but unable to express it, had preceded her.

Despite her health's continuing corrosion, Merle did her best to maintain her strength. At a public luncheon she attended that October, she asked that the paparazzi refrain from taking her picture. She wanted to be remembered as she once was. Merle then agreed to a taped interview in her Malibu home with talk-show host Dinah Shore; it would take place on the last Thursday in November, a week after Thanksgiving. She and Robert found and purchased a new Bel Air pad that they would move to the following April, as a new decade was beginning. In November, Merle and Robert were shopping for furniture at a Beverly Hills antiques shop when she was overcome by a sudden spell. Merle told the salesman they'd come back to see it another time. She wasn't feeling well.

★

THANKSGIVING DAY OF 1979 began like any other for Merle. She chatted with friends on the telephone. She took a walk on the beach in Malibu after dinner. She returned home and lit her fireplace. Before retiring to sleep early, she sat at the foot of the bed and told Robert how much she loved him. Just after 9:30 p.m., she started to feel pangs in her chest. It was 10:18 when paramedics rushed into her Malibu home to find her collapsed, though conscious, from a stroke. No matter how much she'd prepared herself for death, she desperately regretted this happening to her. "My poor, poor Robbie," she whimpered to her husband. "I'm letting you down." Emergency personnel took her to Cedars-Sinai, where she had received treatment the previous year. What had seemed like a manageable condition became graver as night bled into morning. She slid into a coma. Robert and her two children were standing beside Merle when she died at three in the afternoon on November 23.

The memorial service at All Saints Episcopal Church in Beverly Hills was held the following Wednesday. About three hundred people were in attendance. William Wyler, who had chewed out Merle just months earlier, was present. Even those who had known her before she became Merle Oberon—such as Anna Lee, who had met Calcutta-bred Queenie Thompson in the early 1930s—were there to say good-bye to the woman loved by many but understood by few. The rectangular plaque indicating Merle's resting place in the hills of Forest Lawn Memorial Park's Garden of Remembrance, in Los Angeles County's Glendale, would note her birth year, incorrectly, as 1917, instead of 1911. The funeral pamphlet included specifics regarding her life's end: Merle passed away on November 23, 1979, in Los Angeles, California. No birth date was included. Her place of birth was, simply, "Tasmania." She took her secrets with her.

Obituaries did not commemorate Merle in the way she would have wished, lingering on her beauty more often than her acting. Both her birthplace of Tasmania as well as her white, European ancestry were repeated with certainty. The condensed summaries of her biography hit the same counterfeit beats that Merle had been taught to master throughout her life: That her British Army officer father had died before she was born. That she was six when she was whisked away to Bombay, eight when she moved to Calcutta. That an uncle took her to England in her teens, and that he left her with a small wad of cash and a steamer ticket back to Calcutta in case she changed her mind. These remembrances wavered even on matters such as how old Merle was, but some excused the discrepancies by reasoning that she lied about her age in 1932 to secure a work permit (she didn't), which was, in her own words, "a very youthful decision and, apparently, a very foolish one since it has haunted me ever since." And these stories barely even mentioned her mother.

★

JUST OVER A YEAR had passed since her firstborn's death when Constance Joyce was sitting in her bedroom in Bombay. It was a February afternoon in 1981, a few days after what would have been Merle's seventieth birthday. She'd had a rough go of it in the months since her girl's passing. Constance Joyce had fallen, breaking her hip, which began her slow descent toward death. She lingered for about a month before her heart gave way. Harry, the fourth of her five children, had made sure that she had everything she needed, even hiring a caretaker to look after her. The employee went to fetch her a glass of Complan, a powdered chocolate milk drink she loved, before noticing that Constance Joyce wasn't responding. She'd had a heart attack.

Eighty-four at the time of her death, Constance Joyce had held onto those small mementos of her daughter's life: Letters Merle had written to her. Documentation of the money she used to send. The pair of earrings that Merle had worn when she was three. She never told her children or her grandkids of her true relationship to Merle. Harry always had difficulty understanding why his mother felt such a pull toward a woman he understood to be her half sister. He did not realize that Constance Joyce was taking a secret with her to her grave, as her daughter had done. As Constance Joyce was dying, she told Harry she could see an image flickering before her as if it were real: Queenie was standing at the foot of her bed, an apparition dressed in white.

Epilogue

IN 1982, THE YEAR AFTER HIS MOTHER'S DEATH, HARRY Selby visited a grotto of government records at the Bombay (now Mumbai) Municipal Building, located near the handsome Victoria Terminus train station, a UNESCO World Heritage site. He was there, with his son-in-law (who did not wish to divulge his name on the record for this book), to find "Aunt Merle's" birth certificate. This place had thousands of them, stretching back to the eighteenth century. Surely, they'd find Merle's. As they leafed through 1911's entries, the men came across the birth certificate of Estelle Merle Thompson, which presented the truth in plainspoken terms: Her race, Eurasian. Her father, Arthur Thompson. Her mother, Constance Thompson. Not Charlotte. Harry was stunned: He and Merle were half-siblings. Trying to swallow his shock, Harry kept this discovery from the writer Charles Higham, who was already at work on a biography of Merle and had enlisted Harry's help in piecing together her early years. Knowing the bombshell that Higham was about to make public about Merle's origins, Harry did not want to disturb his family's sensitivities further.

Why, one might wonder, didn't anyone expose Merle sooner, during her lifetime? Her purported Tasmanian birth was such accepted wisdom that "Birthplace of Merle Oberon" was even a newspaper crossword clue while she was alive. Though some violated this law of *omertà*, she cultivated enormous goodwill within Hollywood. After an initial period of ostracization, she worked hard to become extraordinarily well liked in the industry. Richard Gully, a Golden

Age Hollywood insider, once commented on Merle's protection by those who knew her secret: "In Hollywood, if people liked you, they covered for you." Her charm, along with her ambition, carried her to great heights. Though Merle very much made herself, the fact that she tethered herself to powerful men like the producers Samuel Goldwyn and Alexander Korda—who in turn grandfathered her into this exclusionary racial milieu—helped her soar, however briefly; gossip columnists of the day—Louella Parsons, Hedda Hopper—adored her, and her friendship with them negated any possibility that they'd turn their pens on her. This quorum of allies, along with an absence of powerful enemies, allowed her to have the career she wanted.

The very year Harry made that chilling discovery in the Bombay archives, press reports emerged that Merle had threatened Michael Korda with a lawsuit after reading an advance copy of *Charmed Lives*, in which he divulged that she'd been an Anglo-Indian girl born in Bombay, and that he was now planning to spin the reality of her life into a novel. That same year, Phyllis Beaumont, her old friend from Calcutta, also told journalists the saga of this Anglo-Indian girl named Queenie with the pretty face and scratchy voice. Although the women had lost touch as Queenie morphed into Merle Oberon, Phyllis marveled at how her friend had moved up in the world through her gumption, beauty, and guile. Phyllis insisted she did not talk to the press to arouse prurience befitting a supermarket tabloid. In recounting the facts of Merle's early life in Calcutta, she simply said that Merle, this woman who died so beloved, deserved understanding: "Now I believe Queenie's story will elicit compassion, rather than censure. The truth can only make people appreciate her more. Like Marilyn Monroe, she was a victim, in her early life. But she was brave. She never surrendered."

Phyllis may have been a touch optimistic. By the time Higham and his coauthor, Roy Moseley, published their book on Merle in 1983, it seemed that Hollywood had, indeed, begun to change for the better. The actor Ben Kingsley, born as Krishna Pandit Bhanji to an Indian father and a British mother, won an Academy Award that very year for playing the titular role in Richard Attenborough's *Gandhi* (1982), the production that Merle had been circling. (The Indian actress Rohini Hattangadi played the role that was initially meant for Merle.) But in subsequent years, as more South Asian actors began to populate screens small and large, Merle's memory became flyspecked with distortions about her relationship to her South Asian heritage. Fictional treatments of her life appeared—such as Michael Korda's *Queenie* (eventually published in 1985) and the 1987 ABC miniseries adapted from it (starring the likable but miscast Italian-American Mia Sara as Queenie, surrounded by performers in brownface)—and both went for shock value as they pillaged the very real story of the brown girl who passed for white. In the absence of clear answers, fiction has its allure, but there is danger in that temptation when one involves the life of a real person. Oral fictions circulated, too. As a further insult to Merle's memory, there were still those back in Tasmania who clung to the idea of Merle's birth on that island, despite what had surfaced as the near-ironclad proof of her Indian origins. Why did the belief retain such a feverish hold? Tasmania's people were on "the periphery of the periphery," as the Tasmanian-born writer Cassandra Pybus once astutely observed of this phenomenon, whereas Hollywood seemed like the center of the world. Tasmania, in other words, was a place that existed at the edges of the earth and the imagination, just as Korda had believed back in 1932. To those islanders who felt that their home was a perennial object of neglect, Merle Oberon represented the distinct possibility that one could escape those shackles and make something of oneself.

And racism kept that myth going. "I've known lots of Indian students—boys who come out here with the papers of their dead brother," one Tasmanian journalist—to whom Merle had given her sole press interview during her doomed 1978 visit—told the writer Nicholas Shakespeare when confronted with Merle's Indian birth certificate. "They don't think twice about forging." Another source told Shakespeare that Tasmanians are "truthful people." Underpinning the fallacy of Merle's Tasmanian birth, then, was a belief that Indians were dishonest by nature, and that they probably fabricated any proof of her South Asian provenance just to get their grubby hands on this glittering star. Despite the racism embedded in such charges, I have some sympathy, too, for anyone in Tasmania who may lean on the delusion that Merle was one of their own. There was something about this actress, the mettle of her mien quite evident on screen, that invites such projection for those of us who imagine ourselves on the peripheries, to borrow Pybus's phrase—a belief that allows us to feel she is one of us, that in her we are seeing a reflection of ourselves.

THINKING OF A PERFORMER like Ben Kingsley, one may wonder who the heirs of Merle's legacy are, what the precise nature of that legacy even is. Some might say that she left no legacy, that she was only looking out for herself. Cynics may even be prompted to cast Merle as a craven opportunist, using her white-passing privilege to assimilate, driven only by the selfish pursuit of fame that ultimately caused more harm for acceptance. This perception has always discomfited me, seeming to downplay the racism and classism into which she was born and could barely escape in Britain and America.

What does America want from its stars when they come from the margins? Being one of the few South Asian women in Hollywood during her era, Merle had the misfortune of scarcity. As such, audiences today may look back on her and wish she had been a prouder representative of her people, because they still have so few role models on the Hollywood screen. In that configuration, individuals from marginalized groups had to carry a responsibility so much larger than themselves, their immediate material needs, and their circumstances. Merle came up in an era when she was taught to feel shame in her racial origins. That she did not take obvious public pride in her background has made her a difficult icon to embrace in an era so eager to flatten the valences of human contradiction to maximize virality, to make cardboard cutouts of flesh-and-blood historical figures. Her story's intricacies preclude easy digestion, too much to fit into one

Tumblr post or tweet in the era of understandable, but at times simplistic, cries that representation matters. How unfair it is to look back on this woman's Hollywood career nearly a century ago and reject her because she was an imperfect—by today's standards—delegate of her race when she was simply trying to survive. These pressures are tied to a misguided belief that a star must function as a public servant, that she owes something to the people who watch her. Merle was working to make a better life for herself. Shouldn't her achievement of that goal be enough?

With time, Merle became a convenient scapegoat for misplaced anxieties about the ugly sins of the past. I suspect the reason why she has not had the same wide embrace as her contemporaries— say, Anna May Wong—is that it is far easier for people in these more enlightened ages to besmirch her, a lone individual, rather than try to understand her, which would involve directing their criticism to the system that pushed her into this performance of concealment. During my research, I came across an unusually compassionate letter from the famed Indian radio journalist Melville de Mellow to the *Times of India* after the truth of Merle's heritage surfaced, taking umbrage with the charge—popular among some of my fellow South Asians—that Merle was a calculating renegade trying to get ahead. "She was just human, in wanting to better her prospects and enjoy the good things of life, instead of ending her days as a street-walker in Calcutta," he wrote. (If this attitude toward sex work seems outmoded, consider that it could often be a precarious profession for women in Merle's time as it sometimes remains today, providing them little protection from violence.) What Merle did, de Mellow said, was the only way for her to dodge the stigma that the British would have attached to her because of her racial identity. Those who deserved blame, he argued, "are the people who advised, helped and encouraged her to live that lie—Hollywood included."

The city of Merle's birth, Bombay (now Mumbai), created what is now Bollywood, whose star-making apparatus would come to resemble that of its American counterpart. Even today, names are changed, biographies skewed, backstories fabricated to broaden appeal to audiences. A routine element of Bollywood stardom has long involved participating in ads for fair-skin creams, similar to those that Hollywood forced upon Merle, reflecting the industry's hostility to darker skin. The deeper systemic rot that Merle battled remains alive, globally. The words *forgotten* and *overlooked* get thrown around rather indiscriminately these days, but they apply to Merle: Hers is the precise sort of story that dominant narratives seem determined to efface. Histories of South Asia have tended to shortchange the Anglo-Indian community in which Merle was reared. Within an American context, meanwhile, the fact that she passed for white has made her ripe for knee-jerk dismissal from people unwilling to understand the climate—in Hollywood, and in America more generally—that compelled her to make such a bargain. Today, the culture sees the fact that she wasn't a mascot of ethnic pride as a demerit rather than an invitation to understand how discriminatory this world once was. In the spirit of de Mellow's letter, see this book, then, not only as a chronicle of one woman's trials and triumphs but also as an indictment of the systems in South Asia, in Britain, in America that told Merle that the only way for her to do what she loved was to hide herself.

Merle was a woman who—like Judy Garland and Marilyn Monroe, two of her more famous sisters in art and survival—was exploited by almost everyone around her from girlhood onward, and someone who kept forging ahead nonetheless. Merle's saga has tragic elements due to the miasma of racism, of classism, of xenophobia, of misogyny she faced throughout her lifetime, but I do not want to frame it as a tragedy: Like Garland and Monroe, she persisted in that tinselly jungle where she wanted desperately to make an impression. I marvel, still, at how Merle was able to remake herself, given the ramshackle circumstances of her upbringing, and how she fought to maintain her autonomy against the constrictions of a narrow-minded star system. In doing so, she cast a long shadow and forged a path that others now walk.

★

NOT LONG AFTER I began writing this book, the Malaysian actress Michelle Yeoh would star in the enormous hit *Everything Everywhere All at Once* (2022), earning a 2023 Academy Award nomination for Best Actress in a Leading Role for her deft, register-spanning performance. This made her the second Asian nominee in the history of that category, after Merle's nomination in 1936. Besides Ben Kingsley, the Oscars had recognized South Asian male actors Dev Patel and Riz Ahmed with nominations, far too few. Whether the club will deign to welcome more—and any other South Asian *women*, for that matter—remains to be seen. Days before Yeoh would win the Oscar for Best Actress, she spoke with talk-show host Stephen Colbert about her historic nomination, and she promptly corrected him when he erroneously claimed she was the first Asian Best Actress nominee. Merle Oberon had come before her, Yeoh said, and she had to hide her identity. I nearly cried when I heard Yeoh simply acknowledge that Merle had once existed, that she didn't have it easy.

I fear that, in the years since Merle's death, the fixation on the agony of a life spent in hiding has occluded respect for her craft. One of the pleasures of writing this book was getting to engage, in a tactile way, with Merle's actual art, and I hope it will prompt a similar quest for discovery on the part of you, the reader. Merle's octave was not as limited as some might have you believe: A few films revealed a range for spry comedy, which reflected her generally jocular offscreen personality. I won't pretend that her talent was kaleidoscopic. She was uncomfortable with accent work—a condition of having to tame her own Anglo-Indian timbre, which had always been a source of shame for her—and there were times when she was unable to fully submerge her persona to become the character she played. I'm forever fascinated by that persona, and the tensions that roiled beneath her presentation of stoicism. She's the kind of actress I'd watch in anything, even in swill. (And there's a bit of it, I'm afraid, in her filmography.) At her best, the entirety of her being—her pain and strength—could flood her performances. Perhaps people will continue to spit on Merle's memory, denying she was Asian, omitting her from lists, histories, and narratives to which she belongs. But I hope, ultimately, that some of you readers will be compelled to see Merle Oberon as I first saw her all those years ago, to see her as I have come to believe she saw herself: as an actress who endeavored to show us her humanity on screen, and, through it, helped us better understand our own.

Acknowledgments

THIS BOOK WAS NOT AN EASY ONE TO WRITE, IN NO SMALL PART DUE TO WHAT I perceived as a general apathy toward Merle's life and legacy. Emphatic thanks, then, to my agent, William Callahan, who understood from the outset the personal significance of this project to me, articulated it more cogently than I could, and championed it every step of the way. William: You may not remember that I told you of my ambition to write a biography of Merle Oberon when you first signed me as a twenty-five-year-old in 2017. You told me to wait, patiently, for the right moment. I am glad we found it.

I am grateful to my editor, Melanie Tortoroli, who not only took a gamble on me as I pursued a passion project far beyond the subject of my first book (a book on which we worked together!) but also suffered through the rancid, frankly unreadable early drafts of these chapters and guided me with her patient hand. Equal thanks go to Annabel Brazaitis for her invaluable editorial input throughout, and for fielding my panicked questions about permissions, photographs, and other minutiae. Thank you to everyone else at, or affiliated with, Norton whose hands touched this book—my eagle-eyed copyeditor Kathleen Brandes, project editor Jessica Murphy, project manager Louise Mattarelliano, art director and cover designer Ingsu Liu, and so many others. And a salute of gratitude to my perspicacious fact-checker, Tia Rotolo, who sifted through the dross of misinformation out there on Merle's life and helped us get as close to the truth as possible. You did not have an easy job.

Thank you to the members of the Selby and Korda families who trusted me with Merle's story and opened up to me during a process otherwise filled with dead ends. Equal thanks to the scholars and sources who shared relevant research on Merle with me, including Maree Delofski, Charles Drazin, and John Calendo. Thanks, too, to the archivists and librarians who assisted me in my research: Genevieve Maxwell and Louise Hilton of the Margaret Herrick Library at the Academy of Motion Picture Arts and Sciences; Espen Bale of the British Film Institute; Sandra Garcia-Myers of the USC Cinematic Arts Library and Archives; and Robert Hazle of the Noël Coward Archive Trust, among others. And to those who helped me in obtaining images of Merle, thank you: Terence Pepper, Andrew Howick, Mary Ellen Jensen, Michele Hadlow, Thomas Haggerty.

Thank you to my long-distance-email buddy Rohan Spong, whose ardor for Merle matches my own, and who graciously provided me with prints of films and documentaries that proved indispensable, along with periodic gut checks. My fellow Old Hollywood biographer, Katie Gee Salisbury: Thank you for your guidance throughout this trying process. I am thankful to Devika Girish and Clinton Krute of *Film Comment* for being the first of my editors to greenlight a pitch from me on Merle (the number of editors who said *no* could fill, well, a book), and for taking her story—and my telling of it—seriously.

My trusted friends—you know who you are—I thank you for your love throughout a process that tested my physical and mental health. Thank you to my mother, Kasturi Sen, for listening to me blather on about Merle for years without disowning me, and to my late father, Sakti Sengupta, for instilling in me a love for cinema that would shape my entire life.

And to Queenie herself, Merle Oberon: You may be a biographer's nightmare, yet I am indebted to you, a survivor, for fighting a battle I wish you hadn't had to fight, for creating art that is so lasting and resonant, and for touching many lives—mine included—in the process.

Filmography

THE FOLLOWING IS A LIST OF THE FILMS—THEATRICAL RELEASES AS
well as television plays—in which I've confirmed Merle Oberon appeared.
As stated in the Introduction, I have eliminated titles that have often
been attached to her name in error, such as *The Three Passions* (1928), a
film that came out a year before she left India. Absent from this list, too,
are films that suspended production, such as *I, Claudius* (1937), or television documentaries in which she's a talking head, such as *The Epic That
Never Was* (1965). In an interview published posthumously in the February 1982 issue of *Films in Review,* Merle denied being in either *Never Trouble Trouble* (1931) and *Service for Ladies* (1932), two films widely associated
with her filmography. There is no proof that she was in *Strange Evidence*
(1933), either, despite present-day filmographies claiming she had a bit
part in it. In another interview early in her career, she also claimed to
have been in *Kiss Me Sergeant* (1930), a comedy based in India. As of this
writing, quite a few of these films are available on streaming services, as
are her television appearances on *Four Star Playhouse*. But even her later
titles, *Interval* included, are difficult to find in higher quality. Most of her
television work is fully lost. (Note: An asterisk in this list denotes a title
currently considered lost media.)

Theatrical
Alf's Button (1930)
Kiss Me Sergeant (1930)
A Warm Corner (1930)
Fascination (1931)

For the Love of Mike (1932)

Ebb Tide (1932)*

Aren't We All? (1932)

Wedding Rehearsal (1932)

Men of Tomorrow (1932)*

The Private Life of Henry VIII (1933)

The Battle (1934)

The Broken Melody (1934)

The Private Life of Don Juan (1934)

The Scarlet Pimpernel (1934)

Folies Bergère de Paris (1935)

The Dark Angel (1935)

These Three (1936)

Beloved Enemy (1936)

The Divorce of Lady X (1938)

The Cowboy and the Lady (1938)

Over the Moon (1939)

Wuthering Heights (1939)

The Lion Has Wings (1939)

'Til We Meet Again (1940)

That Uncertain Feeling (1941)

Affectionately Yours (1941)

Lydia (1941)

Forever and a Day (1943)

Stage Door Canteen (1943)

First Comes Courage (1943)

The Lodger (1944)

Dark Waters (1944)

A Song to Remember (1945)

This Love of Ours (1945)

Night in Paradise (1946)

Temptation (1946)

Night Song (1947)

Berlin Express (1948)

Pardon My French (1951)/*Dans la vie tout s'arrange* (1952)

Affair in Monte Carlo (1952)

All Is Possible in Granada (1954)

Désirée (1954)

Deep in My Heart (1954)

The Price of Fear (1956)

Of Love and Desire (1963)

The Oscar (1966)

Hotel (1967)

Interval (1973)

Television

Ford Television Theatre: "Allison, Ltd." (1953)★

Four Star Playhouse: "Sound Off, My Love" (1953)

Playhouse of Stars: "The Journey" (1953)★

Four Star Playhouse: "Love at Sea" (1953)

The Best of Broadway: "The Man Who Came to Dinner" (1954)

Four Star Playhouse: "The Frightened Woman" (1955)

The 20th Century–Fox Hour: "Cavalcade" (1955)

Ford Television Theatre: "Second Sight" (1955)★

The Loretta Young Show: "The Bracelet" (1955)★

Assignment Foreign Legion (1956–1957)

General Electric Theater: "I Will Not Die" (1957)★

Notes

Introduction

xi **invented for her:** Charles Drazin, *Korda: Britain's Movie Mogul* (London: Sidgwick & Jackson, 2002), 87.

xii **a "Hindu":** Grace Wilcox, "The Meaning of 'Glamour'," *Screen & Radio Weekly*, May 19, 1935, 73.

xii **"dusky peril":** "Have We a Dusky Peril?" *Puget Sound American*, September 16, 1906.

xii **mystics:** Shilpa S. Davé, *Indian Accents: Brown Voice and Racial Performance in American Television and Film* (Urbana: University of Illinois Press, 2013), 23.

xii **temptresses:** John Baxter, *Von Sternberg* (Lexington: University Press of Kentucky, 2010), 208.

xiii **"Miss Oberon":** Nelson B. Bell, "The New Screen and Stage Bills in the Picture Houses Present a Fine Variety," *Washington Post*, March 24, 1935.

xiii **first movie:** Reine Davies, "Stars Reminisce," *San Francisco Examiner*, June 30, 1935.

xiv **"too Oriental":** Drazin, *Korda*, 131.

xiv **play a Hindu:** James Robert Parish, *The Glamour Girls* (New Rochelle, NY: Arlington House, 1975), 602.

xiv **"I would die":** Cable from Merle Oberon to Alexander Korda, March 6, 1935, Samuel Goldwyn Papers, Margaret Herrick Library, Academy of Motion Picture Arts and Sciences, Beverly Hills.

xiv **muzzle them:** *E! Mysteries & Scandals*, Season 3, Episode 48, March 14, 2001.

xiv **mistake of suntanning:** Eleanor Nangle, "Through the Looking Glass," *Chicago Daily Tribune*, July 28, 1935.

xiv **skin-bleaching:** Phil Lonergan, "Janet Gaynor's Future," *Picturegoer*, August 31, 1935, 15.

xiv **cry at will:** Sidney Skolsky, "Hollywood," *Daily News*, June 26, 1935.

xiv **"I detest 'exotic'":** John R. Woolfenden, "'I Detest "Exotic" Women,' Says Exotic Merle Oberon," *Los Angeles Times*, September 15, 1935.

xv   **"Miss Oberon":** Andre Sennwald, "The Screen," *New York Times*, September 6, 1935.

xv   **Academy Awards:** Warren G. Harris, *Clark Gable: A Biography* (New York: Three Rivers Press, 2002), 153.

xv   **announced last:** Damien Bona and Mason Wiley, *Inside Oscar: The Unofficial History of the Academy Awards* (New York: Ballantine Books, 1986), 65.

xvii   **"a nothing actress":** James Baldwin, *If Beale Street Could Talk* (London: Michael Joseph Ltd., 1974), 218.

xvii   **"she was often":** David Thomson, *The New Biographical Dictionary of Film* (New York: Knopf, 2002), 643.

xvii   **"What use was Merle":** Nick Davis, "Best Actress Update: 5 More Down, 90 to Go," Nick's Flick Picks, July 30, 2006 (accessed January 30, 2024).

xx   **"a pagoda":** "She Lost Her Head to Get Head Start," *San Francisco Examiner*, September 14, 1965.

xx   **"girl bride":** Harry Carr, "The Lancer," *Los Angeles Times*, April 2, 1935.

xx   **"imperturbable young Buddha":** Florence Fisher Parry, "I Dare Say—Success Is More than Skin Deep," *Pittsburgh Press*, May 20, 1935.

Chapter 1: My Name Is Queenie

1   **comb her hair:** Anil and Sunil Selby, phone interview by author, April 30, 2023.

2   **"my Queen":** Sidney Skolsky, "Tintypes," *Daily News*, April 9, 1935.

2   **half-Sinhalese and half-British:** Anil and Sunil Selby.

2   **Colombo:** Estelle Merle Thompson, Report of Birth in Greater Bombay, February 18, 1911, Municipal Corporation of Greater Bombay.

2   **stepfather:** Maree Delofski, *The Trouble with Merle*, Australian Broadcasting Corporation, 2002.

2   **no memory:** David Ragan, "Dark Secrets of a Great Star," *South China Morning Post*, October 31, 1982.

2   **baptismal certificate:** Estelle Merle Thompson, Baptisms solemnized at Emmanuel Church Girgaum within the Archdeaconry and Diocese of Bombay in the year of our Lord 1911, March 16, 1911.

3   **campaigning:** Uther Charlton-Stevens, *Anglo-India and the End of Empire* (London: C. Hurst & Co. Ltd., 2022), 26.

3   **315,156,396:** E. A. Gait, *Census of India, 1911 Volume 1* (Calcutta: Superintendent Government Printing, India, 1913), 12.

3   **ruling class:** Sunanda Datta-Ray, "Demise of a Gifted Minority," *South China Morning Post*, February 6, 1977.

3   **upper-caste:** "Anglo-Indians And Indo-Anglians," *Times of India*, September 18, 1983.

3   *Eight annas:* R. L., "POSTSCRIPTS," *Jerusalem Post*, January 30, 1977.

4   **dozen kids:** Jimmie Fidler, "Jimmie Fidler in Hollywood," *Los Angeles Times*, May 8, 1940.

5   *Aladdin:* Marguerite Talezaar, "'Anything Behind That Face?' Merle Oberon Proved There Was," *New York Herald Tribune*, February 3, 1935.

5   **social strata:** Ranita Chatterjee, "Cinema in the Colonial City: Early Film Audiences in Calcutta" in *Audiences: Defining and Researching Screen Entertainment Reception*, edited by Ian Christie (Amsterdam: Amsterdam University Press, 2012), 73.

6   **Miss Rose:** Hyacinth, "'Filmindia' Is Different' Says Rose," *Filmindia*, November 1941, 57.

6   **taboo career:** Ranita Chatterjee, "Confessions of Indian Cinema's First Woman Superstar: Kanan Devi's Memoirs, Film History and Digital Archives" in *Indian Film Stars: New Critical Perspectives*, edited by Michael Lawrence (London: Bloomsbury, 2020), 33.

6   **Queenie's ambitions:** Margaret Marsh and Wanda Ronner, *The Fertility Doctor: John Rock and the Reproductive Revolution* (Baltimore: Johns Hopkins University Press, 2008), 329.

6   **her fallopian tubes:** Loretta McLaughlin, *The Pill, John Rock, and the Church: The Biography of a Revolution* (Boston: Little, Brown, 1982), 52.

7   **Phyllis Beaumont:** Ragan, "Dark Secrets."

8   **Derek Jarman:** Derek Jarman, *Dancing Ledge* (London: Quartet, 1984), 37.

9   **Firpo's:** Sunanda K. Datta-Ray, "More than Skin-Deep," *Business Standard*, January 20, 2013.

9   **Calcutta's finest beauties:** Ben Finney, *Feet First* (New York: Crown, 1971), 159.

9   **they suspected:** Niamh Dillon, *Homeward Bound: Return Migration from Ireland and India at the End of the British Empire* (New York: New York University Press, 2022), 183.

10 **1929:** Delofski, *Trouble.*

Chapter 2: I Have No Mother

11 **"a girl of the streets":** Ragan, "Dark Secrets."

11 **washroom of their own:** James Bawden and Ron Miller, *Conversations with Classic Film Stars: Interviews from Hollywood's Golden Era* (Lexington: University Press of Kentucky, 2016), 207.

12 **cold water:** Gregory William Mank, *Women in Horror Films, 1940s* (Jefferson, NC: McFarland, 1999), 351.

12 **her own dresses:** Mollie Merrick, "Coolie Cloth Popular for Sports Wear," *Hartford Courant*, June 10, 1935.

12 **crackers and water:** "Dale Carnegie Says," *Muncie* [IN] *Morning Star,* June 9, 1943.

12 **candy boxes:** Lydia Lane, "Being in the Swim May Drown You," *Los Angeles Times*, April 8, 1956.

12 **Thousands had flocked:** Rochelle Almeida, *Britain's Anglo-Indians: The Invisibility of Assimilation* (Lanham, MD: Lexington, 2017), 3.

12 **estimated five thousand:** Alison Blunt, *Domicile and Diaspora: Anglo-Indian Women and the Spatial Politics of Home* (Malden, MA: Blackwell, 2005), 243.

12 **spotless skies:** Gloria Jean Moore, *The Anglo-Indian Vision* (Melbourne: AE Press, 1986), 123.

12 **auditions for extras:** Merle Oberon, "Merle Oberon's Discovery, Theme in Four Variations," *Pittsburgh Post-Gazette*, March 19, 1935.

12 **gaggle of fifty:** Rosalind Shaffer, "Meet Merle Oberon, Film Find of Year," *Chicago Daily Tribune*, March 31, 1935.

12 **below street level:** Douglas Fairbanks Jr., *The Salad Days* (New York: Doubleday, 1988), 216.

12 **400 Club:** Charles Sweeny with Colonel James A. Goodson, *Sweeny* (Canterbury, UK: Wingham Press, 1990), 38.

13 **proper evening dress:** Michael Winner, *Winner Takes All: A Life of Sorts* (London: Robison, 2004), 19.

13 **she turned nineteen:** Charlotte Breese, *Hutch* (London: Bloomsbury, 1999), 192.

13 **two pounds:** Charles Gay, "Celebrities in Cameo: No. 71. Merle Oberon," *The Bystander*, October 9, 1934, 47.

13 **World War I:** Jeffrey Richards, *The Age of the Dream Palace: Cinema and Society in Britain 1930–1939* (London: Routledge & Kegan Paul, 1984), 34.

14 **Hollywood films:** Steve Chibnall, *Quota Quickies: The Birth of the British 'B' Film* (London: British Film Institute, 2007), viii.

14 **Carl Brisson:** Lupton A. Wilkinson, "'Go Wash Your Face!'," *Atlanta Constitution*, February 25, 1940.

14 **Victor Silvester:** Laurie Henshaw, "Here's One Musical We Could Have Scored First," *Picturegoer*, October 16, 1954, 9.

15 **David Niven:** Sheridan Morley, *The Other Side of the Moon: The Life of David Niven* (New York: Harper & Row, 1985), 63.

15 **Victor Saville:** Peter Underwood, *Death in Hollywood* (London: Judy Piatkus Ltd., 1992), 30.

16 **"Javanese":** Ethel Waters with Charles Samuels, *His Eye Is on the Sparrow: An Autobiography by Ethel Waters with Charles Samuels* (Garden City, NY: Doubleday, 1951), 211.

17 **lumber-mill workers:** Vivek Bald, *Bengali Harlem and the Lost Histories of South Asian America* (Cambridge: Harvard University Press, 2013), 1.

17 **"least desirable":** Erika Lee, *The Making of Asian America: A History* (New York: Simon & Schuster, 2015), 163.

17 **South Asian characters:** Scott Allen Nollen with Yuyun Yuningsih Nollen, *Karloff and the East: Asian, Indian, Middle Eastern and Oceanian Characters and Subjects in His Screen Career* (Jefferson, NC: McFarland, 2021), 27.

18 **most popular actresses:** WM. H. Mooring, "British Public Still Not Serious on Home Product, Poll Shows," *Motion Picture Herald*, May 14, 1932, 20.

19 **Miles Mander:** Miles Mander, "To Hell with Acting," *Hollywood Reporter*, December 31, 1937, 406.

19 **"Queenie? Queenie Thompson?":** Anna Lee with Barbara Roisman Cooper,

Anna Lee: Memoir of a Career on General Hospital *and in Film* (Jefferson, NC: McFarland, 2007), 66.

21 **Merle's eventual funeral:** "Stars Crowd Rites for Merle Oberon," *Boston Globe*, November 29, 1979.

22 **"little black half-caste":** Drazin, *Korda*, 86.

22 **spilled coffee:** Michael Korda, *Charmed Lives: A Family Romance* (New York: Random House, 1979), 101.

22 **"There she is":** Michael Korda, *Another Life: A Memoir of Other People* (New York: Random House, 1999), 444.

22 **foot taller than Queenie:** Karol Kulik, *Alexander Korda: The Man Who Could Work Miracles* (London: W. H. Allen, 1975), 101.

22 **"I want to see":** Paul Tabori, *Alexander Korda* (London: Oldbourne, 1959), 119.

24 **point of origin:** Nicholas Shakespeare, *In Tasmania: Adventures at the End of the World* (London: The Harvill Press, 2004), 297.

24 **British Army officer father:** Corbin Patrick, "Merle Oberon Reaches Hollywood by Way of Tasmania, India, England," *Indianapolis Star*, March 7, 1935.

25 **Tasmania to Bombay:** Philip K. Scheuer, "Intriguing 'Myths' about Merle Oberon All Exploded," *Los Angeles Times*, December 30, 1934.

25 **shooting accident:** "Merle Oberon, Noted Film Beauty, Veteran of 40-Year Screen Career," *Asbury Park* [NJ] *Press*, November 24, 1979.

25 **Irish:** "The Most Promising Player in the World," *The Sketch*, December 13, 1933, 463.

25 **English and French:** "Love or Career?" *San Francisco Examiner*, November 23, 1934.

25 **three weeks:** E. G. Cousins, "'Extras' Get a Break," *Picturegoer*, June 18, 1932, 22.

Chapter 3: Anne *Sans Tête*

27 **West End:** E. G. Cousins, "On the British Sets," *Picturegoer*, May 28, 1932, 24.

28 **car accident:** Kulik, *Alexander*, 129.

28 **Merle became nervous:** Max Breen, "Merle Oberon Takes Stock," *Picturegoer*, December 19, 1936, 8.

28 **Mayfair accent:** Gavin Lambert, *Norma Shearer: A Life* (New York: Knopf, 1990), 218.

29 **"bright and fresh":** Edith Nepean, "Round the British Studios," *Picture Show*, October 8, 1932, 9.

29 **"slightly slanting":** "British Films in the Making," *Film Weekly*, July 15, 1932, 13.

29 **the first of the London Films quota quickies:** Osmond Borradaile with Anita Borradaile Hadley, *Life Through a Lens: Memoirs of a Cinematographer* (Montreal: McGill–Queen's University Press, 2001), 49.

29 **positive reaction:** Edith Nepean, "Round the British Studios," *Picture Show*, November 19, 1932, 6.

30 **tough sell:** Greg Walker, *The Private Life of Henry VIII: The British Film Guide 8* (London: I. B. Tauris & Co., 2003), 3.

30 **incensed:** Talezaar, "'Anything Behind That Face?'"

31 **felt inadequate:** Bill Duncalf, *The Epic That Never Was*, British Broadcasting Corporation, 1965.

31 **"If I don't":** "Merle Oberon Back in England," *Observer* [UK], November 15, 1936.

31 **studied Boleyn:** M. D., "Danger—Actresses at Work," *Answers*, July 23, 1949, 13.

31 **shot near the end:** "First British Colour Feature," *Kinematograph Weekly*, July 6, 1933, 17.

32 **"Were you late?":** Barbara Saltzman, "Merle Oberon: Looking Back," *Los Angeles Times*, October 2, 1979.

32 **"spiritual insight":** "Coming Attractions," *The Globe* [Toronto], December 7, 1933.

32 **"near perfection":** Edwin Schallert, "'Henry VIII' Rated Picture of Quality," *Los Angeles Times*, November 24, 1933.

32 **"as revolutionary":** "Money and Talent Aid British Film Industry," *State Journal* [Frankfort, KY], November 15, 1934.

33 **Hollywood began circling:** "Offers for British Stars," *Daily Film Renter*, November 2, 1933, 18.

33 **took a second look:** Hubbard Keavy, "Merle Oberon Super-Charged with Ambition," *St. Petersburg Times*, December 23, 1934.

33 **"the woman who launched":** Drazin, *Korda*, 128.

33 **"The Most Promising":** "The Most Promising," *The Sketch*.

33 **back to the Café de Paris:** "Town Topics," *The Bystander*, November 8, 1933, 252.

33 **Schiaparelli:** "Turnstyle: Who's Who Among Schiaparelli Clients," *Women's Wear Daily*, February 2, 1934, 3.

Chapter 4: **My One Ambition**

36 **poring over the rushes:** John Loder, "I Don't Want to Be a Star," *Picturegoer*, June 16, 1934, 14.

36 **recommended she test:** John Loder, *Hollywood Hussar: The Life and Times of John Loder* (London: Howard Baker, 1977), 106.

36 **coconut-oil pomade:** "Actress Finds Beauty Secret," *Los Angeles Times*, June 11, 1935.

36 **"a certain scrubbed":** Scheuer, "Intriguing 'Myths.'"

37 **proud of her performance:** Talezaar, "'Anything Behind That Face?'"

37 **hosannas:** Michael Orme, "Criticisms in Cameo: The Cinema," *The Sketch*, April 18, 1934, 127.

37 **"exotically attractive":** Sydney Tremayne, "The Passing Picture Show," *The Bystander*, April 17, 1934, 98.

37 **"convincingly Oriental":** "Pre-Views of the Latest Films: An Anglo-French Triumph," *Picturegoer*, May 5, 1934, 19.

37   *The Broken Melody:* Bernard Vorhaus, *Saved from Oblivion: An Autobiography* (London: Scarecrow, 2000), 75.

38   **"I thought I was dreadful":** Talezaar, "'Anything Behind That Face?'"

39   *The Road to Dishonour:* Charlton-Stevens, *Anglo-India,* 2.

39   **England's most photographed woman:** "Sleeping, Waking, Supping: The Private Life of Merle Oberon in Three Shots," *The Bystander,* October 2, 1934, 4.

40   **French Riviera:** "Sidelights on Stars," *Tatler,* August 15, 1934, 293.

40   **met him once before:** John Betjeman, "Merle Oberon Breaks Engagement," *London Evening Standard,* October 23, 1934.

41   **"a phlegmatic but outspoken":** "Schenck Is Playing 'Fixer' to Pickford and Fairbanks," the *Evansville* [IN] *Courier,* September 2, 1934.

41   **sleeveless blouse:** "He's Done It Again," *Daily News* [NY], August 15, 1934.

42   **cabled the influential producer:** "Joseph Schenck Weds English Film Actress," *Austin* [TX] *Statesman,* August 8, 1934.

42   **Darryl Zanuck:** "Screen: Movie Stars Will Be Swapped Across the Atlantic," *Newsweek,* September 1, 1934, 24.

42   **"Mrs. Schenck":** Louella O. Parsons, "Merle Oberon Will Play Opposite M. Chevalier in 'Folies Bergère de Paris'," *San Francisco Examiner,* September 29, 1934.

42   **she cease acting:** "Schenck So Loves Merle Oberon Tries to Patch Up Doug's Affair," *Toronto Daily Star,* August 8, 1934.

42   **a woman belonged in the home:** Shaffer, "Meet Merle."

43   **considerable self-possession:** Estel Eforgan, *Leslie Howard: The Lost Actor* (London: Vallentine Mitchell, 2010), 106.

43   **waiting for the telephone:** Sheilah Graham, "Hard Luck Has Pursued Merle Oberon," *Hartford Courant,* July 14, 1937.

44   **"Leslie's superb":** Talezaar, "'Anything Behind That Face?'"

44   **her finest performance:** "The Scarlet Pimpernel," *Kinematograph Weekly,* December 27, 1934, 19.

44   **journeyed to London . . . the peculiarities of their pairing:** Details in these paragraphs are drawn from columns by Louella Parsons published between October and December 1934. Full citations are in the bibliography.

44   **too young to retire:** "English Actress Arrives," *Los Angeles Times,* November 25, 1934.

44   **"And now my one ambition":** O. Bristol, "One of the Greatest 'Finds' of the British Screen," *Picture Show,* November 17, 1934.

45   **the care of a nurse:** "Charlotte Constance Thompson," *England & Wales, National Probate Calendar (Index of Wills and Administrations),* 1858–1995, 86.

45   **letters to her daughter:** Delofski, *Trouble.*

45   **see Merle's movies:** Skolsky, "Tintypes," April 9, 1935.

Chapter 5: To See My Mother Again

47 **small thing:** "Love or Career?" *San Francisco Examiner.*

47 **Los Angeles by train:** "Merle Oberon on Way," *Hollywood Reporter,* November 22, 1934, 2.

48 **Leslie Howard's manager:** Sidney Skolsky, "Hollywood," *Daily News* [NY], November 26, 1934.

48 **army of paparazzi:** "Rambling Reporter," *Hollywood Reporter,* November 26, 1934, 2.

48 **fairytale:** Scheuer, "Intriguing 'Myths.'"

48 **anxious to meet stars:** Sidney Skolsky, "Tintypes," *Daily News* [NY], November 28, 1934.

48 **lingering resentment:** Louella O. Parsons, "Movie Go Round," *San Francisco Examiner,* September 8, 1935.

48 **husband-snatcher:** Eileen Percy, "Montgomery Is Becoming Busiest Actor in Hollywood," *Pittsburgh Post-Gazette,* March 13, 1936.

48 **"a ruthless vamp":** Louella O. Parsons, "Merle Oberon Is Likeable," *San Francisco Examiner,* December 9, 1934.

48 **Sheilah Graham:** Sheilah Graham, "Hollywood Today," *Atlanta Constitution,* October 1, 1937.

51 **"parentage is one-half Indian":** Frances Fink, "Films Import World's Brightest Stars," *Washington Post,* January 13, 1935.

51 **forensic level of scrutiny:** Margaret Chute, "Meet Miss Thompson," *Answers,* October 19, 1935, 6.

52 **foreign interloper:** Woolfenden, "'I Detest "Exotic" Women.'"

52 **guest lists:** Warren Reeve, "The Exclusive Inside Story of Merle Oberon's $123,000 Damage Suit," *Photoplay,* July 1936, 21.

52 **miserable Christmas:** Hedda Hopper, "Hedda Hopper's Hollywood," *Los Angeles Times,* December 26, 1939.

52 **Jean Harlow:** "Merle Oberon Hides Scars of Auto Accident," *Washington Post,* July 4, 1937.

52 **hem of her dress:** Sara Hamilton, "Merle Oberon as Only Norma Knows Her," *Picturegoer,* November 7, 1936, 30.

53 **sisterly ally:** Lambert, *Shearer,* 217.

54 **bungalow:** O. Bristol, "Merle Oberon: Hollywood Has Made Her More English than Ever," *Picture Show,* November 16, 1935, 20.

54 **"It is like living":** Wilcox, "'Glamour'."

54 **$20,000:** Harrison Carroll, "Star Yearns for England," *Border Cities' Star* [Windsor, ON], January 9, 1935.

54 **fish skin:** Ruth Reynolds, "They Aren't as Nature Made 'Em," *Daily News* [NY], May 5, 1935.

54 **"a girl from Mars":** "Merle Oberon Is Considered Filmland's Most Successful Guinea Pig," *State Journal* [Frankfort, KY] July 2, 1941.

54 "This girl, the strongest femme": Kauf [pseud.], "Folies Bergere," *Variety*, February 27, 1935, 12.

54 a mask: Sydney Tremayne, "Films of the Day," *The Bystander*, March 20, 1935, 500; "Oberon's Gold Cosmetic," *Journal–Every Evening* [Wilmington, DE], April 4, 1935.

54 *Oriental*: Richard Watts Jr., "On the Screen," *New York Herald Tribune*, February 25, 1935.

54 "Chinese": "New Films," *Daily Boston Globe*, March 9, 1935.

54 "Javanese": Mark Forrest, "Cinema: Another Musical Spectacle," *Saturday Review*, March 16, 1935, 340.

54 Merle recoiled: Mollie Merrick, "Tom Moore in Films Again," *Spokesman-Review* [Spokane, WA], April 6, 1935.

54 eighty million: Thomas Schatz, *The Genius of the System: Hollywood Filmmaking in the Studio Era* (New York: Pantheon, 1989), 177.

55 homesick: "Star Yearns for England," *Border Cities' Star* [Windsor, ON], January 9, 1935.

55 he rebuffed her: Eforgan, *Leslie*, 112.

55 ever be in love again: Graham, "Hard Luck."

55 greatest ever written: Drazin, *Korda*, 130.

56 "girl that could give me": A. Scott Berg, *Goldwyn: A Biography* (London: Hamish Hamilton, 1989), 258.

57 "Now I believe I have discovered": Florence Fisher Parry, " 'I'm Gold Prospector,' says Samuel Goldwyn," *Pittsburgh Press*, September 15, 1935.

58 lapped by the waves: Grace Grandville, "Just a Little Outdoor Girl," *Democrat and Chronicle* [Rochester, NY], October 4, 1936.

58 fished: Louella O. Parsons, "Carole Lombard, Recovering, Will Be Star in 'Swing High–Swing Low'," *San Francisco Examiner*, June 29, 1936.

58 "In my wildest dreams": Merle Oberon, "My Next Door Neighbors," *Atlanta Constitution*, March 29, 1936.

58 young son: Sidney Skolsky, "Hollywood," *Daily News* [NY], July 13, 1935.

58 easygoing outdoorsman: Morley, *Moon*, 63.

58 like a fourteen-year-old: "The News Reel," *Boy's Cinema*, December 28, 1935, 2.

59 David phoned her: Mayme Ober Peak, "Hollywood Is Asking: When Will Merle Oberon and David Niven Wed?" *Daily Boston Globe*, October 12, 1936.

59 getting nervous: "New Merle Oberon in 'Dark Angel'," *Daily Clarion-Ledger* [Jackson, MS], October 23, 1935.

59 "That girl should be": "What the Fans Think," *Picture Play*, August 1935, 7.

59 "Smell of burning incense": Woolfenden, " 'I Detest "Exotic" Women.' "

60 "I do not see why": Yunte Huang, *Daughter of the Dragon: Anna May Wong's Rendezvous with American History* (New York: Liveright, 2023), 180.

60 cry, cry, cry: "Rambling Reporter," *Hollywood Reporter*, July 8, 1935, 2.

60 Gregg Toland: Gabriel Miller, *William Wyler: The Life and Films of Hollywood's Most Celebrated Director* (Lexington: University Press of Kentucky, 2013), 71.

60 **cosmetic creams:** Miriam J. Petty, *Stealing the Show: African American Performers and Audiences in 1930s Hollywood* (Oakland: University of California Press, 2016), 150.

60 **harmful mercury:** Richard M. Swiderski, *Quicksilver: A History of the Use, Lore and Effects of Mercury* (Jefferson, NC: McFarland, 2006), 182.

61 **"something new under":** "Samuel Goldwyn Inaugurates the 1935–36 Season with 'The Dark Angel'," *Los Angeles Times*, September 13, 1935.

61 **"Merle Oberon plays":** "Trio Stars in Gripping Love Story Offered on Fox Screen," *Arizona Republic*, September 15, 1935.

61 **Occidental avatar:** "Old South Is Theme of 'So Red the Rose'," *Tampa Morning Tribune*, December 22, 1935.

61 **elocution:** Sydney Tremayne, "Films of the Day," *The Bystander*, October 9, 1935, 60.

61 **Sunday school:** The Boulevardier, "Reviews of the New Films," *Screen & Radio Weekly*, September 22, 1935, 61.

61 **"The talk about the change":** Drazin, *Korda*, 138.

62 **her Queenie:** Advertisement, *Times of India*, August 30, 1935.

62 **"mainly to see my mother":** A. P. Luscombe Whyte, "Merle Oberon Is Coming Home," *London Evening Standard*, September 13, 1935.

Chapter 6: Papa Goldwyn, Father Korda

63 **royal homecoming:** Bristol, "Merle Oberon: Hollywood Has Made Her More English than Ever."

63 **Café de Paris:** Sabretache, "Pictures in the Fire," *Tatler*, October 9, 1935, 84.

64 **various affairs:** Graham Lord, *Niv: The Authorized Biography of David Niven* (Waterville, ME: Thorndike, 2003), 74.

65 **he could not articulate:** Allan R. Ellenberger, *Miriam Hopkins: Life and Films of a Hollywood Rebel* (Lexington: University Press of Kentucky, 2018), 119.

65 **bunny slippers:** Grace Wilcox, "Good Luck Pieces of the Stars," *Democrat and Chronicle* [Rochester, NY], March 7, 1937.

65 **"I'm having more trouble":** Berg, *Goldwyn*, 270.

65 **leave her ego aside:** "Merle and Miriam Aren't Afraid of Scene-Stealers," *Philadelphia Inquirer*, April 5, 1936.

66 **minimal stage-acting:** "9 of 10 Academy Player Nominees Are from Stage," *Hollywood Reporter*, February 24, 1936, 6.

66 **"I'm still laughing":** Lloyd Pantages, "Grace Moore's London Triumph Indication of Star's Hold Upon Public Affection Everywhere," *San Francisco Examiner*, June 19, 1935.

66 **made him promise:** Harris, *Gable*, 153.

66 **gold flecks:** "Acad Dinner Brings Out Fresh Flurry of Finery in Fash Prom," *Variety*, March 11, 1936, 18.

67 **blackmail:** *E! Mysteries & Scandals.*

67   **reluctant to abandon:** Michael Lawrence, *Sabu* (London: Palgrave Macmillan, 2014), 46.

68   **color test after color test:** "News of the Screen," *New York Times*, June 10, 1936.

68   **Florence Nightingale:** Edwin Schallert, "Merle Oberon Reported Choice for Interpretation of Florence Nightingale," *Los Angeles Times*, December 30, 1935.

68   **another film on Nightingale:** "Merle Oberon Claims £25,000 Damages," *London Evening Standard*, April 15, 1936.

68   **Arizona heat:** Sheilah Graham, "Merle Oberon Shudders at Desert Trip," *Hartford Courant*, March 14, 1936.

68   **Merle looked in color:** Ed Sullivan, "Broadway," *Daily News* [NY], May 15, 1936.

69   **"a real common piece":** Maria Riva, *Marlene Dietrich* (New York: Knopf, 1992), 355.

69   **$125,333.33:** "Miss Oberon Sues Studio," *Los Angeles Times*, April 15, 1936.

69   **she withdrew it:** "Drops Suit," *Pittsburgh Post-Gazette*, March 12, 1940.

69   **"I can't stand idly":** Reeve, "The Exclusive Inside Story of Merle Oberon's $123,000 Damage Suit," 111.

70   **five-year joint contract:** George Shaffer, "Friends Greet Cagney as He Renews Career," *Chicago Daily Tribune*, November 2, 1936.

70   **different visions:** "Merle Oberon's Split Personality," *Atlanta Constitution*, January 10, 1937.

70   **"I'm in the position":** Kate Cameron, "Film Star Has Unique Contract," *Daily News* [NY], December 20, 1936.

70   **with protective concern:** Louella O. Parsons, "'Mr. and Mrs. Washington' to Be Filmed! Rupert Hughes Doing Story for M-G-M," *San Francisco Examiner*, April 3, 1936.

70   **in all of Europe:** Lawrence, *Sabu*, 11.

70   **boathouse:** Drazin, *Korda*, 167.

71   **his most prized assets:** Morley, *Moon*, 73.

71   **Irving Thalberg:** Mark A. Vieira, *Irving Thalberg: Boy Wonder to Producer Prince* (Berkeley: University of California Press, 2010), 365.

72   **strain on Merle's relationship:** Christofer Robin, "In Flicker Land," *Minneapolis Star*, February 10, 1937.

72   **Retaliating against him:** Michael Munn, *David Niven: The Man Behind the Balloon* (London: JR Books, 2010), 67.

72   **"Great Big Star":** David Niven, *The Moon's a Balloon* (London: Hamish Hamilton, 1971), 175.

72   **matter of her race:** Morley, *Moon*, 62.

72   **leaving her Dalmatians:** "First Readers' Views of Latest Books, Fiction and Biography and News of the Radio," *Commercial Appeal*, February 7, 1937.

72   **"You are the son":** Lord, *Niv*, 77.

72   **spend Christmas with her:** Grace Wilcox, "Christmas Comes to Hollywood," *Screen & Radio Weekly*, December 20, 1936.

73   **costume fitting:** Duncalf, *Epic.*

73 **speeding car:** "Merle Oberon Hides Scars of Auto Accident," *Washington Post*, July 4, 1937.

73 **stomping grounds:** "Merle Oberon Back in England," *Observer* [UK].

73 **on par with Dietrich:** Baxter, *Von Sternberg*, 208.

73 **"Can you imagine":** Riva, *Dietrich*, 432.

73 **her role inadequate:** Drazin, *Korda*, 185.

73 **liked her diaphanous dresses:** Graham, "Hard Luck."

73 **"Think Claudius would undo":** Cable from Merle Oberon to Samuel Goldwyn, January 8, 1937, Samuel Goldwyn Papers, Margaret Herrick Library, Academy of Motion Picture Arts and Sciences, Beverly Hills.

75 **sound of her voice:** Korda, *Another*, 445.

75 **unafraid of death:** *E! Mysteries & Scandals*.

Chapter 7: An Accent of My Own

77 **fifty-six:** "Mrs. Constance Thompson," *New York Herald Tribune*, April 24, 1937.

77 **April 23:** Undated photograph, Merle Oberon Papers, Margaret Herrick Library, Academy of Motion Picture Arts and Sciences, Beverly Hills.

77 **barely out of the hospital:** "Star Leaves Hospital," *Daily News* [NY], April 25, 1937.

77 **Regent's Park:** "Chatter," *Variety*, January 27, 1937, 60.

77 **same street:** Elliseva Sayers, "I Meet Merle Oberon," *Answers*, September 9, 1939, 9.

78 **"You see, I'm very much alone":** Graham, "Hard Luck."

78 **Hampshire estate:** Fairbanks Jr., *Salad*, 216.

78 **elocution lessons:** Sheilah Graham, "A Tip for Andrea Leeds—Tickle Joel McCrea's Ears!" *Minneapolis Tribune*, July 5, 1938.

79 **missed her Dalmatians:** Edith Nepean, "My Friends in British Studios," *Picture Show*, December 18, 1937, 6.

79 **spring of 1938:** Louella O. Parsons, "'Shanghai Deadline' Will Star Sanders," *San Francisco Examiner*, October 13, 1937.

79 **ninth most popular:** Malcolm D. Phillips, "The Customer Talks Back," *Picturegoer*, July 3, 1937, 12.

79 **Hollywood brethren:** Lawrence, *Sabu*, 45.

80 **low opinion:** Jan Herman, *A Talent for Trouble: The Life of Hollywood's Most Acclaimed Director, William Wyler* (New York: G. P. Putnam's Sons, 1995), 195.

80 **"I'm so used to seeing":** "Merle Oberon Makes First Comedy Role," *Journal–Every Evening*, March 31, 1938.

81 **sallow:** Ian Coster, "Merle Oberon Under British Colours," *London Evening Standard*, January 8, 1938.

81 **her delicate beauty:** Michael Orme, "Criticisms in Cameo," *The Sketch*, January 19, 1938, 123.

81 **injuring the appeal:** "'Divorce of Lady X' Scores as Smart English Comedy," *Hollywood Reporter*, January 18, 1938, 3.

81   **"I've been working like a beaver":** Drazin, *Korda*, 193.

81   **constant rewrites:** "'Moon' Lags Oberon by Daily Rewriting," *Hollywood Reporter*, February 19, 1938, 7.

81   **wrong pair of gloves:** Stephen Bourne, *Elisabeth Welch: Soft Lights and Sweet Music* (Lanham, MD: Scarecrow Press, 2005), 40.

82   **unflattering to her complexion:** Parish, *Glamour Girls*, 608.

82   **Nineteen thirty-eight:** Drazin, *Korda*, 203.

82   **nose crinkled:** Sidney Skolsky, "Skolsky's Hollywood," *Cincinnati Enquirer*, February 15, 1943.

82   **ask him out to dinner:** Louella O. Parsons, "Merle, as Producer's Wife, Worries about Expenses Now," *Philadelphia Inquirer*, May 4, 1941.

83   **pouncing on tables:** "Two Dogs for Sale," *Bergen* [NJ] *Evening Record*, June 11, 1938.

83   **Their friendship resumed:** Louella O. Parsons, "Movie Go-Round," *San Francisco Examiner*, May 22, 1938.

83   **publicity stills:** Harrison Carroll, "Behind the Scenes in Hollywood," *Evansville* [IN] *Courier*, May 21, 1938.

83   **film preview:** Sheilah Graham, "Sheilah Graham in Hollywood," *Miami Daily News*, June 6, 1938.

83   **starting to regret:** Robbin Coons, "Hollywood Screen Life," *Poughkeepsie* [NY] *Eagle-News*, September 10, 1938.

83   **"I am a split personality":** Ted Farah, "Korda, Goldwyn Share Interest in Fair Oberon," *Calgary Daily Herald*, April 16, 1938.

83   **"I'm an actress without an accent":** "Accent Troubles Merle Oberon," *Detroit Free Press*, August 7, 1938.

84   **"the world's worst businesswoman":** Wilkinson, ""Go Wash!"

84   **legalese in her contracts:** "Merle Oberon Says Taxes Take 90% of Her Income," the *Hartford Courant*, November 17, 1938.

84   **national taxes:** Alma Whitaker, "Merle Oberon Finds Taxes Eat Up Most of Earnings Here and in Britain," *Los Angeles Times*, June 26, 1938.

84   **thousands of pounds:** "Screen Star's Driver Owes Her $25,000," *Pittsburgh Post-Gazette*, May 5, 1938.

84   **fur coats of skunk:** Hedda Hopper, "Hedda Hopper's Hollywood," *Los Angeles Times*, May 20, 1938.

84   **recoup her status:** "Merle Oberon Denies Romance," *Los Angeles Times*, May 9, 1938.

84   **Gary Cooper:** Berg, *Goldwyn*, 315.

84   *Graustark:* Parish, *Glamour Girls*, 610.

85   **heat prostration:** "Heat Fells Actress in Western Thriller," *Pittsburgh Post-Gazette*, August 23, 1938.

85   **"handicapped":** George Marsden, "London Entertainment," *Country Life*, January 21, 1939.

Chapter 8: I *Am* Heathcliff!

88 **Katharine Hepburn:** Draft of telegram, August 17, 1938, William Wyler Papers, Margaret Herrick Library, Academy of Motion Picture Arts and Sciences, Beverly Hills.

89 **possibly Parsi or Bengali:** Alan Strachan, *Dark Star: A Biography of Vivien Leigh* (London: I. B. Tauris, 2019), 3.

89 **a similarly parental outlook:** Drazin, *Korda*, 160.

90 **more vividly in tragic parts:** Sayers, "I Meet."

90 **"This actor has to be the ugliest":** Stanley Eichelbaum, "Glamor Still Attracts a Crowd," *San Francisco Examiner*, October 5, 1971.

90 **"a little pick-up":** Lord, *Niv*, 93.

90 **"You spat":** Herman, *Trouble*, 195.

91 **"Over with your tantrum":** Philip Ziegler, *Olivier* (London: MacLehose Press, 2013), 67.

92 **corset stays:** Jimmie Fidler, "Hard-hearted Director Cheers as Merle Oberon Is Stabbed in Back," *Minneapolis Star*, January 20, 1939.

92 **she could barely eat:** Grace Wilcox, "For Women Only," *Screen & Radio Weekly*, February 26, 1939.

92 **winds toppled her portable dressing room:** "Oberon's Ankle Hurt on 'Heights' Location," *Hollywood Reporter*, December 9, 1938, 2.

92 **injured her foot:** "Shoot Around Oberon," *Hollywood Reporter*, December 24, 1938, 5.

92 **drafty soundstage:** Milton Harker, "Glamor Gal Dunked in Dishabille State All for Art's Sake," *Austin Statesman*, February 8, 1939.

92 **eggbeater:** Alexander Kahn, "At the Movies—Taking Bath in Public Not So Easy," *Knoxville News-Sentinel*, January 25, 1939.

92 **Filming Cathy's death:** Grace Wilcox, "Hollywood Reporter," *Screen & Radio Weekly*, March 5, 1939.

92 **"a little bit more":** Saltzman, "Merle Oberon."

93 **her role didn't stand out:** Sheilah Graham, "No Synthetic Love Affairs for Actress," *Calgary Herald*, March 25, 1939.

93 **Olivier's pyrotechnics:** Edward H. Holmes, "'Wuthering Heights' Well Cast," *Courier-Journal* [Louisville, KY], April 14, 1939.

93 **lacking intensity:** James Agate, "The Cinema," *Tatler*, May 10, 1939, 240.

93 **turn a profit until 1963:** Parish, *Glamour Girls*, 622.

93 **started to lose faith:** Berg, *Goldwyn*, 334.

94 **exchange of words:** Drazin, *Korda*, 205.

94 **cabochon emeralds:** Hans Nadelhoffer, *Cartier* (San Francisco: Chronicle, 2007), 257.

94 **the children's room:** Anil and Sunil Selby.

94 **Alexander's brothers resented her:** Korda, *Another*, 443.

95 **"that black bitch":** Chris Chase, "Charming Album of a Film Family," *Chicago Tribune*, November 4, 1979.

95 **daily occurrence:** June Provines, "Front Views and Profiles," *Chicago Daily Tribune*, October 6, 1939.

95 **air-raid alarms:** "Actress Here," *Chicago Daily Tribune*, October 6, 1939.

95 **"But lots of times at night":** Bosley Crowther, "About a Film Star Doing Her Bit," *New York Times*, October 8, 1939.

96 **L-shaped lounge:** "A British Film Star Settles Down in California," *Tatler & Bystander*, January 28, 1942, 123.

96 **ship her furniture:** "Rambling Reporter," *Hollywood Reporter*, February 16, 1940, 2.

96 **her true feelings for her husband:** Drazin, *Korda*, 221.

97 **diversions:** Thomas S. Hischak, *1939: Hollywood's Greatest Year* (Lanham, MD: Rowman & Littlefield, 2017), xii.

97 **Warner Brothers:** "Hollywood News," *New York Herald Tribune*, October 19, 1939.

98 **throat infection:** *E! Mysteries & Scandals*.

98 **"feel the tragedy":** Boyd Martin, "Merle Oberon Captures Honors in Romantic 'Til We Meet Again," *Courier-Journal* [Louisville, KY], May 4, 1940.

98 **Spencer Tracy:** Brian McFarlane, *Real and Reel: The Education of a Film Critic* (Manchester, UK: Manchester University Press, 2012), 119.

Chapter 9: My Dearest Joy

99 **Merle was miserable:** Louella O. Parsons, "3d Steinbeck Story Bought for Screen," *Philadelphia Inquirer*, April 9, 1940.

99 **sulfa drugs:** Louella O. Parsons, "Merle Oberon Has Operation for Removal of Facial Scars," *San Francisco Examiner*, June 27, 1949.

100 **"a make-up infection":** Jimmie Fidler, "Jimmie Fidler in Hollywood," *Los Angeles Times*, April 1, 1941.

100 **doctors warning her:** Sheilah Graham, "Hollywood Today," *Hartford Courant*, February 7, 1941.

100 **dark, candlelit room:** Eleanor Lambert, "Why We All Watch Merle," *San Francisco Examiner*, June 4, 1968.

100 **end her own life:** *E! Mysteries & Scandals*.

100 **India began to fade:** H. H. Niemeyer, "Tasmania's Gift to Movies," *St. Louis Post-Dispatch*, February 9, 1940.

100 **Alexander decided to move to Hollywood:** Drazin, *Korda*, 229.

101 **"a brown frog":** Lawrence, *Sabu*, 27.

101 **"Korda's chief instrument":** Baburao Patel, "Korda's Libel on India," *Filmindia*, October 1938, 24.

101 **banned in many parts:** Prem Chowdhry, *Colonial India and the Making of Empire Cinema: Image, Ideology and Identity* (Manchester, UK: Manchester University Press, 2000), 108.

102 **"Turbans do things":** Meenasarani Linde Murugan, " 'Turbans Do Things for You'," in *Our Stories: An Introduction to South Asian America* (Philadelphia: South Asian American Digital Archive, 2021), 75.

102 **bond with Sabu:** "Movie-Go-Round," *San Francisco Examiner*, February 18, 1940.

103 **summer of 1940:** Louella O. Parsons, "Merle Oberon Now Almost All Well," *Philadelphia Inquirer*, July 9, 1940.

103 **soap containing sulfur:** Sheilah Graham, "Hollywood Today: Movie Complexions Are 'World's Worst'," *Courier-Journal* [Louisville, KY], December 8, 1946.

103 **fatigued by cinematic fantasies:** Lambert, *Shearer*, 298.

103 **$100,000:** Sheilah Graham, "Hollywood Today," *Hartford Courant*, January 24, 1941.

103 **muttering to himself:** Paul Harrison, "Behind Camera, Lubitsch Runs Gamut of Emotions," *Cincinnati Post*, December 6, 1940.

103 **enacted her role:** Harrison Carroll, "Behind the Scenes in Hollywood," *Vineland* [NJ] *Times*, December 9, 1940.

104 **"If I wore a sarong":** Robbin Coons, "Hollywood," *Daily News–Journal* [Murfreesboro, TN], January 16, 1941.

104 **"sparkle":** "That Uncertain Feeling," *Sun*, April 26, 1941.

104 **opted out of a vacation:** Louella O. Parsons, "Ruby Keeler Signs for 'Betty Co-ed'," *Philadelphia Inquirer*, January 1, 1941.

104 **Tony Gaudio:** "With Truesdell in Hollywood," *Cincinnati Enquirer*, January 25, 1941.

104 **"What Miss Oberon has":** H. W. W., " 'Ziegfeld Girl' Is Typical Metro-Goldwyn-Mayer Extravaganza," *The Gazette* [Montreal], May 24, 1941.

106 **"I never really acted":** Parish, *Glamour Girls*, 627.

106 **hair had gone gray:** Kulik, *Alexander*, 226.

106 **her second wedding anniversary:** Louella O. Parsons, "Republic Has Role for Miriam Hopkins," *Philadelphia Inquirer*, June 5, 1941.

106 **on par with *Wuthering Heights*:** Hedda Hopper, "Merle the Merrier," *Chicago Daily Tribune*, August 18, 1946.

107 **$19.4 million:** Schatz, *Genius*, 298.

107 **refugee kid:** Jimmie Fidler, "Jimmie Fidler in Hollywood," *Los Angeles Times*, April 12, 1941.

107 **"My husband does not think":** Sheilah Graham, "Merle Oberon Forsakes Film Career to Do Part in Nation's War Effort," *Hartford Courant*, January 17, 1942.

108 **Greer Garson:** Schatz, *Genius*, 362.

108 **"The thought of what we are giving up":** Corinne Hardesty, "No-Sugar-for-Duration Club Formed by Merle Oberon and Eddie Cantor," *Philadelphia Inquirer*, January 27, 1942.

108 **Rudyard Kipling's stories:** Tom MacPherson, "Radio Chart Listening Post," *Ithaca* [NY] *Journal*, February 7, 1942.

108 **granted him citizenship:** "Sabu Is Admitted to U.S. Citizenship," *Washington Post*, January 5, 1944.

109   **work in New York:** Grace Turner, "Thursday-Night Specials," *Cincinnati Enquirer*, September 7, 1941.

109   **"raised scarcely":** Michael Burn, *Mary and Richard: A True Story of Love and War* (New York: Arbor House, 1988), 141.

109   **Toronto:** "Merle Escapes Ellis Island Trip," *Daily News* [NY], August 6, 1941.

109   **She hadn't known she needed one:** "Merle Oberon Ill, So Alien Hearing Waits," *Daily News* [NY], August 5, 1941.

109   **her hotel room:** "Inquiry Canceled on Merle Oberon," *Democrat and Chronicle* [Rochester, NY], August 6, 1941.

110   **Fiorello La Guardia:** Dorothy Kilgallen, "Broadway," *Mansfield* [OH] *News-Journal*, August 19, 1941.

110   **To return the favor:** Louella O. Parsons, "Merle Oberon Pays Back a Favor by Offering Service to Defense," *Atlanta Constitution*, January 6, 1942.

110   **difficult life:** Anil and Sunil Selby.

111   **"My dearest Joy":** Delofski, *Trouble*.

111   **Constance Joyce would carry gratitude:** Sheilah Graham, "Sheilah Graham in Hollywood," *Miami News*, July 19, 1960.

Chapter 10: I Wasn't Born Heroic

114   **mobbed by men in uniform:** "Everything's on the House at Stage Door Canteen," *Bergen* [NJ] *Evening Record*, April 24, 1942.

114   **twenty-one shows:** Jerry Mason, "Merle for Morale," *Sun*, July 11, 1943.

114   **"I began to appreciate":** William Amundson, "Merle Oberon Impressed by Caravan Tour Crowds," *Minneapolis Morning Tribune*, May 9, 1942.

114   **Valentine's Day:** Antoinette Donnelly, "Diet, Exercise, No Dessert, Formula for Easter Figure," *Daily News* [NY], February 23, 1942.

114   **valued her independence:** Drazin, *Korda*, 264.

114   **"Yes, oh yes":** Kulik, *Alexander*, 230.

114   **to Alexander's surprise:** "Korda Surprised about Knighting," *Austin Statesman*, June 12, 1942.

114   **Romanoff's:** Sidney Skolsky, "Skolsky's Hollywood," *Cincinnati Enquirer*, June 26, 1942.

115   **British loyalism:** Charlton-Stevens, *Anglo-India*, 219.

115   **she watched him glide:** Louella O. Parsons, "Lana Turner Boasts Too Much Glamor for Typical American Girl," *Atlanta Constitution*, October 7, 1942.

115   **"God Save the King":** H. C. Norris, "Merle Oberon Vividly Tells of Her Knight Fright as Husband Was Called Before King," *Philadelphia Inquirer*, March 28, 1943.

115   **chill of animosity:** John Truesdell, "In Hollywood," *Des Moines Register*, October 12, 1942.

115   **her allegiance to the Allied war effort:** "Merle Oberon Wants to Appear Only in War Films for Duration," *Philadelphia Inquirer*, August 22, 1943.

116 **steamrolled over Arzner:** Wheeler Winston Dixon, *Film Noir and the Cinema of Paranoia* (Edinburgh: Edinburgh University Press, 2009), 37.

117 **contracted pneumonia:** Judith Mayne, *Directed by Dorothy Arzner* (Bloomington: Indiana University Press, 1994), 77.

117 **minimize her time in the sun:** "Merle Has Short Lease on Tan," *Pittsburgh Press*, April 21, 1943.

117 **hooklike:** James Carson, "They're not all perfect!" *Modern Screen*, November 1940, 60.

117 **delayed shooting for a week:** Sheilah Graham, "Actors Obtain Leave to Make British Movie," *Atlanta Constitution*, May 4, 1943.

117 **"I have never seen such beauty":** Ruth Waterbury, "The Lady and the Cameraman," *Photoplay*, August 1945, 100.

117 **to be a movie star himself:** Harold V. Cohen, "Hollywood," *Pittsburgh Post-Gazette*, July 11, 1945.

118 **didn't think news photographs captured:** Marjory Adams, "Merle Oberon on Honeymoon, Here Without Wedding Ring," *Boston Globe*, October 31, 1945.

118 **Obie:** J. Randy Taraborrelli, *The Secret Life of Marilyn Monroe* (New York: Grand Central, 2009), 178.

118 **"hopelessly miscast":** Edgar Anstey, "The Cinema," *The Spectator*, February 18, 1944, 147.

119 **Malibu ranch:** Harold Heffernan, "Hollywood Horizon," *Bergen* [NJ] *Evening Record*, August 28, 1943.

119 **the nearest telephone was ten miles away:** Paul Prowler, "Can Merle Get Her Count?" *National Police Gazette*, June 1, 1949, 22.

119 **promised to help Merle find a director:** Alain Silver, "André de Toth (1913–2002) – An Interview," *Senses of Cinema*, March 2003 (accessed January 30, 2024).

119 **"the biggest piece of shit":** Drazin, *Korda*, 265.

119 **"But I made Merle":** Andre de Toth, *Fragments: Portraits from the Inside* (London: Faber & Faber, 1994), 301.

119 **"If the audience suffers as much as I do":** Jimmie Fidler, "Jimmie Fidler in Hollywood," *Indianapolis News*, August 1, 1944.

120 **that year's sleeper hits:** Parish, *Glamour Girls*, 629.

121 **bundles of posies:** Walter Winchell, "Winchell Says," *Nashville Tennessean*, March 8, 1945.

121 **until the war's end:** Sheilah Graham, "Hollywood News Flashes," *Cincinnati Enquirer*, November 5, 1944.

121 **negotiating with gossip columnists:** Isabella Taves, "Writer Explodes Many Myths about Louella Parsons," *San Francisco Examiner*, October 8, 1950.

121 **worth the risk:** Louella O. Parsons, "Merle Oberon Relinquished Title and Wealth for Love," *Philadelphia Inquirer*, July 29, 1945.

121 **"Mamma":** Hopper, "Merrier."

121 **hunting trip:** Liza, "Merle's Studio Romance," *Screenland*, November 1945, 99.

Chapter 11: I Ruled My Own Life

123 **Visitors to Merle's homes:** Lambert, *Shearer*, 314.

124 **"dark-complexioned":** Sidney Buchman, Script for *Song to Remember*, November 27, 1934, 40, Merle Oberon Papers, Margaret Herrick Library, Academy of Motion Picture Arts and Sciences, Beverly Hills.

125 **finest since *Wuthering Heights*:** Hedda Hopper, "Star Broadway Bound," *Washington Post*, November 29, 1944.

125 **applause thundering through theaters:** Parish, *Glamour Girls*, 631.

125 **Samuel Goldwyn called her:** Hedda Hopper, "Hollywood," *Daily News* [NY], July 6, 1944.

125 **"I had to pull up strength":** Interview with Merle Oberon, British Broadcasting Corporation, October 20, 1974.

125 **childhood fantasy:** Maxine Garrison, "Merle Portrays Persian Princess, Role She Always Yearned to Play," *Pittsburgh Press*, March 11, 1945.

125 **no need to study her face:** "Lucky Merle," *Pittsburgh Press*, October 31, 1945.

125 **package deal:** Louella O. Parsons, "Show Is Arranged for Mickey Rooney, Also MGM Movies," *Courier-Post* [Cherry Hill, NJ], June 11, 1945.

125 **decline any assignments:** Jimmie Fidler, "In Hollywood," *Fort Myers News-Press*, August 20, 1948.

126 **a locale favored by the Hollywood elite:** Trish Long, " 'Quickie' Juárez divorces ended in 1970," *El Paso Times*, August 3, 2017.

126 **two Mexican stand-ins:** "Actress, Cameraman Use Stand-Ins at Wedding," *Albuquerque Journal*, June 27, 1945.

126 **newspapermen started calling:** Julian Hartt, "Star Plans to Meet Her Own 'Bride'," *Austin Statesman*, August 13, 1946.

126 **growing desperate:** McLaughlin, *Pill*, 52.

127 **fallopian tubes:** Marsh, *Fertility*, 134.

127 **great fanfare by the press:** Earl Wilson, "Hip Hip Hooray for Marie—She Swells Beyond Bacall," *Miami Daily News*, November 21, 1945.

127 **maintaining the surface stance:** Louella O. Parsons, "Hollywood," *Philadelphia Inquirer*, December 15, 1945.

127 **bracing herself:** Sheilah Graham, "Hollywood Today," *Asbury Park Evening Press*, January 10, 1946.

127 **cross-country car trip:** Hedda Hopper, "Looking at Hollywood," *Chicago Daily Tribune*, January 21, 1946.

127 **their young marriage's foundation:** Beatrice Lubitz Cole, "Inside Hollywood," *Movieland*, February 1949, 12.

127 **autograph-seekers:** C. F. ("Bede") Armstrong, "Actress Merle Oberon, Husband Guests of Local Hotel Sunday," *Jackson* [MS] *Sun*, December 31, 1945.

127 **"Please have a baby":** Sheilah Graham, "In Hollywood Today," *Indianapolis Star*, May 22, 1946.

128 **flubbing her lines:** Harold Heffernan, "In Hollywood Today," *Evening Citizen* [Ottawa, ON], June 24, 1946.

128 **"How our grandmothers":** "Johnson in Hollywood," *Lancaster* [OH] *Eagle-Gazette*, June 21, 1946.

128 **Oscar consideration:** Merle Oberon radio spot, circa 1946, Merle Oberon Papers, Margaret Herrick Library, Academy of Motion Picture Arts and Sciences, Beverly Hills.

128 **"rheumatic":** "Critics Pass Off 'Girl,' 'Temptation'," *Hollywood Reporter*, December 30, 1946, 6.

128 **$122 million:** Schatz, *Genius*, 298.

129 **considered curbing:** Virginia MacPherson, "Oberon Packs and Plans Long Vacation with Play," *Indianapolis Star*, August 18, 1946.

129 **Valley Center:** "Merle Oberon Acquires Ranch near Escondido," *Los Angeles Times*, June 3, 1945.

129 **"thinks she'll enjoy it better":** Sheilah Graham, "In Hollywood Today," *Indianapolis Star*, July 27, 1946.

129 **three thousand:** Grace Pusey, "Today in History: Luce-Celler Act Signed in 1946," South Asian American Digital Archive, July 2, 2014 (accessed January 30, 2024).

130 **Tens of thousands:** Datta-Ray, "Demise."

130 **a convenient professional excuse:** Bob Thomas, "Swinging Film Cycle to Less Costly Output," *Daily Advertiser* [Lafayette, LA], June 5, 1947.

131 **"forgets her accent":** Hedda Hopper, "Looking at Hollywood," *Chicago Daily Tribune*, April 9, 1948.

131 **libel:** Dorothy Kilgallen, "Broadway," *Pittsburgh Post-Gazette*, April 27, 1948.

131 **sabotaged her:** Beatrice Lubitz Cole, "Inside Hollywood," *Movieland*, September 1948, 16.

131 **Her fights with Lucien:** J. R. Jones, *The Lives of Robert Ryan* (Middletown, CT: Wesleyan University Press, 2015), 68.

131 **sport a wire:** Bob Thomas, "Hollywood Notes," *Asbury Park* [NJ] *Evening Press*, September 26, 1947.

131 **battered jaw:** Cole, "Inside," February 1949, 12.

131 **RKO demanded:** Bob Thomas, "Health of Bette Davis to Determine Next Film," *Alexandria* [VA] *Daily Town Talk*, November 26, 1947.

131 **having dipped from $122 million:** Schatz, *Genius*, 435.

132 **the very first flat:** Hugh Dixon, "Hollywood," *Pittsburgh Post-Gazette*, June 29, 1948.

132 **their third wedding anniversary:** Dorothy Manners, "Frank Buck Plans New Animal Film in British Deal," *Evening Courier*, July 2, 1948.

132 **boarded a yacht in Capri:** Cholly Knickerbocker, "Gotham Society Hears Dan Toppings in Rift," *San Francisco Examiner*, September 12, 1948.

Chapter 12: **To Belong to This Country**

133 **she belonged to him:** Elsa Maxwell, "Ill-Fated Love Story," *Photoplay*, May 1950, 63.

133 **total catch . . . aristocratic wife:** Details in this paragraph are drawn from articles by the columnist Cholly Knickerbocker published between September 1948 and September 1949. (Full citations are in the bibliography.)

134 **"incompatibility":** Telegram from Merle Oberon to Hedda Hopper, August 5, 1948, Hedda Hopper Papers, Margaret Herrick Library, Academy of Motion Picture Arts and Sciences, Beverly Hills.

134 **the Excelsior:** Drazin, *Korda*, 305.

134 **terms of her divorce:** Dorothy Kilgallen, "The Voice of Broadway," *Elmira* [NY] *Star-Gazette*, November 18, 1948.

134 **her contract with RKO:** Louella O. Parsons, "Goldwyn Buys Original Story by Clare Luce," *San Francisco Examiner*, November 29, 1948.

135 **$250,000:** Sheilah Graham, "Hollywood Today," *Indianapolis Star*, December 7, 1948.

135 **Norma Shearer:** Lambert, *Shearer*, 323.

135 **damaged goods:** "Playboy Italian Count May Wed Merle Oberon," *Los Angeles Times*, February 18, 1949.

135 **an example Merle planned to follow:** Erskine Johnson, "'Living Legends League' Member Reports She Will Retire Soon," *Marshfield* [WI] *News-Herald*, August 27, 1951.

135 **tussling with Lucien:** Sheilah Graham, "Demand Is Big for Jean Arthur," *Spokesman-Review* [Spokane, WA], December 20, 1948.

135 **Shangri-La:** Hedda Hopper, "Jane Russell, Bob Mitchum Will Co-Star," *Evansville* [IN] *Courier*, January 20, 1949.

135 **jetting to Paris:** Louella O. Parsons, "Merle Oberon in Paris," *San Francisco Examiner*, February 14, 1949.

136 **a violent scuffle:** "On Worldwide News Front," *Minneapolis Star*, April 21, 1949.

136 **worried that her nose:** Dorothy Kilgallen, "The Voice of Broadway," *Elmira* [NY] *Star-Gazette*, May 3, 1949.

136 **plastic surgeon:** "Whodunit?" *Detroit Free Press*, April 21, 1949.

136 **lingering scars:** Parsons, "Merle Oberon Has Operation."

136 **comedians would crack jokes:** David Galligan, "Joan Rivers," *Advocate*, February 22, 1978, 32.

136 **revive the silent movies:** Danton Walker, "Broadway," *Daily News*, May 28, 1949.

136 **Europe's plushest resorts:** "Actress Merle Oberon Loses Lover in French Plane Crash," *Great Falls* [MT] *Tribune*, September 1, 1949.

136 **leave for Venice:** "Merle Oberon Watches as Plane Strikes Tree Killing Two Friends," *Pittsburgh Press*, August 31, 1949.

137 **"look like those of a dolphin":** Franco Rol, *The Unbelievable Gustavo Adolfo Rol* (Morrisville, NC: Lulu Press, 2014), 473.

137 "Couldn't you take a train?": "Merle Oberon Sees Friend, Count Cini, Killed in Crash at French Airport," *Courier-Journal* [Louisville, KY], September 1, 1949.

137 handkerchief: Dorothy Kilgallen, "On Broadway," *Pittsburgh Post-Gazette*, September 26, 1949.

137 then she heard: "Miss Oberon Sees Count Die in Plane," *Washington Post*, September 1, 1949.

137 struggling to gain altitude: "Merle Oberon Watches as Plane Strikes Tree, Killing Two Friends," *Pittsburgh Press*.

137 "My life is finished": "Merle Oberon Sees Friend and Pilot Die in Plane Crash," *Chicago Daily Tribune*, September 1, 1949.

137 she contemplated suicide: Roderick Mann, "Beautiful Merle Oberon Can Easily Face Her Mirrors," *Albuquerque Tribune*, June 6, 1969.

137 femme fatale: Drazin, *Korda*, 267.

137 flickered in and out of consciousness: Cholly Knickerbocker, "Roulette Wheel Whirls Ali into the Red," *San Francisco Examiner*, September 17, 1949.

137 a sanatorium to recover: Dorothy Manners, "Defore Seeks Robinson for Baseball Film," *Philadelphia Inquirer*, September 5, 1949.

138 stay in the next room: "Love Is a Spirit," *Detroit Free Press*, January 21, 1950.

138 remained under medical care: Dorothy Manners, "Jackie Robinson Baseball Career Will Be Screened," *San Francisco Examiner*, September 5, 1949.

138 a recluse: Hedda Hopper, "'Lend Me Your Ears' Planned in Rome; Sothern Is Thrilled at Royal Reception," *Miami Daily News*, December 16, 1949.

138 strapped for cash: Harrison Carroll, "Behind the Scenes in Hollywood," *Lancaster* [OH] *Eagle-Gazette*, December 22, 1949.

138 her torpor . . . quiet and calm, but not all there: Details in these paragraphs are drawn from columns by Sheilah Graham published between December 1949 and January 1950. (Full citations are in the bibliography.)

138 a dubbing coach: "Coach for Oberon," *Hollywood Reporter*, April 7, 1950, 8.

139 "If I had once started crying": Armand Archerd, "Merle Oberon Finds Surcease from Grief over Tragic End of Romance in Film Work," *Daily News-Journal* [Murfreesboro, TN], October 4, 1951.

139 faces smudged with grime: Vorhaus, *Oblivion*, 118.

139 didn't cheer up Merle: Hedda Hopper, "Astaire to Make 'Belle of New York' with Romance Set in Chinatown," *Miami Daily News*, May 16, 1950.

139 its reported $300,000 budget: Harrison Carroll, "Behind the Scenes in Hollywood," *Lancaster* [OH] *Eagle-Gazette*, March 29, 1950.

140 started attending seances again: Louella O. Parsons, "'Father of the Bride' Has Made Tracy One of MGM's Top Drawing Cards," *Albuquerque Journal*, August 1, 1950.

140 Overworked and fatigued: Cholly Knickerbocker, "Cholly Knickerbocker Observes," *San Francisco Examiner*, April 8, 1950.

140 a Swiss sanatorium: Walter Winchell, "Walter Winchell On Broadway," *Courier-Post* [Cherry Hill, NJ], May 16, 1950.

140 **Biarritz:** Sheilah Graham, "Hollywood," *Pittsburgh Post-Gazette*, April 13, 1950.

140 **"ungracious":** Brog, "Pardon My French," *Variety*, August 22, 1951, 10.

140 **wander alone through the Biarritz spas:** Cholly Knickerbocker, "Cholly Knickerbocker Observes," *San Francisco Examiner*, April 28, 1950.

140 **terrified of having to face the press:** Sheilah Graham, "Miss Dru Seeks Change of Role," *Spokesman-Review* [Spokane, WA], April 15, 1950.

140 **thought of selling all her Hollywood holdings:** Dorothy Kilgallen, "On Broadway," *Pittsburgh Post-Gazette*, March 29, 1950.

140 **stay near the site of Giorgio's crash:** Sheilah Graham, "Hollywood," *Pittsburgh Post-Gazette*, March 21, 1950.

140 **stories about her visits:** Dorothy Manners, "Pidgeon Gets British Blonde as Co-Star," *Philadelphia Inquirer*, August 2, 1950.

140 **back on the studio lot:** Hedda Hopper, "Hollywood," *Daily News* [NY], January 5, 1951.

140 **owed the studio two pictures:** Sheilah Graham, "Shirley Happy as Housewife," *Spokesman-Review* [Spokane, WA], January 6, 1951.

140 **she could just go back to France:** Louella Parsons, "Louella Parsons in Hollywood," *Courier-Post* [Cherry Hill, NJ], January 25, 1951.

140 **her old Bel Air home:** Harrison Carroll, "Behind the Scenes in Hollywood," *Lancaster* [OH] *Eagle-Gazette*, January 10, 1951.

140 **a transparently fragile thing:** Hedda Hopper, "Looking at Hollywood," *Chicago Daily Tribune*, January 4, 1951.

141 **"Well . . . I'm living":** "Actress Recalled from Seclusion to Resume Contract," *Muncie* [IN] *Evening Press*, January 1, 1951.

141 **everything she wanted in a man:** Leonard Lyons, "The Lyons Den," *Pittsburgh Post-Gazette*, May 10, 1951.

141 **moneyed, handsome:** Dorothy Kilgallen, "On Broadway," *Pittsburgh Post-Gazette*, July 19, 1951.

141 **tall:** Cholly Knickerbocker, "Cholly Knickerbocker Observes," *San Francisco Examiner*, November 21, 1951.

141 **Viennese waltzes:** Louella Parsons, "Modesty Wins Good Roles for Widmark," *Philadelphia Inquirer*, April 5, 1951.

141 **hosting dinner parties:** Sheilah Graham, "Hollywood," *Pittsburgh Post-Gazette*, July 11, 1951.

141 **a picture she now regretted:** Hedda Hopper, "Gene Fowler Finds Skelton a Big Hit in London Palladium," *Chicago Daily Tribune*, July 12, 1951.

141 **"Why are pictures so bad":** Johnson, "'Living Legends."

142 **"Millions of people love":** Merle Oberon letter to Rex Ross, October 14, 1951, Cedric Gibbons and Hazel Brooks Papers, Margaret Herrick Library, Academy of Motion Picture Arts and Sciences, Beverly Hills.

142 **"seems more maternal":** G. K., "Tin Mining Sets Stage for 'Old Hat'," *Los Angeles Times*, September 12, 1953.

143 **Punta del Este:** Louella O. Parsons, "Hollywood Today," *Arizona Republic*, January 11, 1952.

143 **labeled her birth country as India:** Immigration card for Estelle Merle O'Brien Ballard, January 19, 1952, Rio de Janeiro, Brazil, Immigration Cards, 1900–1965.

143 **Madhubala:** Katijia Akbar, *I Want to Live: The Story of Madhubala* (New Delhi: Hay House, 1997).

144 **Korla Pandit:** Michael J. Altman, *Hinduism in America: An Introduction* (New York: Routledge, 2022), 4.

144 **"I have come to the happy conclusion":** Louella Parsons, "Monday Morning Gossip of the Nation," *Philadelphia Inquirer*, February 16, 1953.

144 **getting cold feet:** Ragan, "Dark Secrets."

Chapter 13: Like a Virus

145 **disregard her contract with RKO:** Louella O. Parsons, "Hollywood Today," *Arizona Republic*, December 26, 1952.

145 **acting on television:** Erskine Johnson, "Glamorous Merle Oberon Is Beaming over First Telefilm," *Marshfield* [WI] *News-Herald*, February 25, 1953.

145 **a snob's skepticism:** "Television Chatter," *Variety*, March 12, 1952, 40.

146 **worry that his film career had petered out:** Munn, *Niven*, 160.

146 **February 1953:** "Merle Oberon TV Debut," *Hollywood Reporter*, February 11, 1953, 14.

146 **"transparent idiocy":** Dan Jenkins, "On the Air," *Hollywood Reporter*, February 16, 1953, 6.

146 **drew $4,000 checks:** "Prices Soaring for Film Names; Seen Curbing Coast Telepix Pacts," *Variety*, April 8, 1953, 24.

146 **without even telling Merle:** Leonard Lyons, "Gossip of the Nation," *Philadelphia Inquirer*, August 20, 1953.

146 **at the same hotel:** Wallace Reyburn, "The Queen and Duke Play a Game of Spotting the Television Birdie," *Courier-Journal* [Louisville, KY], July 4, 1953.

147 **"I want love":** Merle Oberon letter to Rex Ross, June 8, 1953, Cedric Gibbons and Hazel Brooks Papers, Margaret Herrick Library, Academy of Motion Picture Arts and Sciences, Beverly Hills.

147 **a son on whom he doted:** Hedda Hopper, "Piersall Provides Basis Plan Baseball Story," *Pittsburgh Press*, September 8, 1955.

147 **"I think you are one of those people":** Merle Oberon letter to Rex Ross, June 19, 1953, Cedric Gibbons and Hazel Brooks Papers, Margaret Herrick Library, Academy of Motion Picture Arts and Sciences, Beverly Hills.

147 **Spain in September:** Hedda Hopper, "Hollywood," *Daily News*, September 21, 1953.

147 **"She'll have to go over the Panama Canal":** Earl Wilson, "It Happened Last Night," *Newsday*, August 21, 1953.

147 **January of 1954:** Merle Oberon letter to Rex Ross, January 14, 1954, Cedric

Gibbons and Hazel Brooks Papers, Margaret Herrick Library, Academy of Motion Picture Arts and Sciences, Beverly Hills.

147 **to the industry's surprise:** Parish, *Glamour Girls*, 636.

147 **the grace of her performance:** Jack Moffitt, " 'Deep in My Heart' Is Top Musical with Big B.O. Draw," *Hollywood Reporter*, December 1, 1954, 3.

148 **"sultry and theatrical":** Daniel Taradash, Script for *Désirée*, April 5, 1954, Merle Oberon Papers, Margaret Herrick Library, Academy of Motion Picture Arts and Sciences, Beverly Hills, 35.

148 **Merle's ardor for Rex had cooled:** Dorothy Kilgallen, "Voice of Broadway," *Washington Post*, March 21, 1954.

149 **"The only roles open to me":** Darwin Porter, *Brando Unzipped* (New York: Blood Moon, 2005), 467.

149 **"Miss Merle Oberon, on the other hand":** Winn Fanning, " 'Desiree'," *Pittsburgh Post-Gazette*, November 19, 1954.

149 **$12,500 paycheck:** "TV Behind the Scenes Gets More Like Movies," *Birmingham Post-Herald*, October 25, 1954.

150 **"suffered brutally":** Lawrence Laurent, "It's the Same Old Woolley, But Not the Same Old 'Man'," *Washington Post*, October 15, 1954.

150 **"All I want to do":** Hedda Hopper, "Merle Comes Back," *Chicago Daily Tribune*, August 22, 1954.

150 **"within the careful limits of good taste":** Thomas Doherty, *Hollywood's Censor: Joseph I. Breen & the Production Code Administration* (New York: Columbia University Press), 319.

150 **an Oscar nomination:** Edwin Schallert, "Forecast of Academy Awards Made by Times Drama Editor," *Los Angeles Times*, January 16, 1955.

151 **"swelled with pride":** Donald Bogle, *Dorothy Dandridge: A Biography* (New York: Amistad, 1997), 320.

151 **pink silk saris:** "Emerald Green Floor Length Sheaths Popular at Fan Ball," *Women's Wear Daily*, November 15, 1954.

151 *Harper's Bazaar*: "The Far East Influence," *Harper's Bazaar,* January 1954, 123.

151 **Marilyn Monroe:** Kaspar Monahan, "Marilyn and Gwen Vie for Attention," *Pittsburgh Press*, July 10, 1955.

152 **an unsympathetic role:** Ron Burton, "Film Shop," *Daily World*, January 17, 1956.

152 **substituted narration:** Sheilah Graham, "Brando Turns Down Role," *Miami Daily News,* March 12, 1956.

152 **critics dinged her:** Jack Moffitt, " 'Emergency Hospital' Good; 'Price of Fear' Misses Mark," *Hollywood Reporter*, March 20, 1956, 3.

152 *Assignment Foreign Legion:* Louella O. Parsons, "Merle Oberon Plans TV Series in London," *Philadelphia Inquirer,* January 10, 1956.

152 **locked its grip on Merle:** Edwin Schallert, "Korda Started Many on Way to Film Fame," *Los Angeles Times*, January 24, 1956.

152 **She sobbed before reporters:** "Film Capital Mourns Korda," *Calgary Herald*, January 24, 1956.

152 **he eliminated her from his will:** "Korda Passes Up Oberon in Will," *Palm Beach Post*, May 19, 1956.

152 **"Acting is like a virus":** Walter Ames, "Merle Oberon Will Star in TV Series on Foreign Legion," *Los Angeles Times*, April 1, 1956.

153 **French Army officers:** Leon Morse, "Pilot Review," *Billboard*, December 1, 1956, 12.

153 **Nazi informers:** Barbara Delatiner, "New Suspense Series Lays Real (Time) Bomb," *Newsday*, October 2, 1957.

153 **She'd ask journalists:** Anne Sharpley, "'Tell Me How to Be a Reporter,' said Merle Oberon," *London Evening Standard*, April 7, 1956.

153 **"When one is very young":** Lane, "Being in the Swim."

154 **Kashfi's parents were Anglo-Indian:** Sarah Broughton, *Brando's Bride* (Cardigan, UK: Parthian, 2019), 247.

154 **alleged Black ancestry:** Charlton-Stevens, *Anglo-India*, 15.

Chapter 14: Being Mrs. Pagliai

157 **hovering over her table:** Earl Wilson, "It Happened Last Night," *Pittsburgh Post-Gazette*, December 6, 1957.

157 **December 1956:** "Mexican Fiesta Attends Preem of Hilton's Latest," *Variety*, December 12, 1956, 2.

157 **emeralds and diamonds . . . the White House:** Details in these paragraphs about Merle's jewelry, and Bruno's Mexico City home, are drawn from Hedda Hopper columns published between December 1956 and February 1957. (Full citations are in the bibliography.)

158 **Hernán Cortés's palace:** Merle Oberon de Pagliai, "Cuernavaca, 'Eternal Springtime'," *Vogue*, January 15, 1967, 43.

158 **Merle found him charming:** "A Surprise for Merle," *Modern Screen*, May 1957, 21.

158 **she wanted stability:** E! *Mysteries & Scandals*.

158 **he'd met her a decade earlier:** Parish, *Glamour Girls*, 637.

158 **too old to fall in love again:** Joan Hanauer, "Merle Oberon in Prime of Life," *Daily Defender*, December 9, 1957.

158 **New Year's Eve:** Hedda Hopper, "Looking at Hollywood," *Chicago Daily Tribune*, January 14, 1957.

158 **guest of honor:** Louella O. Parsons, "Louella's Movie-Go-'Round," *Albuquerque Journal*, January 21, 1957.

159 **25-karat:** Mike Connolly, "Hollywood," *Pittsburgh Post-Gazette*, April 26, 1957.

159 **she could wear it on a chain:** Cliff Eisen and Dominic McHugh, *The Letters of Cole Porter* (New Haven, CT: Yale University Press, 2019), 569.

159 **Mata Hari:** Leo Guild, "On the Air," *Hollywood Reporter*, March 18, 1957, 18.

159 **hours before her execution:** "Miss Oberon Will Star on GE Show," *Orlando Sentinel*, April 28, 1957.

159 **"My marriage will come first"**: Erskine Johnson, "This Is Hollywood," *Times Recorder* [Marshfield, WI], April 18, 1957.

159 **"I didn't quit the movies to be bothered"**: "Merle Oberon Marries in Rome," *Daily News* [NY], July 29, 1957.

159 **"My career is being Mrs. Pagliai"**: Louella O. Parsons, "Hollywood Today," *Arizona Republic*, December 6, 1957.

160 **white-brick wonderland**: "Merle Oberon's Mexico," *San Francisco Examiner*, July 15, 1962.

160 **pool fountain**: "Living in Mexico," *Town & Country*, July 1959, 47.

160 **grand New Year's Eve bash**: Hedda Hopper, "Karloff Starts a New Frankenstein Film," *Chicago Daily Tribune*, January 9, 1958.

160 **Miguel Alemán**: Cholly Knickerbocker, "Greek Prince Likes 'Em Buxom," *Philadelphia Inquirer*, December 17, 1957.

160 **adopt children**: Wilson, "It Happened."

160 **looked a bit like Merle**: Hedda Hopper, "Looking at Hollywood," *Chicago Daily Tribune*, August 22, 1959.

160 **an irrational paranoia**: Louella O. Parsons, "Douglas Third Star in New Wilder Film," *Bergen* [NJ] *Evening Record*, August 17, 1959.

160 **"When they are with me"**: Maggie Savoy, "In Two Lands," *Los Angeles Times*, March 2, 1969.

160 **"If Miss Gabor"**: Walter Ames, "Zsa Zsa Sputters Like a Model-T after Bolting Dinner for Ford," *Los Angeles Times*, November 3, 1959.

161 **her children present at these gatherings**: "Inside Hollywood," *Detroit Free Press*, December 13, 1959.

161 *Vogue*: "Children Are to Enjoy," *Vogue*, August 15, 1963, 94.

161 **Mexico City's elevation**: Earl Wilson, "Married Merle Is Happy Lady," *Indianapolis Star*, March 25, 1977.

161 **tell her kids the same stories**: *E! Mysteries & Scandals*.

162 **"educated all four"**: Sheilah Graham, "Sheilah Graham in Hollywood," *Miami News*, July 19, 1960.

162 **By September 1960**: Louella O. Parsons, "Goetz Gets Remarque's Novel, 'Borrowed Time' for New Film," *Record*, September 28, 1960.

162 **Selby House**: Wanda Henderson, "Confetti: A Visit with Merle," *Los Angeles Times*, August 12, 1962.

162 **Anna Lee**: Lee, *Anna Lee*, 67.

162 **her hair grow down to her waist**: Mike Connolly, "Rambling Reporter," *Hollywood Reporter*, September 14, 1960, 2.

162 **"Guess the old gal"**: J. C. Brossier, "Hush Puppies," *Orlando Sentinel*, October 25, 1960.

162 **kept her in the spotlight**: Parish, *Glamour Girls*, 638.

163 **$15,000 sable coat**: Leonard Lyons, "In The Lyons Den," *Morning Call*, December 6, 1961.

163 **talked to Louella Parsons every day:** Louella Parsons, "Joanie Benny in TV Bow," *San Francisco Examiner,* April 8, 1961.

163 **the demon child's grandmother:** Barry Paris, *Audrey Hepburn* (New York: G. P. Putnam's Sons, 1996), 176.

163 **"Actresses should retire" . . . end of 1961 . . . Cables were strewn:** Details in these paragraphs are drawn from columns by Louella Parsons published between December 1959 and August 1962. (Full citations are in the bibliography.)

164 **the first day of shooting:** William Glover, "Homes Turned into Set for Film Return," *Austin American,* August 4, 1963.

165 **"Styles have changed":** "Merle Oberon Making Comeback," *St. Louis Post-Dispatch,* July 22, 1962.

165 **trouble finding a distributor:** Dave Freeman, "The TV Ticker," *Evening Press,* October 22, 1962.

165 **the following April:** Louella Parsons, "Zanuck Buys Oberon Film," *San Francisco Examiner,* April 8, 1963.

165 **"nasty, overwhelmingly stupid":** Bryan Barney, "Canadian Weekly at the Movies," *The Gazette* [Montreal], October 12, 1963.

165 **gauzy linoleum:** Elspeth Grant, "Films Films Films," *She,* April 1964, 38.

165 **pirouetting around in a bikini:** Welton Jones, "Seat on the Aisle," *Shreveport Times,* January 10, 1964.

165 **"embarrassing and pitiful":** Walter Scott, "Walter Scott's Personality Parade," *Detroit Free Press,* October 20, 1963.

165 **"sadly worn":** Bosley Crowther, "Screen: Romantic Middle-Aged Men and Women," *New York Times,* September 12, 1963.

165 **"I feel that artists":** "Newsmakers," *Newsweek,* October 21, 1963, 72–73.

166 **the lines under her eyes:** Earl Wilson, "It Happened Last Night," *Newsday,* October 15, 1963.

166 **disliked smoking:** Shirley Henin, "Actress Close to Fountain of Youth," *Arizona Republic,* July 11, 1963.

166 **swam daily:** Mildred Schroeder, "Still Glamorous After 50," *San Francisco Examiner,* September 4, 1963.

166 **"The only time I stay up late":** "A Beauty Recipe," *Sydney Morning Herald,* September 1, 1963.

166 **questions about Merle's origins:** Mike Connolly, "Best of Hollywood," *Philadelphia Inquirer,* December 5, 1963.

167 **"Can you tell me":** Scott, "Personality Parade."

167 **Gayatri Devi:** Maurice Richardson, "Electra Rocks the Box," *Observer,* December 2, 1962.

167 **"Singh dress":** Advertisement, *Harper's Bazaar,* October 1962, 109.

168 **"Both my parents were English":** "Miss Oberon Ends Some Old Illusions," *Sydney Morning Herald,* January 19, 1965.

Chapter 15: **The Last of the Great Faces**

169   **Taj Mahal:** Sally Kirkland, "In a Swinging Resort the Star Is Merle Oberon," *Life,* January 27, 1967, 62A.

169   **"fond memories":** Hermine Mariaux, "Romance with Acapulco," *Town & Country,* February 1967, 72.

170   **October 1965:** Eugenia Sheppard, "Moving Day for Merle Oberon—Into Four Houses," *Gazette,* October 27, 1965.

170   **manmade lagoons:** Maxine Cheshire, "Lynda Bird's home for Mexican Visit Is Named 'To Love'," *Philadelphia Inquirer,* January 1, 1967.

170   **lemon and mango trees:** Betty Beale, "Life with the Pagliais," *San Francisco Examiner,* March 31, 1968.

170   **macaws, parakeets, and parrots:** Merle Oberon de Pagliai, "Travel," *Vogue,* January 1, 1966, 57.

170   *Vogue:* "Mrs. Bruno Pagliai at Home," *Vogue,* November 15, 1965, 129.

170   **solicitations of producers:** Gord Atkinson, "Gord Atkinson's Show Business," *Ottawa Citizen,* April 24, 1965.

170   **$500,000 worth of her own jewelry:** Earl Wilson, "Falk Tells Lawyers: 'Relax'," *Detroit Free Press,* October 9, 1965.

171   **she was fifteen:** "She Lost Her Head," *San Francisco Examiner,* September 14, 1965.

171   **"I'm the last":** Sheilah Graham, "Inside Hollywood," *Paterson* [NJ] *Evening News,* July 26, 1965.

171   *Town & Country:* "The Pleasure of Your Company Is Requested at a Series of Interviews with Today's Leading International Hostesses," *Town & Country,* May 1965, 98.

171   **The citation horrified her:** Philip K. Scheuer, "Merle in Films to Fulfill Dream," *Los Angeles Times,* July 10, 1966.

172   **flowers and notes from well-wishers:** "Merle Returns," *Detroit Free Press,* July 20, 1966.

172   **dressing rooms:** Harold Heffernan, "Merle Oberon Returning," *Morning Call,* July 22, 1966.

172   **costume baubles:** Sheilah Graham, "'Hamilton' Switches Locale, Will Now Film in New York," *Edmonton Journal,* August 26, 1966.

172   **gun-toting guard:** Dorothy Manners, "Merle's Gem Guardian," *San Francisco Examiner,* July 23, 1966.

172   **Merle wore $350,000 worth:** "Merle Oberon Feels a Duty to Look Young," *San Francisco Examiner,* July 15, 1966.

172   **struggling with some dialogue:** Kevin Thomas, "Actor Turned Director Is No Longer a Rarity," *Des Moines Register,* August 29, 1966.

172   **"I see the Countess as":** Jeanne Miller, "Merle—'A Woman Should Look Better with Age'," *San Francisco Examiner,* September 16, 1966.

172   **Miami in January 1967:** Terry Clifford, "Tell Us, Miss Oberon, What Brings You to Miami Beach This Time of Year?" *Chicago Tribune,* March 12, 1967.

172 **"I'm sick":** Dan Lewis, "Oberon Shrieks in Rage," *Morning Call,* January 23, 1967.

173 **glamour walk-through:** Sheilah Graham, "Sheilah Graham," *Pittsburgh Press,* May 20, 1967.

173 **a duchess or an empress:** Dorothy Manners, "Silly Gossip about Eddie," *San Francisco Examiner,* August 21, 1967.

173 **"Duchess" or "Queen":** "Broadway," *Variety,* March 8, 1967.

173 **"They don't need me":** Ruth Olis, "People-Watching Is a Change of Pace," *Courier-Post* [Cherry Hill, NJ], July 11, 1967.

173 **the 1968 Academy Awards:** Mark Harris, *Pictures at a Revolution* (New York: Penguin, 2008), 1.

175 **"Did you ever hear":** Lambert, "Why We All."

175 **six to eight Acapulco dinners:** Charlotte Curtis, "For Rich Nomads, Acapulco Is Siesta Time," *New York Times,* March 31, 1968.

175 **Hollywood's heyday:** Jerry Hulse, "Mexico: That's the Way the Jet Sets," *Los Angeles Times,* April 20, 1969.

175 *The Killing of Sister George:* Marian Christy, "Merle Oberon Making a Success of Marriage," *Boston Globe,* October 26, 1969.

175 **Her husband was usually away:** Jerry Parker, "Merle Oberon: Taking the Script to Heart," *Newsday,* June 24, 1973.

175 **sold off her precious Selby House:** Bob Thomas, "Movie Stars Changing Life Style," *Marion* [OH] *Star,* April 2, 1971.

175 **"a prison":** William Otterburn-Hall, "The World of Stars," *Star-Phoenix,* April 7, 1973.

176 **a pool, a library:** Linda Ashland, "On Giving Yourself," *Town & Country,* December 1970, 121.

176 **"I did a lot":** Joyce Haber, "'Spangled Girl' Casting Completed," *Los Angeles Times,* April 21, 1971.

176 **rough and virile:** Molly Haskell, *From Reverence to Rape: The Treatment of Women in the Movies* (Baltimore: Penguin, 1974), 34.

176 **Grand Guignol:** Parish, *Glamour Girls,* 644.

176 **"I'd rather be":** Marian Christy, "Fashion Profile," *Boston Globe,* June 24, 1973.

176 **Gavin Lambert:** "Q and A Session with Merle, Rex," *Los Angeles Times,* October 12, 1971.

177 **reflection of herself:** "Oberon Stars in and Directs 'Interval'," *Miami News,* June 11, 1973.

Chapter 16: Where I Belong

179 **"own miserable little":** Parker, "Merle Oberon."

180 **Ghalal up for sale:** Joyce Haber, "Cambridge to Cut Out Fattening Films," *Los Angeles Times,* November 3, 1971.

180 **stretch on for years:** "Acapulco Manor Is Sold to Shah?" *Boston Globe,* January 15, 1979.

180   **Rochester, New York, in 1959:** Paris, *Hepburn*, 288.

180   **"He may have great promise":** Alexander Walker, *Audrey: Her Real Story* (New York: St. Martin's Griffin, 1994), 254.

180   **intense heat of Yucatán:** Dorothy Manners, "Minnelli Leaves New Oberon Film," *Indianapolis Star*, January 19, 1972.

180   **Lambert's patchwork script:** Rex Reed, "Ageless Merle Oberon Starts Anew, Again," *Courier-Journal*, June 24, 1973.

181   **"nonsense":** Karin Winner, "Merle Oberon, 'Not at All What You'd Expect of Me'," *Women's Wear Daily*, November 8, 1972, 4.

181   **"All that these movements":** "Australia Ducky for Expatriate Farmer," *Los Angeles Times*, June 6, 1971.

181   **"shudder":** Norma Lee Browning, "Merle Doing War Dance over 'Tango'," *Chicago Tribune*, March 12, 1973.

181   **depressed her:** Barbara Cloud, "Love Story Screened before Interview: Merle to Wed Young Co-star in February," *Pittsburgh Press*, June 24, 1973.

181   **"I don't really relate":** Parker, "Merle Oberon."

181   **insisted upon a tragic ending:** Rebecca Morehouse, "Older Woman, Younger Man: Life Imitating Art for Couple," *Sun*, June 20, 1973.

181   **"I wanted to prove":** Roderick Mann, "A Noted Hostess, but 'Parties Bore Me'," *San Francisco Examiner*, February 23, 1973.

182   **demeanor was so respectful:** Burn, *Mary*, 140.

182   **the core of Lambert's script:** Eugenia Sheppard, "Woman Dominates Film's Production," *Austin Statesman*, January 10, 1973.

182   **rental for an English cottage:** Suzy, "Oberon's Abode," *Chicago Tribune*, July 11, 1972.

183   **"beautiful and secure":** Vernon Scott, "Merle Makes a Movie," *Courier-Post* [Cherry Hill, NJ], June 11, 1973.

183   **Joseph E. Levine:** Joyce Haber, "Disney Films for Misses Hayes, Rush," *Los Angeles Times*, September 27, 1972.

183   **"a Hollywood Comeback":** Karin Winner, "A Long Interval," *Women's Wear Daily*, March 5, 1973, 4.

183   **David Niven and Laurence Olivier:** Charles McHarry, "On the Town," *Daily News* [NY], December 28, 1972.

183   **"When this is all over":** Winner, "A Long Interval."

184   **Her marriage's collapse:** Suzy, "Merle and Bruno Part," *Daily News*, March 11, 1973.

184   **on the fingers of a single hand:** Otterburn-Hall, "World of Stars."

184   **"It's wrong to put down the Oscars":** Joyce Haber, "Merle Oberon: Her Life, Her Loves," *Los Angeles Times*, June 10, 1973.

184   **"I like to be":** Christy, "Fashion Profile."

185   **"half-Indian beauty":** Toni Kosover, "Focus: Charles Revson on Women," *Women's Wear Daily*, March 12, 1971, 18.

185   **"new type of beauty":** Jamie Sue Spurgeon, "Begin by Evolving Your Total Personality," *Cincinnati Enquirer*, April 18, 1973.

185   **her comfort food to be curry:** Johna Blinn, "Celebrity Cookbook: Merle Oberon's Specialty: Curry Stew," *Chicago Tribune*, June 28, 1973.

185   **luncheons at her Malibu home:** Jody Jacobs, "Invitation to the Ball that Wasn't," *Los Angeles Times*, November 19, 1975; Jody Jacobs, "Casbah Chow for the Chips," *Los Angeles Times*, June 3, 1977.

185   **"Javanese flower":** Otterburn-Hall, "World of Stars."

186   **"It's not a very big part":** "Merle Oberon's First and Final Pic Prod.," *Variety*, May 16, 1973, 118.

186   **snickering at its melodramatic flourishes:** Marilou Berry, "A Beauty at Any Age," *Evansville* [IN] *Press*, July 8, 1973.

186   **hackneyed:** "Buying & Booking Guide: INTERVAL (PG)," *Independent Film Journal*, June 25, 1973, 61.

186   **travelogue:** Jerry Parker, "Archaeological Melodrama," *Newsday*, June 15, 1973.

186   **soap opera:** "Film Reviews: Interval," *Variety*, June 20, 1973, 28.

186   **"as sweet as a $1 valentine":** J. Oliver Prescott, "Don't Get Caught in This Interval," *St. Petersburg Times*, August 14, 1973.

186   **"aura of an empty perfume bottle":** Howard Kissel, "Films: 'Interval'," *Women's Wear Daily*, June 15, 1973, 14.

186   **Kleenex:** Kevin Kelly, "Merle Oberon Acts Her Age," *Boston Globe*, July 14, 1973.

186   **"vanity production":** Parker, "Archaeological Melodrama."

186   **"ego trip":** Barbara Cloud, "Merle to Wed Young Co-star in February," *Pittsburgh Press*, June 24, 1973.

187   *preserved:* Derek Malcolm, "Cosmo Sees the Films," *Cosmopolitan*, November 1973, 8.

187   **frequent facelifts:** Ellie Schultz, "Fashion Folio: Self-Identification Result of Impromptu Make-over," *Arizona Republic*, August 7, 1973.

187   **"polyethylene face":** Kelly, "Merle Oberon."

187   **"She has the expressions":** Gary Arnold, "The Art Didn't Imitate Life," *Washington Post*, November 27, 1973.

187   **"There was never such a movie":** Roger Greenspun, "The Screen: An Almost Sublime 'Interval' Opens," *New York Times*, June 16, 1973.

187   **practiced yoga:** Mallen De Santis, "Young and Beautiful into Your 40's and 50's," *Cosmopolitan*, January 1970, 105.

187   **cold salt water:** Bob Thomas, "Even Glamorous Entertainers Are Slaves to Rigorous Diets," *Morning Call*, October 1, 1973.

187   **tennis:** Arlene Dahl, "Pisceans' Secrets," *Morning Call*, March 14, 1970.

187   **forty-five minutes:** "My Pet Beauty Secret," *Cosmopolitan*, October 1971, 110.

187   **"I think they've been conditioned":** Parker, "Merle Oberon."

188   **"I feel the world":** Christine Anderson, "At the Fashion Shows: Merle Oberon Shares Romantic Interval," *Knoxville* [TN] *News-Sentinel*, June 20, 1973.

188   **after three weeks:** Parish, *Glamour Girls*, 643.

188   **Merle ultimately lost money:** "Merle Oberon Secretly Wed to Actor, 38," *Globe and Mail*, February 5, 1975.

189   **Captain Harry Selby:** Delofski, *Trouble.*

190   **half of his salary:** Anil and Sunil Selby.

Chapter 17: Local Girl Makes Good!

193   **rethinking her lifestyle:** "Oberon Planning to Marry," *Leader Post* [Regina, SK], November 17, 1973.

194   **auctioned off:** Suzy, "A Capital Couple!" *Chicago Tribune,* November 7, 1973.

194   **wooden carousel horse:** Joyce Haber, "Sculpture Makes Mike Swing into Auction," *Philadelphia Inquirer,* November 16, 1973.

194   **"I think it's disgraceful":** "Eye," *Women's Wear Daily,* January 8, 1974, 12.

194   **draft her will:** Paris, *Hepburn,* 290.

194   **Norma Shearer:** Lambert, *Shearer,* 350.

194   **round-the-world cruise:** "Polling the Newsmakers on 1974," *Los Angeles Times,* January 1, 1974.

194   **fearful of disembarking:** Anil and Sunil Selby.

194   **white sari:** "On Fashion," *Los Angeles Times,* March 11, 1976.

194 **"We sure hope":** Robin Adams Sloan, "The Gossip Column," *News Journal,* July 17, 1973.

194   **Robin:** Wilson, "Married Merle."

195   **"Regardless of the fact":** "Love Is Ageless," *Pittsburgh Press,* November 15, 1973.

195   **"He has given my life":** Walker, *Audrey,* 255.

195   **"from failing her terminal ambition":** Jack O'Brian, "Voice of Broadway," *Asbury Park* [NJ] *Evening Press,* March 29, 1973.

195   **"boredom lying in bed":** Nickie McWhirter, "Overnight, Front and Rear Just Go Pop! Pop! Pop!" *Detroit Free Press,* May 21, 1978.

195   **"looks like she's been dead":** Roger Ebert, "'The Sunshine Boys' Are Still at It," *Boston Globe,* January 1, 1976.

195   **"I said, 'Merle Oberon'":** Galligan, "Joan Rivers."

195   **three-month decompression:** Suzy, "Hip, Hip, Beret!" *Daily News,* April 24, 1974.

195   **local summer stock:** Tom Mankiewicz and Robert Crane, *My Life as a Mankiewicz: An Insider's Journey Through Hollywood* (Lexington: University Press of Kentucky, 2012), 124.

195   **a set of watercolors:** Beth Twiggar, "A Stage Role, and No Retakes, Gives Chills to Hollywood Star," *New York Herald Tribune,* September 14, 1941.

196   **Leslie Stevens:** Walter Kohner, Paul Kohner, Inc., note, November 6, 1974, with a letter to Oberon from Leslie Stevens, November 5, 1974, Merle Oberon Papers, Margaret Herrick Library, Academy of Motion Picture Arts and Sciences, Beverly Hills.

196   **his association with Merle:** Edward Z. Epstein, *Audrey and Bill: A Romantic Biography of Audrey Hepburn and William Holden* (Philadelphia: Running Press, 2015), 196.

196 **scaled-down wedding:** Maggie Daly, "Maggie Daly," *Chicago Tribune,* May 26, 1974.

196 **the Netherlands:** Gerry Nadel, "The Ball Game," *Women's Wear Daily,* September 10, 1974, 5.

196 **birth certificate:** Joyce Haber, "Rob and Merle's Best-Kept Secret," *Los Angeles Times,* February 4, 1975.

196 **dinner party:** Delofski, *Trouble.*

197 **left him feeling rejected:** Anil and Sunil Selby.

197 **"partly Indian":** Walter Scott, "Walter Scott's Personality Parade," *Asheville* [NC] *Citizen,* March 23, 1975.

197 **"Isn't she really Indian?":** Walter Scott, "Walter Scott's Personality Parade," *Albuquerque Journal,* April 30, 1978.

197 **"carefully ironed out":** Datta-Ray, "Demise."

198 **Wrest Point:** "Personal Appearances: Tasmania's Wrest Point Casino to Stage Plush Dinner-Theatre Prods.," *Variety,* March 20, 1974, 65.

198 **happier than any other:** Paris, *Hepburn,* 289.

198 **California coast:** Walker, *Audrey,* 255.

198 **fearful of how ridiculous:** *E! Mysteries & Scandals.*

198 **"It is very rewarding":** Radie Harris, "Broadway Ballyhoo," *Hollywood Reporter,* September 7, 1978, 8.

198 **Sammy Awards:** "Australian TV & Film Awards," *Variety,* October 18, 1978, 87.

199 **fits of crying:** Cassandra Pybus, *Till Apples Grow on an Orange Tree* (St. Lucia, Australia: University of Queensland Press, 1998), 109.

199 **"It's probably a bad time":** Delofski, *Trouble.*

200 **passed out:** Shakespeare, *Tasmania,* 300.

Chapter 18: It Has Haunted Me Ever Since

201 **emergency coronary bypass:** "Actress Merle Oberon, 63, Undergoes Heart Surgery," *Chicago Tribune,* November 17, 1978.

202 **seven and a half hours:** Liz Smith, "Those Who Take Beauty Seriously," *Daily News,* November 20, 1978.

202 **scar:** Epstein, *Audrey,* 197.

202 **Malibu beach:** Jody Jacobs, "Diadames' Man of Mystery," *Los Angeles Times,* February 7, 1979.

202 **Francesca's wedding:** Eugenia Sheppard, "Sister Team Has California Show," *Shreveport* [LA] *Times,* May 20, 1979.

202 **Ronald Reagan:** Robert Shogan, "Reagan Takes Big Step Toward 1980 Race," *Los Angeles Times,* March 8, 1979.

202 **nearly two thousand people:** Saltzman, "Merle Oberon."

202 **"I feel well":** Robert Osborne, "Merle Oberon: A Touch of Class," *Los Angeles Times,* December 9, 1979.

203 **"Belated congratulations":** Herman, *Trouble,* 460.

203 **"has stood the test":** Handwritten drafts of William Wyler letter to Merle Oberon, October 1979, William Wyler Papers, Margaret Herrick Library, Academy of Motion Picture Arts and Sciences.

203 **Michael Korda:** Korda, *Another*, 445.

203 **her real name:** Kevin Thomas, " 'Queenie' and the Novel Fact of Oberon's Fiction," *Los Angeles Times*, May 31, 1985.

203 **"beautiful young Tasmanian-born actress":** Korda, *Charmed*, 100.

204 **asked that the paparazzi refrain:** Jody Jacobs, "100 Ways to Make Money," *Los Angeles Times*, October 21, 1979.

204 **Dinah Shore:** Robert Osborne, "Rites Wednesday at All Saints for Merle Oberon," *Hollywood Reporter*, November 26, 1979, 4.

204 **Bel Air pad:** Shirley Eder, "Merle Oberon Always Had a Loyal Following," *Detroit Free Press*, November 27, 1979.

204 **walk on the beach:** Maggie Daly, "Season's Greetings to All the Ships at Sea," *Chicago Tribune*, November 26, 1979.

204 **foot of the bed:** Radie Harris, "Broadway Ballyhoo," *Hollywood Reporter*, November 29, 1979, 6.

204 **10:18:** Richard E. Meyer, "Merle Oberon Suffers Stroke, Is in Coma," *Los Angeles Times*, November 23, 1979.

204 **"My poor, poor Robbie":** Walker, *Audrey*, 255.

204 **Robert and her two children:** "Merle Oberon Dead," *Advocate*, November 24, 1979.

204 **three hundred people:** "Stars Crowd Rites for Merle Oberon," *Boston Globe*.

205 **funeral pamphlet:** Funeral Program for Merle Oberon Wolders, November 28, 1979, Cary Grant Papers, Margaret Herrick Library, Academy of Motion Picture Arts and Sciences.

205 **That she was six:** "Merle Oberon, Noted Film Beauty, Veteran of 40-Year Screen career," *Asbury Park* [NJ] *Press*.

205 **"a very youthful decision":** Osborne, "Rites Wednesday."

205 **February afternoon in 1981:** Anil and Sunil Selby.

206 **dressed in white:** Delofski, *Trouble*.

Epilogue

207 **his family's sensitivities:** Maree Delofski, "Storytelling and Archival Material in 'The Trouble with Merle'," *The Moving Image*, Spring 2006, 91.

207 **"Birthplace of Merle Oberon":** "Crossword Puzzle," *Pittsburgh Post-Gazette*, April 23, 1973.

208 **"In Hollywood, if people liked you":** Amy Fine Collins, "The Man Hollywood Trusted," *Vanity Fair*, April 2001, 298.

208 **press reports emerged:** Ragan, "Dark Secrets."

209 **"the periphery":** Delofski, *Trouble*.

209 **"I've known lots of Indian students":** Shakespeare, *Tasmania*, 305.

211   **"She was just human":** Melville de Mellow, "Letters: Living a Lie," *Times of India*, November 20, 1983.

Filmography

218   **February 1982:** Al Kilgore and Roi Frumkes, "Merle Oberon," *Films in Review*, February 1982, 76.

Selected Bibliography

Archives, libraries, and papers

Cary Grant Papers. Margaret Herrick Library, Academy of Motion Picture Arts and Sciences, Beverly Hills.

Cedric Gibbons and Hazel Brooks Papers. Margaret Herrick Library, Academy of Motion Picture Arts and Sciences, Beverly Hills.

Charles Higham Collection, University of Southern California Cinematic Arts Library, Los Angeles.

Hedda Hopper Papers. Margaret Herrick Library, Academy of Motion Picture Arts and Sciences, Beverly Hills.

Merle Oberon Papers. Margaret Herrick Library, Academy of Motion Picture Arts and Sciences, Beverly Hills.

Samuel Goldwyn Papers. Margaret Herrick Library, Academy of Motion Picture Arts and Sciences, Beverly Hills.

William Wyler Papers. Margaret Herrick Library, Academy of Motion Picture Arts and Sciences, Beverly Hills.

Birth, baptismal, travel, and will documents

"Estelle Thompson." List or Manifest of Alien Passengers for the United States Immigration Officer at Port of Arrival, S.S. *Paris*, Passengers sailing from Plymouth (England), November 14, 1934. Arriving at Port of New York, USA, November 20, 1934. National Archives and Records Administration, Washington, DC; Passenger and Crew Lists of Vessels Arriving at and Departing from Ogdensburg, New York, 5/27/1948–11/28/1972; Microfilm Serial or NAID: T715, 1897–1957.

"Estelle Merle Thompson." List or Manifest of Alien Passengers for the United States Immigration Officer at Port of Arrival, S.S. *Berengaria*, Passengers sailing from Southampton, October 23, 1935. Arriving at Port of New York, USA, October 30, 1935. National Archives and Records Administration; Washington, DC; Passenger and Crew Lists of Vessels Arriving at and Departing from Ogdensburg, New York, 5/27/1948–11/28/1972; Microfilm Serial or NAID: T715, 1897–1957.

Estelle Merle Thompson. Report of Birth in Greater Bombay. February 18, 1911, Municipal Corporation of Greater Bombay.

Estelle Merle Thompson. Baptisms solemnized at Emmanuel Church Girgaum within the Archdeaconry and Diocese of Bombay in the year of our Lord 1911. March 16, 1911.

"Charlotte Constance Thompson." *England & Wales, National Probate Calendar (Index of Wills and Administrations)*, 1858–1995.

Immigration card for Estelle Merle O'Brien Ballard. January 19, 1952, Rio de Janeiro, Brazil, Immigration Cards, 1900–1965.

"Merle Oberon." Pan American Airways Flight 115, Departure date December 20, 1950. Point of Embarkation Orly Airport, Paris [to] New York. Arrival Date December 21, 1950, Arrival Port of New York, USA. Arriving Passenger and Crew Lists (including Castle Garden and Ellis Island), 1820–1957, National Archives and Records Administration, Washington, DC; Passenger and Crew Lists of Vessels Arriving at and Departing from Ogdensburg, New York, 5/27/1948–11/28/1972; Microfilm Serial or NAID: T715, 1897–1957.

Author interviews and emails
Delofski, Maree. June 5, 2022; March 4, 2023.
Drazin, Charles. June 21, 2023.
Korda, Michael. May 23, 2023.
Selby, Anil. Phone interview, April 27, 2023.
Selby, Anil and Sunil. Phone interview, April 30, 2023.

Television documentaries and broadcasts
Delofski, Maree. *The Trouble with Merle*. Australian Broadcasting Corporation, 2002.
Duncalf, Bill. *The Epic That Never Was*. British Broadcasting Corporation, 1965.
E! Mysteries & Scandals. Season 3, Episode 48. March 14, 2001.
Interview with Merle Oberon. British Broadcasting Corporation, October 20, 1974.

Articles, advertisements, and books
"9 Of 10 Academy Player Nominees Are from Stage." *Hollywood Reporter*, February 24, 1936.
"Acad Dinner Brings Out Fresh Flurry of Finery in Fash Prom." *Variety*, March 11, 1936.
"Acapulco Manor Is Sold to Shah?" *Boston Globe*, January 15, 1979.
"Accent Troubles Merle Oberon." *Detroit Free Press*, August 7, 1938.
"Actress, Cameraman Use Stand-Ins at Wedding." *Albuquerque Journal*, June 27, 1945.
"Actress Finds Beauty Secret." *Los Angeles Times*, June 11, 1935.
"Actress Here." *Chicago Daily Tribune*, October 6, 1939.
"Actress Merle Oberon, 63, Undergoes Heart Surgery." *Chicago Tribune*, November 17, 1978.
"Actress Merle Oberon Loses Lover in French Plane Crash." *Great Falls* [MT] *Tribune*, September 1, 1949.
"Actress Recalled from Seclusion to Resume Contract." *Muncie* [IN] *Evening Press*, January 1, 1951.

Adams, Marjory. "Merle Oberon on Honeymoon, Here without Wedding Ring." *Boston Globe*, October 31, 1945.

Advertisement. *Picturegoer*, March 17, 1934.

Advertisement. *Picturegoer*, March 24, 1934.

Advertisement. *Picturegoer*, October 13, 1934.

Advertisement. *Times of India*, August 30, 1935.

Advertisement. *Daily News* [NY], September 6, 1935.

Advertisement. *Los Angeles Times*, September 13, 1935.

Advertisement. *Variety*, October 21, 1953.

Advertisement. *Harper's Bazaar*, October 1962.

Agate, James. "The Cinema." *Tatler*, May 10, 1939.

Akbar, Katijia. *I Want to Live: The Story of Madhubala*. New Delhi: Hay House, 1997.

Almeida, Rochelle. *Britain's Anglo-Indians: The Invisibility of Assimilation*. Lanham, MD: Lexington, 2017.

Altman, Michael J. *Hinduism in America: An Introduction*. New York: Routledge, 2022.

Ames, Walter. "Merle Oberon Will Star in TV Series on Foreign Legion." *Los Angeles Times*, April 1, 1956.

———. "Zsa Zsa Sputters Like a Model-T after Bolting Dinner for Ford." *Los Angeles Times*, November 3, 1959.

Amundson, William. "Merle Oberon Impressed by Caravan Tour Crowds." *Minneapolis Morning Tribune*, May 9, 1942.

Anderson, Christine. "At the Fashion Shows: Merle Oberon Shares Romantic Interval." *Knoxville* [TN] *News-Sentinel*, June 20, 1973.

"Anglo-Indians and Indo-Anglians." *Times of India*, September 18, 1983.

Anstey, Edgar. "The Cinema." *The Spectator*, February 18, 1944.

Archerd, Armand. "Merle Oberon Finds Surcease from Grief over Tragic End of Romance in Film Work." *Daily News-Journal* [Murfreesboro,TN], October 4, 1951.

Armstrong, C. F. ("Bede"). "Actress Merle Oberon, Husband Guests of Local Hotel Sunday." *Jackson* [TN] *Sun*, December 31, 1945.

Arnold, Gary. "The Art Didn't Imitate Life." *Washington Post*, November 27, 1973.

Ashland, Linda. "On Giving Yourself." *Town & Country*, December 1970.

Atkinson, Gord. "Gord Atkinson's Show Business." *Ottawa Citizen*, April 24, 1965.

"Australia Ducky for Expatriate Farmer." *Los Angeles Times*, June 6, 1971.

"Australian TV & Film Awards." *Variety*, October 18, 1978.

Bald, Vivek. *Bengali Harlem and the Lost Histories of South Asian America*. Cambridge: Harvard University Press, 2013.

Baldwin, James. *If Beale Street Could Talk*. London: Michael Joseph Ltd., 1974.

Barney, Bryan. "Canadian Weekly at the Movies." *The Gazette* [Montreal], October 12, 1963.

Bawden, James, and Ron Miller. *Conversations with Classic Film Stars: Interviews from Hollywood's Golden Era*. Lexington: University Press of Kentucky, 2016.

Baxter, John. *Von Sternberg*. Lexington: University Press of Kentucky, 2010.

Beale, Betty. "Life with the Pagliais." *San Francisco Examiner*, March 31, 1968.

"A Beauty Recipe." *Sydney Morning Herald*, September 1, 1963.

Bell, Nelson B. "The New Screen and Stage Bills in the Picture Houses Present a Fine Variety." *Washington Post*, March 24, 1935.

Berg, A. Scott. *Goldwyn: A Biography*. London: Hamish Hamilton, 1989.

Berry, Marilou. "A Beauty at any Age." *Evansville* [IN] *Press*, July 8, 1973.

Betjeman, John. "Merle Oberon Breaks Engagement." *London Evening Standard*, October 23, 1934.

Blinn, Johna. "Celebrity Cookbook: Merle Oberon's Specialty: Curry Stew." *Chicago Tribune*, June 28, 1973.

Blunt, Alison. *Domicile and Diaspora: Anglo-Indian Women and the Spatial Politics of Home*. Malden, MA: Blackwell, 2005.

Bogle, Donald. *Dorothy Dandridge: A Biography*. New York: Amistad, 1997.

Bona, Damien, and Mason Wiley. *Inside Oscar: The Unofficial History of the Academy Awards*. New York: Ballantine Books, 1986.

Borradaile, Osmond, with Anita Borradaile Hadley. *Life Through a Lens: Memoirs of a Cinematographer*. Montreal: McGill-Queen's University Press, 2001.

Boulevardier, The. "Reviews of the New Films." *Screen & Radio Weekly*, September 22, 1935.

Bourne, Stephen. *Elisabeth Welch: Soft Lights and Sweet Music*. Lanham, MD: Scarecrow Press, 2005.

Breen, Max. "Merle Oberon Takes Stock." *Picturegoer*, December 19, 1936.

Breese, Charlotte. *Hutch*. London: Bloomsbury, 1999.

Bristol, O. "One of the Greatest 'Finds' of the British Screen." *Picture Show*, November 17, 1934.

———. "Merle Oberon: Hollywood Has Made Her More English than Ever." *Picture Show*, November 16, 1935.

"A British Film Star Settles Down in California." *Tatler & Bystander*, January 28, 1942.

"British Films in the Making." *Film Weekly*, July 15, 1932.

"Broadway." *Variety*, March 8, 1967.

Brog. "Pardon My French." *Variety*, August 22, 1951.

Brossier, J. C. "Hush Puppies." *Orlando Sentinel*, October 25, 1960.

Broughton, Sarah. *Brando's Bride*. Cardigan, UK: Parthian, 2019.

Browning, Norma Lee. "Merle Doing War Dance over 'Tango'." *Chicago Tribune*, March 12, 1973.

Burn, Michael. *Mary and Richard: A True Story of Love and War*. New York: Arbor House, 1988.

Burton, Ron. "Film Shop." *Daily World* [Opelousas, LA], January 17, 1956.

"Buying & Booking Guide: INTERVAL (PG)." *Independent Film Journal*, June 25, 1973.

Cameron, Kate. "Film Star Has Unique Contract." *Daily News* [NY], December 20, 1936.

Carr, Harry. "The Lancer." *Los Angeles Times*, April 2, 1935.

Carroll, Harrison. "Star Yearns for England." *Border Cities' Star* [Windsor, ON], January 9, 1935.

———. "Behind the Scenes in Hollywood." *Evansville* [IN] *Courier*, May 21, 1938.

―――. "Behind the Scenes in Hollywood." *Vineland* [NJ] *Times*, December 9, 1940.

―――. "Behind the Scenes in Hollywood." *Lancaster* [OH] *Eagle-Gazette*, December 22, 1949.

―――. "Behind the Scenes in Hollywood." *Lancaster Eagle-Gazette*, March 29, 1950.

―――. "Behind the Scenes in Hollywood." *Lancaster Eagle-Gazette*, January 10, 1951.

Carson, James. "They're Not All Perfect!" *Modern Screen*, November 1940.

Charlton-Stevens, Uther. *Anglo-India and the End of Empire*. London: C. Hurst & Co. Ltd., 2022.

Chase, Chris. "Charming Album of a Film Family." *Chicago Tribune*, November 4, 1979.

"Chatter." *Variety*, January 27, 1937.

Chatterjee, Ranita. "Cinema in the Colonial City: Early Film Audiences in Calcutta." In *Audiences: Defining and Researching Screen Entertainment Reception*, edited by Ian Christie. Amsterdam: Amsterdam University Press, 2012.

―――. "Confessions of Indian Cinema's First Woman Superstar: Kanan Devi's Memoirs, Film History and Digital Archives." In *Indian Film Stars: New Critical Perspectives*, edited by Michael Lawrence. London: Bloomsbury, 2020.

Cheshire, Maxine. "Lynda Bird's Home for Mexican Visit Is Named 'To Love'." *Philadelphia Inquirer*, January 1, 1967.

Chibnall, Steve. *Quota Quickies: The Birth of the British "B" Film*. London: British Film Institute, 2007.

"Children Are to Enjoy." *Vogue*, August 15, 1963.

Chowdhry, Prem. *Colonial India and the Making of Empire Cinema: Image, Ideology and Identity*. Manchester, UK: Manchester University Press, 2000.

Christy, Marian. "Merle Oberon Making a Success of Marriage." *Boston Globe*, October 26, 1969.

―――. "Fashion Profile." *Boston Globe*, June 24, 1973.

Chute, Margaret. "Meet Miss Thompson." *Answers*, October 19, 1935.

Clifford, Terry. "Tell Us, Miss Oberon, What Brings You to Miami Beach This Time of Year?" *Chicago Tribune*, March 12, 1967.

Cloud, Barbara. "Love Story Screened Before Interview: Merle to Wed Young Co-star in February." *Pittsburgh Press*, June 24, 1973.

"Coach for Oberon." *Hollywood Reporter*, April 7, 1950.

Cohen, Harold V. "Hollywood." *Pittsburgh Post-Gazette*, July 11, 1945.

Cole, Beatrice Lubitz. "Inside Hollywood." *Movieland*, September 1948.

―――. "Inside Hollywood." *Movieland*, February 1949.

Collins, Amy Fine. "The Man Hollywood Trusted." *Vanity Fair*, April 2001.

"Coming Attractions." *Boston Globe*, December 7, 1933.

Connolly, Mike. "Hollywood." *Pittsburgh Post-Gazette*, April 26, 1957.

―――. "Rambling Reporter." *Hollywood Reporter*, September 14, 1960.

―――. "Best of Hollywood." *Philadelphia Inquirer*, December 5, 1963.

Coons, Robbin. "Hollywood Screen Life." *Poughkeepsie* [NY] *Eagle-News*, September 10, 1938.

―――. "Hollywood." *Daily News-Journal* [Murfreesboro, TN], January 16, 1941.

Coster, Ian. "Merle Oberon Under British Colours." *London Evening Standard*, January 8, 1938.

Cousins, E. G. "On the British Sets." *Picturegoer*, May 28, 1932.

———. " 'Extras' Get a Break." *Picturegoer*, June 18, 1932.

"Critics Pass Off 'Girl,' 'Temptation'." *Hollywood Reporter*, December 30, 1946.

"Crossword Puzzle." *Pittsburgh Post-Gazette*, April 23, 1973.

Crowther, Bosley. "About a Film Star Doing Her Bit." *New York Times*, October 8, 1939.

———. "Screen: Romantic Middle-Aged Men and Women." *New York Times*, September 12, 1963.

Curtis, Charlotte. "For Rich Nomads, Acapulco Is Siesta Time." *New York Times*, March 31, 1968.

Dahl, Arlene. "Pisceans' Secrets." *Morning Call*, March 14, 1970.

"Dale Carnegie Says." *Muncie* [IN] *Morning Star*, June 9, 1943.

Daly, Maggie. "Maggie Daly." *Chicago Tribune*, May 26, 1974.

———. "Season's Greetings to All the Ships at Sea." *Chicago Tribune*, November 26, 1979.

Datta-Ray, Sunanda. "Demise of a Gifted Minority." *South China Morning Post*, February 6, 1977.

———. "More than Skin-Deep." *Business Standard*, January 20, 2013.

Davé, Shilpa S. *Indian Accents: Brown Voice and Racial Performance in American Television and Film*. Urbana: University of Illinois Press, 2013.

Davies, Reine. "Stars Reminisce." *San Francisco Examiner*, June 30, 1935.

Davis, Nick. "Best Actress Update: 5 More Down, 90 to Go." *Nick's Flick Picks*, July 30, 2006.

de Mellow, Melville. "Letters: Living a Lie." *Times of India*, November 20, 1983.

de Pagliai, Merle Oberon. "Travel," *Vogue*, January 1, 1966.

———. "Cuernavaca, 'Eternal Springtime'." *Vogue*, January 15, 1967.

De Santis, Mallen. "Young and Beautiful into Your 40's and 50's." *Cosmopolitan*, January 1970.

de Toth, Andre. *Fragments: Portraits from the Inside*. London: Faber & Faber, 1994.

Delatiner, Barbara. "New Suspense Series Lays Real (Time) Bomb." *Newsday*, October 2, 1957.

Delofski, Maree. "Storytelling and Archival Material in 'The Trouble with Merle'." *The Moving Image*, Spring 2006.

Dillon, Niamh. *Homeward Bound: Return Migration from Ireland and India at the End of the British Empire*. New York: New York University Press, 2022.

" 'Divorce of Lady X' Scores as Smart English Comedy." *Hollywood Reporter*, January 18, 1938.

Dixon, Hugh. "Hollywood." *Pittsburgh Post-Gazette*, June 29, 1948.

Dixon, Wheeler Winston. *Film Noir and the Cinema of Paranoia*. Edinburgh: Edinburgh University Press, 2009.

Doherty, Thomas. *Hollywood's Censor: Joseph I. Breen & the Production Code Administration*. New York: Columbia University Press.

Donnelly, Antoinette. "Diet, Exercise, No Dessert, Formula for Easter Figure." *Daily News* [NY], February 23, 1942.

Drazin, Charles. *Korda: Britain's Movie Mogul*. London: Sidgwick & Jackson, 2002.

"Drops Suit." *Pittsburgh Post-Gazette*, March 12, 1940.

Ebert, Roger. " 'The Sunshine Boys' Are Still at It." *Boston Globe*, January 1, 1976.

Eder, Shirley. "Merle Oberon Always Had a Loyal Following." *Detroit Free Press*, November 27, 1979.

Eforgan, Estel. *Leslie Howard: The Lost Actor*. London: Vallentine Mitchell, 2010.

Eichelbaum, Stanley. "Glamor Still Attracts a Crowd," *San Francisco Examiner*, October 5, 1971.

Eisen, Cliff, and Dominic McHugh. *The Letters of Cole Porter*. New Haven: Yale University Press, 2019.

Ellenberger, Allan R. *Miriam Hopkins: Life and Films of a Hollywood Rebel*. Lexington: University Press of Kentucky, 2018.

"Emerald Green Floor Length Sheaths Popular at Fan Ball." *Women's Wear Daily*, November 15, 1954.

"English Actress Arrives." *Los Angeles Times*, November 25, 1934.

Epstein, Edward Z. *Audrey and Bill: A Romantic Biography of Audrey Hepburn and William Holden*. Philadelphia: Running Press, 2015.

"Everything's On the House at Stage Door Canteen." *Bergen* [NJ] *Evening Record*, April 24, 1942.

"Eye." *Women's Wear Daily*, January 8, 1974.

Fairbanks Jr., Douglas. *The Salad Days*. New York: Doubleday, 1988.

Fanning, Winn. " 'Desiree'." *Pittsburgh Post-Gazette*, November 19, 1954.

Farah, Ted. "Korda, Goldwyn Share Interest in Fair Oberon." *Calgary Daily Herald*, April 16, 1938.

Fidler, Jimmie. "Hard-hearted Director Cheers as Merle Oberon Is Stabbed in Back." *Minneapolis Star*, January 20, 1939.

———. "Jimmie Fidler in Hollywood." *Los Angeles Times*, May 8, 1940.

———. "Jimmie Fidler in Hollywood." *Los Angeles Times*, April 1, 1941.

———. "Jimmie Fidler in Hollywood." *Los Angeles Times*, April 12, 1941.

———. "Jimmie Fidler in Hollywood." *Indianapolis News*, August 1, 1944.

———. "In Hollywood." *Fort Myers News-Press*, August 20, 1948.

"Film Capital Mourns Korda." *Calgary Herald*, January 24, 1956.

"Film Reviews: Interval." *Variety*, June 20, 1973.

Fink, Frances. "Films Import World's Brightest Stars." *Washington Post*, January 13, 1935.

Finney, Ben. *Feet First*. New York: Crown, 1971.

"First British Colour Feature." *Kinematograph Weekly*, July 6, 1933.

"First Readers' Views of Latest Books, Fiction and Biography and News of the Radio." *Commercial Appeal* [Memphis, TN], February 7, 1937.

Forrest, Mark. "Cinema: Another Musical Spectacle." *Saturday Review*, March 16, 1935.

Freeman, Dave. "The TV Ticker." *Evening Press* [Binghamton, NY], October 22, 1962.

Gait, E. A. *Census of India, 1911, Vol. 1.* Calcutta: Office of the Superintendent of Government Printing, 1913.

Galligan, David. "Joan Rivers." *Advocate,* February 22, 1978.

Garrison, Maxine. "Merle Portrays Persian Princess, Role She Always Yearned to Play." *Pittsburgh Press,* March 11, 1945.

Gay, Charles. "Celebrities in Cameo: No. 71. Merle Oberon." *The Bystander,* October 9, 1934.

G. K. "Tin Mining Sets Stage for 'Old Hat'." *Los Angeles Times,* September 12, 1953.

Glover, William. "Homes Turned into Set for Film Return." *Austin* [TX] *American,* August 4, 1963.

Graham, Sheilah. "Merle Oberon Shudders at Desert Trip." *Hartford Courant,* March 14, 1936.

———. "Hard Luck Has Pursued Merle Oberon." *Hartford Courant,* July 14, 1937.

———. "Hollywood Today." *Atlanta Constitution,* October 1, 1937.

———. "Sheilah Graham in Hollywood." *Miami Daily News,* June 6, 1938.

———. "A Tip for Andrea Leeds—Tickle Joel McCrea's Ears!" *Minneapolis Tribune,* July 5, 1938.

———. "No Synthetic Love Affairs for Actress." *Calgary Herald,* March 25, 1939.

———. "Hollywood Today." *Hartford Courant,* January 24, 1941.

———. "Hollywood Today." *Hartford Courant,* February 7, 1941.

———. "Merle Oberon Forsakes Film Career to Do Part in Nation's War Effort." *Hartford Courant,* January 17, 1942.

———. "Actors Obtain Leave to Make British Movie." *Atlanta Constitution,* May 4, 1943.

———. "Hollywood News Flashes." *Cincinnati Enquirer,* November 5, 1944.

———. "Hollywood Today." *Asbury Park* [NJ] *Evening Press,* January 10, 1946.

———. "In Hollywood Today." *Indianapolis Star,* May 22, 1946.

———. "In Hollywood Today." *Indianapolis Star,* July 27, 1946.

———. "Hollywood Today: Movie Complexions Are 'World's Worst'." [Louisville, KY] *Courier-Journal,* December 8, 1946.

———. "Hollywood Today." *Indianapolis Star,* December 7, 1948.

———. "Demand Is Big for Jean Arthur." *Spokesman-Review* [Spokane, WA], December 20, 1948.

———. "Benny's Singers Doing All Right." *Spokesman-Review,* December 17, 1949.

———. "Appeals Flood Maureen O'Hara." *Spokesman-Review,* January 25, 1950.

———. "Hollywood." *Pittsburgh Post-Gazette,* March 21, 1950.

———. "Hollywood." *Pittsburgh Post-Gazette,* April 13, 1950.

———. "Miss Dru Seeks Change of Role." *Spokesman-Review,* April 15, 1950.

———. "Shirley Happy as Housewife." *Spokesman-Review,* January 6, 1951.

———. "Hollywood." *Pittsburgh Post-Gazette,* July 11, 1951.

———. "Brando Turns Down Role." *Miami Daily News,* March 12, 1956.

———. "Sheilah Graham in Hollywood." *Miami News,* July 19, 1960.

———. "Inside Hollywood." *Paterson* [NJ] *Evening News,* July 26, 1965.

———. "Hamilton Switches Locale, Will Now Film in New York." *Edmonton* [Alberta] *Journal,* August 26, 1966.

————. "Sheilah Graham." *Pittsburgh Press*, May 20, 1967.

Grandville, Grace. "Just a Little Outdoor Girl." *Democrat and Chronicle* [Rochester, NY], October 4, 1936.

Grant, Elspeth. "Films Films Films." *She*, April 1964.

Greenspun, Roger. "The Screen: An Almost Sublime 'Interval' Opens." *New York Times*, June 16, 1973.

Guild, Leo. "On the Air." *Hollywood Reporter*, March 18, 1957.

Haber, Joyce. "'Spangled Girl' Casting Completed." *Los Angeles Times*, April 21, 1971.

————. "Cambridge to Cut Out Fattening Films." *Los Angeles Times*, November 3, 1971.

————. "Disney Films for Misses Hayes, Rush." *Los Angeles Times*, September 27, 1972.

————. "Merle Oberon: Her Life, Her Loves." *Los Angeles Times*, June 10, 1973.

————. "Sculpture Makes Mike Swing into Auction." *Philadelphia Inquirer*, November 16, 1973.

————. "Rob and Merle's Best-Kept Secret." *Los Angeles Times*, February 4, 1975.

Hamilton, Sara. "Merle Oberon as Only Norma Knows Her." *Picturegoer*, November 7, 1936.

Hanauer, Joan. "Merle Oberon in Prime of Life." *Daily Defender* [Chicago], December 9, 1957.

Hardesty, Corinne. "No-Sugar-for-Duration Club Formed by Merle Oberon and Eddie Cantor." *Philadelphia Inquirer*, January 27, 1942.

Harker, Milton. "Glamor Gal Dunked in Dishabille State All for Art's Sake." *Austin* [TX] *Statesman*, February 8, 1939.

Harris, Mark. *Pictures at a Revolution*. New York: Penguin, 2008.

Harris, Radie. "Broadway Ballyhoo." *Hollywood Reporter*, September 7, 1978.

————. "Broadway Ballyhoo." *Hollywood Reporter*, November 29, 1979.

Harris, Warren G. *Clark Gable: A Biography*. New York: Three Rivers Press, 2002.

Harrison, Paul. "Behind Camera, Lubitsch Runs Gamut of Emotions." *Cincinnati Post*, December 6, 1940.

Hartt, Julian. "Star Plans to Meet Her Own 'Bride'." *Austin Statesman*, August 13, 1946.

Haskell, Molly. *From Reverence to Rape: The Treatment of Women in the Movies*. Baltimore: Penguin, 1974.

"Have We a Dusky Peril?" *Puget Sound American*, September 16, 1906.

"He's Done It Again." *Daily News* [NY], August 15, 1934.

"Heat Fells Actress in Western Thriller." *Pittsburgh Post-Gazette*, August 23, 1938.

Heffernan, Harold. "Hollywood Horizon." *Bergen* [NJ] *Evening Record*, August 28, 1943.

————. "In Hollywood Today." *Evening Citizen* [Ottawa, ON], June 24, 1946.

————. "Merle Oberon Returning." *Morning Call*, July 22, 1966.

Henderson, Wanda. "Confetti: A Visit with Merle." *Los Angeles Times*, August 12, 1962.

Henin, Shirley. "Actress Close to Fountain of Youth." *Arizona Republic*, July 11, 1963.

Henshaw, Laurie. "Here's One Musical We Could Have Scored First." *Picturegoer*, October 16, 1954.

Herman, Jan. *A Talent for Trouble: The Life of Hollywood's Most Acclaimed Director, William Wyler*. New York: G. P. Putnam's Sons, 1995.

Hischak, Thomas S. *1939: Hollywood's Greatest Year.* Lanham, MD: Rowman & Littlefield, 2017.

"Hollywood News." *New York Herald Tribune,* October 19, 1939.

Holmes, Edward H. "'Wuthering Heights' Well Cast." *Courier-Journal* [Louisville, KY], April 14, 1939.

Hopper, Hedda. "Hedda Hopper's Hollywood." *Los Angeles Times,* May 20, 1938.

———. "Hedda Hopper's Hollywood." *Los Angeles Times,* December 26, 1939.

———. "Looking at Hollywood." *Chicago Daily Tribune,* August 5, 1942.

———. "Hollywood." *Daily News* [NY], July 6, 1944.

———. "Star Broadway Bound." *Washington Post,* November 29, 1944.

———. "Looking at Hollywood." *Chicago Daily Tribune,* January 21, 1946.

———. "Merle the Merrier." *Chicago Daily Tribune,* August 18, 1946.

———. "Looking at Hollywood." *Chicago Daily Tribune,* April 9, 1948.

———. "Jane Russell, Bob Mitchum Will Co-Star." *Evansville* [IN] *Courier,* January 20, 1949.

———. "'Lend Me Your Ears' Planned in Rome; Sothern Is Thrilled at Royal Reception." *Miami Daily News,* December 16, 1949.

———. "Astaire to Make 'Belle of New York' with Romance Set in Chinatown." *Miami Daily News,* May 16, 1950.

———. "Looking at Hollywood." *Chicago Daily Tribune,* January 4, 1951.

———. "Hollywood." *Daily News* [NY], January 5, 1951.

———. "Gene Fowler Finds Skelton a Big Hit in London Palladium." *Chicago Daily Tribune,* July 12, 1951.

———. "Hollywood." *Daily News* [NY], September 21, 1953.

———. "Piersall Provides Basis Plan Baseball Story." *Pittsburgh Press,* September 8, 1955.

———. "Merle Comes Back." *Chicago Daily Tribune,* August 22, 1954.

———. "Looking at Hollywood." *Newark Advocate,* December 19, 1956.

———. "Looking at Hollywood." *Chicago Daily Tribune,* January 14, 1957.

———. "Merle Oberon Engaged to Mexico Industrialist." *Los Angeles Times,* February 6, 1957.

———. "Karloff Starts a New Frankenstein Film." *Chicago Daily Tribune,* January 9, 1958.

———. "Looking at Hollywood." *Chicago Daily Tribune,* August 22, 1959.

Huang, Yunte. *Daughter of the Dragon: Anna May Wong's Rendezvous with American History.* New York: Liveright, 2023.

Hulse, Jerry. "Mexico: That's the Way the Jet Sets." *Los Angeles Times,* April 20, 1969.

H. W. W. "'Ziegfeld Girl' Is Typical Metro-Goldwyn-Mayer Extravaganza." *The Gazette* [Montreal], May 24, 1941.

Hyacinth. "'Filmindia Is Different' Says Rose." *Filmindia,* November 1941.

"Inquiry Canceled on Merle Oberon." *Democrat and Chronicle* [Rochester, NY], August 6, 1941.

"Inside Hollywood." *Detroit Free Press,* December 13, 1959.

Jacobs, Jody. "Invitation to the Ball That Wasn't." *Los Angeles Times*, November 19, 1975.

———. "Casbah Chow for the Chips." *Los Angeles Times*, June 3, 1977.

———. "Diadames' Man of Mystery." *Los Angeles Times*, February 7, 1979.

———. "100 Ways to Make Money." *Los Angeles Times*, October 21, 1979.

Jarman, Derek. *Dancing Ledge*. London: Quartet, 1984.

Jenkins, Dan. "On the Air." *Hollywood Reporter*, February 16, 1953.

Johnson, Erskine. "'Living Legends League' Member Reports She Will Retire Soon." *Marshfield* [WI] *News-Herald*, August 27, 1951.

———. "Glamorous Merle Oberon Is Beaming over First Telefilm." *Marshfield News-Herald*, February 25, 1953.

———. "This Is Hollywood." *Times Recorder* [Marshfield, WI], April 18, 1957.

"Johnson in Hollywood." *Lancaster* [OH] *Eagle-Gazette*, June 21, 1946.

Jones, J. R. *The Lives of Robert Ryan*. Middletown, CT: Wesleyan University Press, 2015.

Jones, Welton. "Seat on the Aisle." *Shreveport* [LA] *Times*, January 10, 1964.

"Joseph Schenck Weds English Film Actress." *Austin* [TX] *Statesman*, August 8, 1934.

Kahn, Alexander. "At the Movies—Taking Bath in Public Not So Easy." *Knoxville* [TN] *News-Sentinel*, January 25, 1939.

Kauf [pseud.]. "Folies Bergere." *Variety*, February 27, 1935.

Keavy, Hubbard. "Merle Oberon Super-Charged with Ambition." *St. Petersburg Times*, December 23, 1934.

Kelly, Kevin. "Merle Oberon Acts Her Age." *Boston Globe*, July 14, 1973.

Kilgallen, Dorothy. "Broadway." *Mansfield* [OH] *News-Journal*, August 19, 1941.

———. "Broadway." *Pittsburgh Post-Gazette*, April 27, 1948.

———. "The Voice of Broadway." *Elmira* [NY] *Star-Gazette*, November 18, 1948.

———. "The Voice of Broadway." *Elmira Star-Gazette*, May 3, 1949.

———. "On Broadway." *Pittsburgh Post-Gazette*, September 26, 1949.

———. "On Broadway." *Pittsburgh Post-Gazette*, March 29, 1950.

———. "On Broadway." *Pittsburgh Post-Gazette*, July 19, 1951.

———. "Voice of Broadway." *Washington Post*, March 21, 1954.

Kilgore, Al, and Roi Frumkes. "Merle Oberon." *Films in Review*, February 1982.

Kirkland, Sally. "In a Swinging Resort, the Star Is Merle Oberon." *Life*, January 27, 1967.

Kissel, Howard. "Films: 'Interval'." *Women's Wear Daily*, June 15, 1973.

Knickerbocker, Cholly. "Gotham Society Hears Dan Toppings in Rift." *San Francisco Examiner*, September 12, 1948.

———. "The Smart Set." *Palm Beach Post*, September 17, 1948.

———. "Cholly Again Peers at Principals in Romances." *San Francisco Examiner*, January 2, 1949.

———. "Strange Warning Precedes Count Cini Plane Crash." *San Francisco Examiner*, September 9, 1949.

———. "Roulette Wheel Whirls Ali into the Red." *San Francisco Examiner*, September 17, 1949.

———. "Cholly Knickerbocker Observes." *San Francisco Examiner*, April 8, 1950.

———. "Cholly Knickerbocker Observes." *San Francisco Examiner*, April 28, 1950.

———. "Cholly Knickerbocker Observes." *San Francisco Examiner*, November 21, 1951.

———. "Greek Prince Likes 'Em Buxom." *Philadelphia Inquirer*, December 17, 1957.

Korda, Michael. *Charmed Lives: A Family Romance*. New York: Random House, 1979.

———. *Another Life: A Memoir of Other People*. New York: Random House, 1999.

"Korda Passes Up Oberon in Will." *Palm Beach Post*, May 19, 1956.

"Korda Surprised about Knighting." *Austin* [TX] *Statesman*, June 12, 1942.

Kosover, Toni. "Focus: Charles Revson On Women." *Women's Wear Daily*, March 12, 1971.

Kulik, Karol. *Alexander Korda: The Man Who Could Work Miracles*. London: W. H. Allen, 1975.

Lambert, Eleanor. "Why We All Watch Merle." *San Francisco Examiner*, June 4, 1968.

Lambert, Gavin. *Norma Shearer: A Life*. New York: Knopf, 1990.

Lane, Lydia. "Being in the Swim May Drown You." *Los Angeles Times*, April 8, 1956.

Laurent, Lawrence. "It's the Same Old Woolley, But Not the Same Old 'Man'." *Washington Post*, October 15, 1954.

Lawrence, Michael. *Sabu*. London: Palgrave Macmillan, 2014.

Lee, Anna, with Barbara Roisman Cooper. *Anna Lee: Memoir of a Career on General Hospital and in Film*. Jefferson, NC: McFarland, 2007.

Lee, Erika. *The Making of Asian America: A History*. New York: Simon & Schuster, 2015.

Lewis, Dan. "Oberon Shrieks in Rage." *Morning Call*, January 23, 1967.

"Living in Mexico." *Town & Country*, July 1959.

Liza. "Merle's Studio Romance." *Screenland*, November 1945.

Loder, John. "I Don't Want to Be a Star." *Picturegoer*, June 16, 1934.

———. *Hollywood Hussar: The Life and Times of John Loder*. London: Howard Baker, 1977.

Lonergan, Phil. "Janet Gaynor's Future." *Picturegoer*, August 31, 1935.

Long, Trish. " 'Quickie' Juárez Divorces Ended in 1970." *El Paso Times*, August 3, 2017.

Lord, Graham. *Niv: The Authorized Biography of David Niven*. Waterville, ME: Thorndike, 2003.

"Love Is Ageless." *Pittsburgh Press*, November 15, 1973.

"Love Is a Spirit." *Detroit Free Press*, January 21, 1950.

"Love or Career?" *San Francisco Examiner*, November 23, 1934.

"Lucky Merle." *Pittsburgh Press*, October 31, 1945.

Lyons, Leonard. "The Lyons Den." *Pittsburgh Post-Gazette*, May 10, 1951.

———. "Gossip of the Nation." *Philadelphia Inquirer*, August 20, 1953.

———. "In The Lyons Den." *Morning Call*, December 6, 1961.

MacPherson, Tom. "Radio Chart Listening Post." *Ithaca* [NY] *Journal*, February 7, 1942.

MacPherson, Virginia. "Oberon Packs and Plans Long Vacation with Play." *Indianapolis Star*, August 18, 1946.

Malcolm, Derek. "Cosmo Sees the Films." *Cosmopolitan*, November 1973.

Mander, Miles. "To Hell with Acting." *Hollywood Reporter*, December 31, 1937.

Mank, Gregory William. *Women in Horror Films, 1940s*. Jefferson, NC: McFarland, 1999.

Mankiewicz, Tom, and Robert Crane. *My Life as a Mankiewicz: An Insider's Journey Through Hollywood*. Lexington: University Press of Kentucky, 2012.

Mann, Roderick. "Beautiful Merle Oberon Can Easily Face Her Mirrors," *Albuquerque Tribune*, June 6, 1969.

———. "A Noted Hostess, but 'Parties Bore Me'." *San Francisco Examiner*, February 23, 1973.

Manners, Dorothy. "Frank Buck Plans New Animal Film in British Deal." *Evening Courier* [Camden, NJ], July 2, 1948.

———. "Defore Seeks Robinson for Baseball Film." *Philadelphia Inquirer*, September 5, 1949.

———. "Jackie Robinson Baseball Career Will Be Screened." *San Francisco Examiner*, September 5, 1949.

———. "Pidgeon Gets British Blonde as Co-Star." *Philadelphia Inquirer*, August 2, 1950.

———. "Merle's Gem Guardian." *San Francisco Examiner*, July 23, 1966.

———. "Silly Gossip about Eddie." *San Francisco Examiner*, August 21, 1967.

———. "Minnelli Leaves New Oberon Film." *Indianapolis Star*, January 19, 1972.

Mariaux, Hermine. "Romance with Acapulco." *Town & Country*, February 1967.

Marsden, George. "London Entertainment." *Country Life*, January 21, 1939.

Marsh, Margaret, and Wanda Ronner. *The Fertility Doctor: John Rock and the Reproductive Revolution*. Baltimore: Johns Hopkins University Press, 2008.

Martin, Boyd. "Merle Oberon Captures Honors in Romantic 'Til We Meet Again'." *Courier-Journal* [Louisville, KY], May 4, 1940.

Mason, Jerry. "Merle for Morale." *Sun*, July 11, 1943.

Maxwell, Elsa. "Ill-Fated Love Story." *Photoplay*, May 1950.

Mayne, Judith. *Directed by Dorothy Arzner*. Bloomington: Indiana University Press, 1994.

McFarlane, Brian. *Real and Reel: The Education of a Film Critic*. Manchester, UK: Manchester University Press, 2012.

McHarry, Charles. "On the Town." *Daily News* [NY], December 28, 1972.

McLaughlin, Loretta. *The Pill, John Rock, and the Church: The Biography of a Revolution*. Boston: Little, Brown, 1982.

McWhirter, Nickie. "Overnight, Front and Rear Just Go Pop! Pop! Pop!" *Detroit Free Press*, May 21, 1978.

M. D. "Danger–Actresses at Work." *Answers*, July 23, 1949.

"Merle and Miriam Aren't Afraid of Scene-Stealers." *Philadelphia Inquirer*, April 5, 1936.

"Merle Escapes Ellis Island Trip." *Daily News* [NY], August 6, 1941.

"Merle Oberon Feels a Duty to Look Young." *San Francisco Examiner*, July 15, 1966.

"Merle Has Short Lease on Tan." *Pittsburgh Press*, April 21, 1943.

"Merle Oberon Acquires Ranch near Escondido." *Los Angeles Times*, June 3, 1945.

"Merle Oberon Back in England." *Observer* [London], November 15, 1936.

"Merle Oberon Claims £25,000 Damages." *London Evening Standard*, April 15, 1936.

"Merle Oberon Dead." *Advocate* [Newark, OH], November 24, 1979.

"Merle Oberon Denies Romance." *Los Angeles Times*, May 9, 1938.

"Merle Oberon Ill, So Alien Hearing Waits." *Daily News* [NY], August 5, 1941.

"Merle Oberon Hides Scars of Auto Accident." *Washington Post*, July 4, 1937.

"Merle Oberon Is Considered Filmland's Most Successful Guinea Pig." *State Journal* [Frankfort, KY], July 2, 1941.

"Merle Oberon Makes First Comedy Role." *Journal–Every Evening* [Wilmington, DE], March 31, 1938.

"Merle Oberon Marries in Rome." *Daily News* [NY], July 29, 1957.

"Merle Oberon, Noted Film Beauty, Veteran of 40-Year Screen Career." *Asbury Park* [NJ] *Press*, November 24, 1979.

"Merle Oberon On Way." *Hollywood Reporter*, November 22, 1934.

"Merle Returns." *Detroit Free Press*, July 20, 1966.

"Merle Oberon Says Taxes Take 90% of Her Income." *Hartford Courant*, November 17, 1938.

"Merle Oberon Secretly Wed to Actor, 38." *Globe and Mail* [Toronto], February 5, 1975.

"Merle Oberon Sees Friend and Pilot Die in Plane Crash." *Chicago Daily Tribune*, September 1, 1949.

"Merle Oberon Sees Friend, Count Cini, Killed in Crash at French Airport." *Courier-Journal* [Louisville, KY], September 1, 1949.

"Merle Oberon's First and Final Pic Prod." *Variety*, May 16, 1973.

"Merle Oberon's Mexico." *San Francisco Examiner*, July 15, 1962.

"Merle Oberon's Split Personality." *Atlanta Constitution*, January 10, 1937.

"Merle Oberon TV Debut." *Hollywood Reporter*, February 11, 1953.

"Merle Oberon Wants to Appear Only in War Films for Duration." *Philadelphia Inquirer*, August 22, 1943.

"Merle Oberon Watches as Plane Strikes Tree, Killing Two Friends." *Pittsburgh Press*, August 31, 1949.

Merrick, Mollie. "Tom Moore in Films Again." *Spokesman-Review* [Spokane, WA], April 6, 1935.

———. "Coolie Cloth Popular for Sports Wear." *Hartford Courant*, June 10, 1935.

"Mexican Fiesta Attends Preem of Hilton's Latest." *Variety*, December 12, 1956.

Meyer, Richard E. "Merle Oberon Suffers Stroke, Is in Coma." *Los Angeles Times*, November 23, 1979.

Miller, Gabriel. *William Wyler: The Life and Films of Hollywood's Most Celebrated Director.* Lexington: University Press of Kentucky, 2013.

Miller, Jeanne. "Merle—'A Woman Should Look Better with Age'." *San Francisco Examiner*, September 16, 1966.

"Miss Oberon Ends Some Old Illusions." *Sydney* [Australia] *Morning Herald*, January 19, 1965.

"Miss Oberon Sees Count Die in Plane." *Washington Post*, September 1, 1949.

"Miss Oberon Sues Studio." *Los Angeles Times*, April 15, 1936.

"Miss Oberon Will Star on GE Show." *Orlando Sentinel*, April 28, 1957.

Moffitt, Jack. "'Deep in My Heart' Is Top Musical with Big B.O. Draw." *Hollywood Reporter*, December 1, 1954.

———. "'Emergency Hospital' Good; 'Price of Fear' Misses Mark." *Hollywood Reporter*, March 20, 1956.

Monahan, Kaspar. "Marilyn and Gwen Vie for Attention." *Pittsburgh Press*, July 10, 1955.

"Money and Talent Aid British Film Industry." *State Journal* [Frankfort, KY], November 15, 1934.

"'Moon' Lags Oberon by Daily Rewriting." *Hollywood Reporter*, February 19, 1938.

Moore, Gloria Jean. *The Anglo-Indian Vision*. Melbourne: AE Press, 1986.

Mooring, Wm. H. "British Public Still Not Serious on Home Product, Poll Shows." *Motion Picture Herald*, May 14, 1932.

Morehouse, Rebecca. "Older Woman, Younger Man: Life Imitating Art for Couple." *Sun*, June 20, 1973.

Morley, Sheridan. *The Other Side of the Moon: The Life of David Niven*. New York: Harper & Row, 1985.

Morse, Leon. "Pilot Review." *Billboard*, December 1, 1956.

"Movie-Go-'Round." *San Francisco Examiner*, February 18, 1940.

"Mrs. Bruno Pagliai at Home." *Vogue*, November 15, 1965.

"Mrs. Constance Thompson." *New York Herald Tribune*, April 24, 1937.

Munn, Michael. *David Niven: The Man Behind the Balloon*. London: JR Books, 2010.

Murugan, Meenasarani Linde. "'Turbans Do Things for You.'" In *Our Stories: An Introduction to South Asian America*. Philadelphia: South Asian American Digital Archive (SAADA), 2021.

"My Pet Beauty Secret." *Cosmopolitan*, October 1971.

Nadel, Gerry. "The Ball Game." *Women's Wear Daily*, September 10, 1974.

Nadelhoffer, Hans. *Cartier*. San Francisco: Chronicle, 2007.

Nangle, Eleanor. "Through the Looking Glass." *Chicago Daily Tribune*, July 28, 1935.

Nepean, Edith. "Round the British Studios." *Picture Show*, October 8, 1932.

———. "Round the British Studios." *Picture Show*, November 19, 1932.

———. "My Friends in British Studios." *Picture Show*, December 18, 1937.

"New Films." *Daily Boston Globe*, March 9, 1935.

"New Merle Oberon in 'Dark Angel'." *Daily Clarion-Ledger* [Jackson, MS], October 23, 1935.

"News of the Screen." *New York Times*, June 10, 1936.

"Newsmakers." *Newsweek*, October 21, 1963.

"The News Reel." *Boy's Cinema*, December 28, 1935.

Niemeyer, H. H. "Tasmania's Gift to Movies." *St. Louis Post-Dispatch*, February 9, 1940.

Niven, David. *The Moon's a Balloon*. London: Hamish Hamilton, 1971.

Nollen, Scott Allen, with Yuyun Yuningsih Nollen. *Karloff and the East: Asian, Indian, Middle Eastern and Oceanian Characters and Subjects in His Screen Career*. Jefferson, NC: McFarland, 2021.

Norris, H. C. "Merle Oberon Vividly Tells of Her Knight Fright as Husband Was Called Before King." *Philadelphia Inquirer*, March 28, 1943.

O'Brian, Jack. "Voice of Broadway." *Asbury Park* [NJ] *Evening Press*, March 29, 1973.

"Oberon Planning to Marry." *Leader Post* [Regina, SK], November 17, 1973.

"Oberon's Ankle Hurt on 'Heights' Location." *Hollywood Reporter*, December 9, 1938.

"Oberon's Gold Cosmetic." *Journal–Every Evening* [Wilmington, DE], April 4, 1935.

"Oberon Stars in and Directs 'Interval'." *Miami News*, June 11, 1973.

Oberon, Merle. "Merle Oberon's Discovery, Theme in Four Variations." *Pittsburgh Post-Gazette*, March 19, 1935.

———. "The Debts I Owe." *Picturegoer*, October 5, 1935.

———. "My Next Door Neighbors." *Atlanta Constitution*, March 29, 1936.

"Offers for British Stars." *Daily Film Renter*, November 2, 1933.

"Old South Is Theme of 'So Red the Rose'." *Tampa Morning Tribune*, December 22, 1935.

Olis, Ruth. "People-Watching Is a Change of Pace." *Courier-Post* [Cherry Hill, NJ], July 11, 1967.

"On Fashion." *Los Angeles Times*, March 11, 1976.

"On Worldwide News Front." *Minneapolis Star*, April 21, 1949.

Orme, Michael. "Criticisms in Cameo: The Cinema." *The Sketch*, April 18, 1934.

———. "Criticisms in Cameo." *The Sketch*, January 19, 1938.

Osborne, Robert. "Rites Wednesday at All Saints for Merle Oberon." *Hollywood Reporter*, November 26, 1979.

———. "Merle Oberon: A Touch of Class." *Los Angeles Times*, December 9, 1979.

Otterburn-Hall, William. "The World of Stars." *Saskatoon StarPhoenix*, April 7, 1973.

Pantages, Lloyd. "Grace Moore's London Triumph Indication of Star's Hold upon Public Affection Everywhere." *San Francisco Examiner*, June 19, 1935.

Paris, Barry. *Audrey Hepburn*. New York: G. P. Putnam's Sons, 1996.

Parish, James Robert. *The Glamour Girls*. New Rochelle, NY: Arlington House, 1975.

Parker, Jerry. "Merle Oberon: Taking the Script to Heart." *Newsday*, June 24, 1973.

———. "Archaeological Melodrama." *Newsday*, June 15, 1973.

Parry, Florence Fisher. "I Dare Say—Success Is More than Skin Deep." *Pittsburgh Press*, May 20, 1935.

———. "'I'm Gold Prospector,' Says Samuel Goldwyn." *Pittsburgh Press*, September 15, 1935.

Parsons, Louella O. "Merle Oberon Will Play Opposite M. Chevalier in 'Folies Bergere de Paris'." *San Francisco Examiner*, September 29, 1934.

———. "Helen Gahagan Cast for Opera and Lyda Roberti in 'Scandals'; Snapshots of Hollywood Folk." *Philadelphia Inquirer*, October 16, 1934.

———. "Introducing!" *Cincinnati Enquirer*, December 9, 1934.

———. "Merle Oberon Is Likeable." *San Francisco Examiner*, December 9, 1934.

———. "Movie-Go-'Round." *San Francisco Examiner*, September 8, 1935.

———. "'Mr. and Mrs. Washington' to Be Filmed! Rupert Hughes Doing Story for M-G-M." *San Francisco Examiner*, April 3, 1936.

———. "Carole Lombard, Recovering, Will Be Star in 'Swing High, Swing Low'." *San Francisco Examiner*, June 29, 1936.

———. "'Shanghai Deadline' Will Star Sanders." *San Francisco Examiner*, October 13, 1937.

———. "Movie-Go-'Round." *San Francisco Examiner*, May 22, 1938.

———. "3d Steinbeck Story Bought for Screen." *Philadelphia Inquirer*, April 9, 1940.

————. "Merle Oberon Now Almost All Well." *Philadelphia Inquirer*, July 9, 1940.

————. "Ruby Keeler Signs for 'Betty Co-ed'." *Philadelphia Inquirer*, January 1, 1941.

————. "Merle, as Producer's Wife, Worries about Expenses Now." *Philadelphia Inquirer*, May 4, 1941.

————. "Republic Has Role for Miriam Hopkins." *Philadelphia Inquirer*, June 5, 1941.

————. "Merle Oberon Pays Back a Favor by Offering Service to Defense." *Atlanta Constitution*, January 6, 1942.

————. "Lana Turner Boasts Too Much Glamor for Typical American Girl." *Atlanta Constitution*, October 7, 1942.

————. "Show Is Arranged for Mickey Rooney, Also MGM Movies." *Courier-Post* [Cherry Hill, NJ], June 11, 1945.

————. "Merle Oberon Relinquished Title and Wealth for Love." *Philadelphia Inquirer*, July 29, 1945.

————. "Hollywood." *Philadelphia Inquirer*, December 15, 1945.

————. "Goldwyn Buys Original Story by Clare Luce." *San Francisco Examiner*, November 29, 1948.

————. "Merle Oberon in Paris." *San Francisco Examiner*, February 14, 1949.

————. "Merle Oberon Has Operation for Removal of Facial Scars." *San Francisco Examiner*, June 27, 1949.

————. "'Father of the Bride' Has Made Tracy One of MGM's Top Drawing Cards." *Albuquerque Journal*, August 1, 1950.

————. "Louella Parsons in Hollywood." *Courier-Post* [Cherry Hill, NJ], January 25, 1951.

————. "Modesty Wins Good Roles for Widmark." *Philadelphia Inquirer*, April 5, 1951.

————. "Hollywood Today." *Arizona Republic*, January 11, 1952.

————. "Hollywood Today." *Arizona Republic*, December 26, 1952.

————. "Monday Morning Gossip of the Nation." *Philadelphia Inquirer*, February 16, 1953.

————. "Merle Oberon Plans TV Series in London." *Philadelphia Inquirer*, January 10, 1956.

————. "Louella's Movie-Go-'Round." *Albuquerque Journal*, January 21, 1957.

————. "Hollywood Today." *Arizona Republic*, December 6, 1957.

————. "Douglas Third Star in New Wilder Film." *Bergen* [NJ] *Evening Record*, August 17, 1959.

————. "Retirement Suits Merle Oberon." *San Francisco Examiner*, December 12, 1959.

————. "Goetz Gets Remarque's Novel, 'Borrowed Time,' for New Film." *The Record* [Bergen, NJ], September 28, 1960.

————. "Joanie Benny in TV Bow." *San Francisco Examiner*, April 8, 1961.

————. "Merle Oberon to Return to Screen." *San Francisco Examiner*, December 19, 1961.

————. "Merle Oberon: First Film in Seven Years." *San Francisco Examiner*, August 26, 1962.

————. "Zanuck Buys Oberon Film." *San Francisco Examiner*, April 8, 1963.

Patel, Baburao. "Korda's Libel on India." *Filmindia*, October 1938.

Patrick, Corbin. "Merle Oberon Reaches Hollywood by Way of Tasmania, India, England." *Indianapolis Star*, March 7, 1935.

Peak, Mayme Ober. "Hollywood Is Asking: When Will Merle Oberon and David Niven Wed?" *Daily Boston Globe*, October 12, 1936.

Percy, Eileen. "Montgomery Is Becoming Busiest Actor in Hollywood." *Pittsburgh Post-Gazette*, March 13, 1936.

"Personal Appearances: Tasmania's Wrest Point Casino to Stage Plush Dinner-Theatre Prods." *Variety*, March 20, 1974.

Petty, Miriam J. *Stealing the Show: African American Performers and Audiences in 1930s Hollywood*. Oakland: University of California Press, 2016.

Phillips, Malcolm D. "The Customer Talks Back." *Picturegoer*, July 3, 1937.

"Playboy Italian Count May Wed Merle Oberon." *Los Angeles Times*, February 18, 1949.

"The Pleasure of Your Company Is Requested at a Series of Interviews with Today's Leading International Hostesses." *Town & Country*, May 1965.

"Polling the Newsmakers on 1974." *Los Angeles Times*, January 1, 1974.

Porter, Darwin. *Brando Unzipped*. New York: Blood Moon, 2005.

Prescott, J. Oliver. "Don't Get Caught in This Interval." *St. Petersburg Times*, August 14, 1973.

"Pre-Views of the Latest Films: An Anglo-French Triumph." *Picturegoer*, May 5, 1934.

"Prices Soaring for Film Names; Seen Curbing Coast Telepix Pacts." *Variety*, April 8, 1953.

Provines, June. "Front Views and Profiles." *Chicago Daily Tribune*, October 6, 1939.

Prowler, Paul. "Can Merle Get Her Count?" *National Police Gazette*, June 1, 1949.

Pusey, Grace. "Today in History: Luce-Celler Act Signed in 1946." South Asian American Digital Archive (SAADA), July 2, 2014.

Pybus, Cassandra. *Till Apples Grow on an Orange Tree*. St. Lucia, Australia: University of Queensland Press, 1998.

"Q and A Session with Merle, Rex." *Los Angeles Times*, October 12, 1971.

Ragan, David. "Dark Secrets of a Great Star." *South China Morning Post*, October 31, 1982.

"Rambling Reporter." *Hollywood Reporter*, November 26, 1934.

———. July 8, 1935.

———. February 16, 1940.

Reed, Rex. "Ageless Merle Oberon Starts Anew, Again." *Courier-Journal* [Louisville, KY], June 24, 1973.

Reeve, Warren. "The Exclusive Inside Story of Merle Oberon's $123,000 Damage Suit." *Photoplay*, July 1936.

Reyburn, Wallace. "The Queen and Duke Play a Game of Spotting the Television Birdie." *Courier-Journal* [Louisville, KY], July 4, 1953.

Reynolds, Ruth. "They Aren't as Nature Made 'Em." *Daily News* [NY], May 5, 1935.

Richards, Jeffrey. *The Age of the Dream Palace: Cinema and Society in Britain 1930–1939*. London: Routledge & Kegan Paul, 1984.

Richardson, Maurice. "Electra Rocks the Box." *Observer* [UK], December 2, 1962.

Riva, Maria. *Marlene Dietrich*. New York: Knopf, 1992.

R. L. "POSTSCRIPTS." *Jerusalem Post*, January 30, 1977.

Robin, Christofer. "In Flicker Land." *Minneapolis Star*, February 10, 1937.

Rol, Franco. *The Unbelievable Gustavo Adolfo Rol*. Morrisville, NC: Lulu Press, 2014.

Sabretache. "Pictures in the Fire." *Tatler*, October 9, 1935.

"Sabu Is Admitted to U.S. Citizenship." *Washington Post*, January 5, 1944.

Saltzman, Barbara. "Merle Oberon: Looking Back." *Los Angeles Times*, October 2, 1979.

"Samuel Goldwyn Inaugurates the 1935–36 Season with 'The Dark Angel'." *Los Angeles Times*, September 13, 1935.

Savoy, Maggie. "In Two Lands." *Los Angeles Times*, March 2, 1969.

Sayers, Elliseva. "I Meet Merle Oberon." *Answers*, September 9, 1939.

Schallert, Edwin. "'Henry VIII' Rated Picture of Quality." *Los Angeles Times*, November 24, 1933.

———. "Merle Oberon Reported Choice for Interpretation of Florence Nightingale." *Los Angeles Times*, December 30, 1935.

———. "Forecast of Academy Awards Made by Times Drama Editor." *Los Angeles Times*, January 16, 1955.

———. "Korda Started Many on Way to Film Fame." *Los Angeles Times*, January 24, 1956.

Schatz, Thomas. *The Genius of the System: Hollywood Filmmaking in the Studio Era*. New York: Pantheon, 1989.

"Schenck Is Playing 'Fixer' to Pickford and Fairbanks." *Evansville* [IN] *Courier*, September 2, 1934.

"Schenck So Loves Merle Oberon Tries to Patch Up Doug's Affair." *Toronto Daily Star*, August 8, 1934.

Scheuer, Philip K. "Intriguing 'Myths' about Merle Oberon All Exploded." *Los Angeles Times*, December 30, 1934.

———. "Merle in Films to Fulfill Dream." *Los Angeles Times*, July 10, 1966.

Schroeder, Mildred. "Still Glamorous after 50." *San Francisco Examiner*, September 4, 1963.

Schultz, Ellie. "Fashion Folio: Self-Identification Result of Impromptu Make-over." *Arizona Republic*, August 7, 1973.

Scott, Verno. "Merle Makes a Movie." *Courier-Post* [Cherry Hill, NJ], June 11, 1973.

Scott, Walter. "Walter Scott's Personality Parade." *Detroit Free Press*, October 20, 1963.

———. "Walter Scott's Personality Parade." *Asheville* [NC] *Citizen*, March 23, 1975.

———. "Walter Scott's Personality Parade." *Albuquerque Journal*, April 30, 1978.

"Screen: Movie Stars Will Be Swapped Across the Atlantic." *Newsweek*, September 1, 1934.

"Screen Star's Driver Owes Her $25,000." *Pittsburgh Post-Gazette*, May 5, 1938.

Sennwald, Andre. "The Screen." *New York Times*, September 6, 1935.

Shaffer, George. "Friends Greet Cagney as He Renews Career." *Chicago Daily Tribune*, November 2, 1936.

Shaffer, Rosalind. "Meet Merle Oberon, Film Find of Year." *Chicago Daily Tribune*, March 31, 1935.

Shakespeare, Nicholas. *In Tasmania: Adventures at the End of the World*. London: Harvill Press, 2004.

Sharpley, Anne. " 'Tell Me How to Be a Reporter,' said Merle Oberon." *London Evening Standard*, April 7, 1956.

"She Lost Her Head to Get Head Start." *San Francisco Examiner*, September 14, 1965.

Sheppard, Eugenia. "Moving Day for Merle Oberon—Into Four Houses." *Gazette* [Montreal], October 27, 1965.

———. "Woman Dominates Film's Production." *Austin Statesman*, January 10, 1973.

———. "Sister Team Has California Show." *Shreveport Times*, May 20, 1979.

Sherwood, Lydia E. "Alexander Korda: Man of Destiny." *Vogue*, September 1, 1936.

Shogan, Robert. "Reagan Takes Big Step Toward 1980 Race." *Los Angeles Times*, March 8, 1979.

"Shoot Around Oberon." *Hollywood Reporter*, December 24, 1938.

"Sidelights on Stars." *Tatler*, August 15, 1934.

Silver, Alain. "André de Toth (1913–2002)—An Interview." *Senses of Cinema*, March 2003.

Skolsky, Sidney. "Hollywood." *Daily News* [NY], November 26, 1934.

———. "Tintypes," *Daily News*, November 28, 1934.

———. "Tintypes." *Daily News*, April 9, 1935.

———. "Hollywood." *Daily News*, June 26, 1935.

———. "Hollywood." *Daily News*, July 13, 1935.

———. "Skolsky's Hollywood." *Cincinnati Enquirer*, June 26, 1942.

———. "Skolsky's Hollywood." *Cincinnati Enquirer*, February 15, 1943.

"Sleeping, Waking, Supping: The Private Life of Merle Oberon in Three Shots." *The Bystander*, October 2, 1934.

Sloan, Robin Adams. "The Gossip Column." *News Journal*, July 17, 1973.

Smith, Liz. "Those Who Take Beauty Seriously." *Daily News*, November 20, 1978.

Spurgeon, Jamie Sue. "Begin by Evolving Your Total Personality." *Cincinnati Enquirer*, April 18, 1973.

"Star Leaves Hospital." *Daily News*, April 25, 1937.

"Star Yearns for England." *Border Cities' Star* [Windsor, ON], January 9, 1935.

"Stars Crowd Rites for Merle Oberon." *Boston Globe*, November 29, 1979.

Strachan, Alan. *Dark Star: A Biography of Vivien Leigh*. London: I. B. Tauris, 2019.

Sullivan, Ed. "Broadway." *Daily News*, May 15, 1936.

"A Surprise for Merle." *Modern Screen*, May 1957.

Suzy. "Oberon's Abode." *Chicago Tribune*, July 11, 1972.

———. "Merle and Bruno Part." *Daily News* [NY], March 11, 1973.

———. "A Capital Couple!" *Chicago Tribune*, November 7, 1973.

———. "Hip, Hip, Beret!" *Daily News* [NY], April 24, 1974.

Sweeny, Charles, with Colonel James A. Goodson. *Sweeny*. Canterbury, UK: Wingham Press, 1990.

Swiderski, Richard M. *Quicksilver: A History of the Use, Lore and Effects of Mercury*. Jefferson, NC: McFarland, 2006.

Taraborrelli, J. Randy. *The Secret Life of Marilyn Monroe*. New York: Grand Central Publishing, 2009.

Tabori, Paul. *Alexander Korda*. London: Oldbourne, 1959.

Talezaar, Marguerite. "'Anything Behind That Face?' Merle Oberon Proved There Was." *New York Herald Tribune*, February 3, 1935.

Taves, Isabella. "Writer Explodes Many Myths about Louella Parsons." *San Francisco Examiner*, October 8, 1950.

"Television Chatter." *Variety*, March 12, 1952.

"That Uncertain Feeling." *Sun*, April 26, 1941.

"The Far East Influence." *Harper's Bazaar,* January 1954.

"The Most Promising Player in the World." *The Sketch*, December 13, 1933.

"The Scarlet Pimpernel." *Kinematograph Weekly*, December 27, 1934.

"The Turban Winds Up with Fame." *Vogue*, May 1939.

Thomas, Bob. "Swinging Film Cycle to Less Costly Output." *Daily Advertiser* [Lafayette, LA], June 5, 1947.

———. "Hollywood Notes." *Asbury Park* [NJ] *Evening Press*, September 26, 1947.

———. "Health of Bette Davis to Determine Next Film." *Alexandria* [VA] *Daily Town Talk*, November 26, 1947.

———. "Merle Oberon Making Comeback." *St. Louis Post-Dispatch*, July 22, 1962.

———. "Movie Stars Changing Life Style." *Marion* [OH] *Star*, April 2, 1971.

———. "Even Glamorous Entertainers Are Slaves to Rigorous Diets." *Morning Call*, October 1, 1973.

Thomas, Kevin. "Actor Turned Director Is No Longer a Rarity." *Des Moines Register*, August 29, 1966.

———. "'Queenie' and the Novel Fact of Oberon's Fiction." *Los Angeles Times*, May 31, 1985.

Thomson, David. *The New Biographical Dictionary of Film*. New York: Knopf, 2002.

"Town Topics." *The Bystander*, November 8, 1933.

Tremayne, Sydney. "The Passing Picture Show." *The Bystander*, April 17, 1934.

———. "Films of the Day." *The Bystander*, March 20, 1935.

———. "Films of the Day." *The Bystander*, October 9, 1935.

"Trio Stars in Gripping Love Story Offered on Fox Screen." *Arizona Republic*, September 15, 1935.

Truesdell, John. "In Hollywood." *Des Moines Register*, October 12, 1942.

Turner, Grace. "Thursday-Night Specials." *Cincinnati Enquirer*, September 7, 1941.

"Turnstyle: Who's Who Among Schiaparelli Clients." *Women's Wear Daily*, February 2, 1934.

"TV Behind the Scenes Gets More Like Movies." *Birmingham Post-Herald*, October 25, 1954.

Twiggar, Beth. "A Stage Role, and No Retakes, Gives Chills to Hollywood Star." *New York Herald Tribune*, September 14, 1941.

"Two Dogs for Sale." *Bergen* [NJ] *Evening Record*, June 11, 1938.

Underwood, Peter. *Death in Hollywood*. London: Judy Piatkus Ltd., 1992.

Vieira, Mark A. *Irving Thalberg: Boy Wonder to Producer Prince*. Berkeley: University of California Press, 2010.

Vorhaus, Bernard. *Saved from Oblivion: An Autobiography*. London: Scarecrow, 2000.

Walker, Alexander. *Audrey: Her Real Story*. New York: St. Martin's Griffin, 1994.

Walker, Danton. "Broadway." *Daily News*, May 28, 1949.

Walker, Greg. *The Private Life of Henry VIII: The British Film Guide 8*. London: I. B. Tauris & Co., 2003.

Waterbury, Ruth. "The Lady and the Cameraman." *Photoplay*, August 1945.

Waters, Ethel, with Charles Samuels. *His Eye Is on the Sparrow: An Autobiography by Ethel Waters with Charles Samuels*. Garden City, NY: Doubleday, 1951.

Watts Jr., Richard. "On the Screen." *New York Herald Tribune*, February 25, 1935.

"What the Fans Think." *Picture Play*, August 1935.

Whitaker, Alma. "Merle Oberon Finds Taxes Eat Up Most of Earnings Here and in Britain." *Los Angeles Times*, June 26, 1938.

"Whodunit?" *Detroit Free Press*, April 21, 1949.

Whyte, A. P. Luscombe. "Merle Oberon Is Coming Home." *London Evening Standard*, September 13, 1935.

Wilcox, Grace. "The Meaning of 'Glamour'." *Screen & Radio Weekly*, May 19, 1935.

———. "Christmas Comes to Hollywood." *Screen & Radio Weekly*, December 20, 1936.

———. "Good Luck Pieces of the Stars." *Democrat and Chronicle* [Rochester, NY], March 7, 1937.

———. "For Women Only." *Screen & Radio Weekly*, February 26, 1939.

———. "Hollywood Reporter." *Screen & Radio Weekly*, March 5, 1939.

Wilkinson, Lupton A. "'Go Wash Your Face!'." *Atlanta Constitution*, February 25, 1940.

Wilson, Earl. "Hip Hip Hooray for Marie—She Swells Beyond Bacall." *Miami Daily News*, November 21, 1945.

———. "It Happened Last Night." *Newsday*, August 21, 1953.

———. "It Happened Last Night." *Pittsburgh Post-Gazette*, December 6, 1957.

———. "It Happened Last Night." *Newsday*, October 15, 1963.

———. "Falk Tells Lawyers: 'Relax'." *Detroit Free Press*, October 9, 1965.

———. "Married Merle Is Happy Lady." *Indianapolis Star*, March 25, 1977.

Winchell, Walter. "Winchell Says." *Nashville Tennessean*, March 8, 1945.

———. "Walter Winchell On Broadway." *Courier-Post* [Cherry Hill, NJ], May 16, 1950.

Winner, Karin. "Merle Oberon . . . 'Not at All What You'd Expect of Me'." *Women's Wear Daily*, November 8, 1972.

———. "A Long Interval." *Women's Wear Daily*, March 5, 1973.

Winner, Michael. *Winner Takes All: A Life of Sorts*. London: Robison, 2004.

"With Truesdell in Hollywood." *Cincinnati Enquirer*, January 25, 1941.

Woolfenden, John R. "'I Detest "Exotic" Women,' Says Exotic Merle Oberon." *Los Angeles Times*, September 15, 1935.

Ziegler, Philip. *Olivier*. London: MacLehose Press, 2013.

Illustration Credits

Index

Page numbers in italics refer to illustrations.

ABOUT THE AUTHOR

Mayukh Sen is the James Beard and IACP Award–winning author of *Taste Makers: Seven Immigrant Women Who Revolutionized Food in America*, and a Class of 2025 Fellow at New America, where he has been named the inaugural Shourie Family Fellow. His work has been published in outlets such as *The New Yorker*, *New York Times*, *Washington Post*, and *Atlantic*, and has been anthologized in four editions of *The Best American Food and Travel Writing*. He teaches journalism at New York University and lives in Brooklyn, New York.